# Media Literacy for Young Children

## Teaching Beyond the Screen Time Debates

Faith Rogow

National Association for the Education of Young Children
Washington, DC

National Association for the
Education of Young Children

1401 H Street NW, Suite 600
Washington, DC 20005
202-232-8777 • 800-424-2460
NAEYC.org

**NAEYC Books**
**Senior Director, Publishing & Content Development**
*Susan Friedman*

**Director, Books**
*Dana Battaglia*

**Senior Editor**
*Holly Bohart*

**Editor II**
*Rossella Procopio*

**Senior Creative Design Manager**
*Charity Coleman*

**Senior Creative Design Specialist**
*Gillian Frank*

**Publishing Business Operations Manager**
*Francine Markowitz*



**Photo Credits**

Copyright © Getty Images: cover

All other photos credited throughout the book.



Library of Congress Control Number: 2021932761

ISBN: 978-1-938113-97-0

Item: 1158

# Contents

# Acknowledgments

This book is the product of more than 30 years of work in educational media and media literacy education. There isn't enough space in these pages to name everyone who has helped along the way, but that doesn't diminish my appreciation for every single one of them. I've been fortunate to be surrounded by an amazing professional community.

To the scholars I have never met in person but whose work has inspired me; to WSKG and the early PBS Ready to Learn station outreach specialists, series producers, and national staff; to those with whom I have been honored to share my media literacy journey, including Cyndy Scheibe, Chris Sperry, and Sox Sperry at Project Look Sharp, Renee Hobbs at the Media Education Lab, and NAMLE—especially the leaders who served with me when we founded the organization and all the members whose energy and creativity are making media literacy education a "fact on the ground" in countless schools and communities; to Chip Donohue and Roberta Schomburg and all the other persistent and wise folks who fought for NAEYC's position statement on technology in early childhood education; to the team at NAEYC, with a special shout-out to my editor, Dana Battaglia, whose insight and advocacy made this a better book; to all the social justice warriors and to everyone who cares for children enough to try to make their world better.

And finally, my deepest gratitude always to Del "Child Whisperer" Brown, who sustains me—body, mind, and spirit.

Faith Rogow
Ithaca, New York

# Start Here

**This is a book about teaching.**

It's also a book about learning and acting on what we learn.

And it's about thinking and reflection.

And young children.

And media.

And us.

**This is a book for**

- People who are curious about media literacy and how to introduce its complex skills and concepts to children who are still so young that tying their own shoes is a major accomplishment
- Grown-ups who care about the ways that young children are shaped by their interactions with media
- Early childhood professionals or people interested in becoming an early childhood professional who aren't satisfied with a "just say no" approach to children and technology but who have concerns about digital media
- Educators who are committed to the task of preparing children for their digital future rather than our analog past
- People who believe that critical thinking is essential for a healthy democracy and vibrant planet

If any of this sounds like you, **welcome to the journey.**

# What to Expect: Media Literacy Is Literacy

People use the label *media literacy* to describe a lot of different things. This book approaches media literacy as *literacy*. Depending on what you currently think about media and literacy, this approach may include some surprises.

You probably already have an intuitive sense of what literacy is—you are, after all, reading print media right now. So, you won't have far to go to understand media literacy. When pared down to its core, media literacy is primarily an expansion of traditional literacy that includes *all* the ways we communicate today—digital media to be sure, but also printed books, posters, product packaging, logos, jigsaw puzzles, songs, signs, and so much more. Any form of communication that is mediated—with something between the sender and receiver of a message—is media. We want children to learn to apply critical inquiry and reflection skills to all of them.

Approaching media literacy as *literacy* means that it is about much more than technology integration or attempts to persuade children that media time is less valuable than other activities in their lives. Like traditional literacy, media literacy includes learning how to decode symbol systems that allow us to "read" and "write" using multiple forms of media.

It also extends beyond mastery of mechanics or techniques to encompass making connections and discovering the ways that a shared symbol system allows us to learn from one another's ideas and stories. Finland's Ministry of Education and Culture describes it this way:

> Media literacy is more than simply acquiring means of understanding and creating content for media. Media literacy is strongly connected to matters of personal growth, creativity, critical thinking, being literate and part of society and cultures. (2019, 5)

Framed as literacy, media literacy includes emotional awareness, ethics, discernment, and complex concepts such as

- Epistemology—uncovering the sources of our ideas
- Metacognition—awareness of how we know what we know and how we learn
- Reason—using evidence and logic to arrive at conclusions

Even young children can engage in these very substantive pursuits, especially if, like traditional literacy, we weave media literacy into nearly everything we teach rather than limit it to an occasional, isolated lesson. In this aspect, media literacy is as much a method as it is a subject area.

As you become comfortable with its strategies, you'll discover that teaching media literacy is like using a kaleidoscope—there is a fixed set of skills and knowledge that you can turn and jiggle into an infinite variety of intriguing combinations. The results can be inspiring . . . and fun!

# What to Pack

As you prepare to embark on the media literacy education journey, here's what you'll need to bring along:

## WONDER

What do you wonder about?

Are you surprised that the first question in a media literacy book is about things in the world that pique your curiosity? Maybe you expected a question about your use of digital devices or your favorite childhood video game or TV character. Or perhaps you weren't anticipating a question at all, expecting instead a concerning statistic about screen use or an amazing story about kids using cameras.

All of these are related to media literacy. But we start with wonder because being literate in today's digital world demands a bear-hug-sized embrace of intellectual curiosity.

Consider for a moment that, in a single week, any major newspaper contains more information than the people who declared US independence were likely to come across in a lifetime (McLoed 2019). And every person who has access to a social media platform also has access to a potential audience of millions, or even billions. Take a moment to ponder how amazing that is—and how challenging.

Despite some popular but misguided ideas about "digital natives," the ability to use devices doesn't automatically include the ability to construct useful knowledge from all that information, nor does it ensure an understanding of how (or why) social media algorithms shape the content or form of media messages. Mastery of reading and writing printed words gives access to part of the available data, but only part. And no device or platform automatically creates ethical users.

Digital technologies are transforming nearly every aspect of our lives in ways both splendid and disquieting. A recent report by the World Economic Forum notes that "65% of children entering primary school today will have jobs that do not yet exist" (2017, 5). Not since the Industrial Revolution displaced a culture centered around artisans and farmers have daily routines and norms been so upended.

And it's not just changes that relate to work. "Smart" phones and wearables, tablets, social networks, search engines, artificial intelligence, voice assistants, big data, and cloud storage are shifting the ways we shop, study, play, and get around. They influence our health and alter the ways that we access health-care services and medical information. They've redefined the meaning of national borders and posed new challenges to democracy. They have forced a re-thinking of the meaning of privacy and money. They even change how we interact socially, with whom, and which words or images we use.

It's not that a digital hurricane has come and gone, and we are survivors tasked with learning the best ways to live in our new digital reality—the storm is ongoing. The continuing upheaval is unsettling and trying to keep up can easily send us into overload. It was just 2008 when MySpace was the largest social network. By 2009, it had been sent into decline by Facebook. Just three years later, Twitter had a 100 million users, and we had Instagram and WhatsApp (both owned by Facebook), and Snapchat. As this book is being written, TikTok has entered the picture and YouTube reigns supreme in the lives of young children in the United States. If you feel like just when you've learned to use one thing it's replaced by something new, you're not alone.

In a world defined by rapid change, our sense of wonder can keep our anxieties in check (or at least in perspective). Wonder allows us to pause and marvel at the novelty and possibilities, even as we assess whether particular changes are in the best interest of children, society, or ourselves. It gives us permission to experiment, knowing that not everything we try will work, but that we'll learn from our attempts. And it centers our lives around questions and the adventure of inquiry and discovery. Not coincidentally, media literacy education is also centered around the practice of inquiry.

### IMAGINATION

Imagination is wonder's close cousin. It allows us to envision a world in which people routinely use media ethically and effectively. From there we can reverse engineer to figure out what young children need to learn to make that vision real.

Early childhood educators especially need imagination because when advocates first described media literacy as the ability "to access, analyze, and produce information for specific outcomes," they mostly had adolescents and young adults in mind (Firestone 1993, 6). Though there have been a few notable efforts to engage primary students in media literacy (e.g., Bazagette, 2010 or ProjectLookSharp.org), we're only recently beginning to explore which practices that are common in teaching older children will need to change in order to engage toddlers and preschoolers.

At this moment in history, the boundaries of media literacy in early childhood education are fluid, which means there are wide open opportunities to forge new pathways. We're like wilderness scouts. To create new trails, we need a clear idea of where we're headed and also knowledge of the existing landscape—in this case, child development, education, and media. Imagination opens us to visions of new paths, especially as the landscape changes and we need to adapt.

## A Guide

This book is premised on the belief that every early childhood professional has the capacity to navigate the profound challenges of preparing young children to thrive in an unpredictable digital future. Equipped with wonder and imagination, you'll be able to use the practice and pedagogy of media literacy education as a field guide. Here's what you'll find in these pages to help:

### Part I—Getting Ready

We're better media literacy teachers when we're media literate ourselves, so we start by examining how we are/have been shaped by media, how our existing ideas about media and literacy influence the ways that we engage children, and how they shape our sense of ourselves as teachers.

### Part II—Defining the Task

All good educational design starts with a clear articulation of purpose and outcomes. We work backwards from the end point to determine the steps needed to get there. So, these chapters outline the general goals and pedagogy of media literacy education, with introductory suggestions about what developmentally appropriate media literacy education looks like in practice.

### Part III—Transforming Pedagogy into Practice

A primary goal of this book is that you walk away with the skills and knowledge you need to create your own media literacy lessons. This section provides examples to help you see the possibilities, and practical suggestions for integrating media literacy into your existing routines, including partnering with families.

Inquiry and reflection are core to the practice and pedagogy of media literacy education, so they will be woven throughout the book. These include designated prompts to pause and ponder, so you can practice the type of contemplation and analysis that is routine in a media literate world.

## A Note About Language Choices

Media—This book uses *media* as a plural noun, rather than the more colloquial singular. That's not just a nod to grammatical accuracy. It's a reminder that even though nearly all major media are owned by only a dozen or so companies, and even though those companies wield a great deal of power, media are actually quite diverse, in both form and content. There is no such thing as a singular, unified entity that is "the media."

TV and Videos—The book uses the term *TV* broadly, to include all the ways that children watch: live, recorded, and on demand. Watching a series on a tablet or phone rather than on a television set doesn't change its identity as a TV show.

The term *videos* generally refers to online videos accessed via services like YouTube. The book does not use the word *video* as a synonym for movie or film.

It's important to understand these two categories—TV and videos—because combined, they account for nearly three-quarters of all screen time for children age 0 to 8 (Rideout & Robb 2020, 3).

Kids—The book uses *kids* as an informal synonym for *children*. Historically, the word may have been used in an insulting way to describe a rambunctious child (by comparing them to a goat), but few people use it that way today. In the author's view, it is a better option than the common alternative *kiddos*, which for many, connotes an intimacy that is inappropriate in the context of this text.

Developmentally Appropriate Practice—The recommendations in this book are intended for engaging children ages 2 to 7. Within that range, the book uses general terms rather than narrow-age specific recommendations:

- *Very young* or the *youngest children* describes 2-, 3-, and sometimes 4-year-olds.
- *Young children* typically denotes 4- and 5-year-olds.
- *Older children* or *school age* refers to kids ages 5, 6 or 7.

These designations are general guides. They should never replace your professional judgment. You know your children and their capabilities. If you try something and it seems to be too frustrating or too easy, move on and try something else. And remember that beliefs about what is developmentally appropriate are not culturally universal. Differences in heritage, culture, nationality, and even necessity create very different expectations.

It's also worth noting that the ideas in this book may be useful to people in many parts of the world—everyone can always learn from others—but it is written from a distinctly American perspective and is focused on early childhood education as it is practiced in the United States. It makes no claims that its approach can or should be generalized to other cultures or education systems.

## The Quest

The genesis for the pages you hold in your hand is a trio of questions:

1. In a digital world, what do children need in order to gain the power that once came with traditional literacy?

   Knowing how to read and write print has been a path to power for centuries. In the United States, for example, the governments of several slaveholding states recognized literacy as so powerful, they feared that literate slaves would revolt. So, to protect the institution of slavery they made it illegal to teach enslaved Black people to read or write. What they understood was that literacy could expand one's world view, increase chances to achieve economic success, and allow for participation in democratic institutions as an informed citizen. In the digital world, print literacy will continue to be important, but it isn't enough. Much of civic life, learning, information sharing, social networking, commerce, and storytelling now routinely takes place in the digital commons. In the online world, print, image, and audio converge. To succeed requires more than the ability to read and write with printed words.

2. Which skills, knowledge, and dispositions will remain central to success no matter how the media landscape changes?

   To learn in a world where so many people have access to nearly unlimited information and audiences, children will need critical thinking and discernment skills and the desire to use them. In 2015, I wrote that to construct education for a digital world, "we need to expand the three Rs to include reasoning and reflection. And we need to do so in ways that foster curiosity, creativity, and collaboration" (Rogow 2015, 91). In addition to critical inquiry and problem-solving skills, we will also need to instill a sense of ethics and social responsibility, so that whether they are online or not, children will remember that they are part of a community.

3. How can we respond to uncertainty with imagination rather than fear?

   Our path forward will be informed by our concerns, but we can't let our fears become quicksand. We need to stretch beyond our instinct to protect. In real life, children aren't knights; they need for us to equip them with more than shields and armor.

I wrote this book because it's time to re-think our educational responses to living in a world where media and digital technologies are woven into the fabric of daily life. As you read, consider yourself part of a community that is crowdsourcing the role that early childhood educators will play in creating a media literate society. Welcome to the conversation. I invite you to share your thoughts, insights, and questions on the NAEYC Hello discussion forum or on Twitter using the hashtag #ECEMediaLit.

PAUSE TO **REFLECT**

The journey to succeed as early childhood educators in an ever-changing digital world will require us to ask and answer many questions. What questions brought you to this book?

## Sources

Bazalgette, C., ed. 2010. *Teaching Media in Primary Schools.* London: Sage & Media Education Association.

Firestone, C. 1993. "Introduction." In "Media Literacy–A Report of the National Leadership Conference on Media Literacy," P. Aufderheide. Proceedings of the Aspen Institute National Leadership Conference. https://eric.ed.gov/?id=ED365294.

*McLoed, S. 2019. "Did You Know 6.0." https://www.youtube.com/watch?v=u06BXgWbGvA.

"Media Literacy in Finland: National Media Education Policy." 2019. Helsinki: Publications of the Ministry of Education and Culture. https://medialukutaitosuomessa.fi/en/category/medialukutaito/

Rideout, V., & M.B. Robb. 2020. *The Common Sense Census: Media Use by Kids Age Zero to Eight, 2020.* San Francisco, CA: Common Sense Media.

Rogow, F. 2015. "Media Literacy in Early Childhood Education: Inquiry-Based Technology Integration." In *Technology and Digital Media in the Early Years: Tools for Teaching and Learning*, ed. C. Donohue. 91-103. New York and Washington, D.C.: Routledge and NAEYC.

World Economic Forum. 2017. "Realizing Human Potential in the Fourth Industrial Revolution: An Agenda for Leaders to Shape the Future of Education, Gender and Work." White paper. Geneva, Switzerland: World Economic Forum. http://www3.weforum.org/docs/WEF_EGW_Whitepaper.pdf.

PART I

# Getting Ready

**Imagine that the beginning of your media literacy journey is like consulting a map app for directions. To know where to go, you first need to understand where you are.**

For media literacy education, understanding where you are requires knowing about

- *The context in which you teach or will be teaching*—Education is always situated in a specific set of circumstances that shape every aspect of your work (and play!), including the rules for licensing, school district policies, available resources, and, importantly, the histories, heritage, and unique needs of the specific families and communities you serve. Education never happens in isolation.
- *Media*—Understanding media structures, methods, and messages helps you determine what's important for children to learn and do.
- *Your existing knowledge and skills*—What you choose to do will be significantly shaped by who you are. That includes all the things you already know or believe about teaching and children, your expectations, and your lifetime of media experiences.

Everyone's *context* is different and specific, so you'll have to fill in those details for yourself. But the last two parts of the trio—*media* and *what you already know*—this book is designed to help with those. By the time you've finished reading and reflecting on Part I, you'll have a solid idea of your current location.

To start, take a moment to ponder this question:

*How would you summarize the role that media and ideas about media play in your life, personally and professionally?*

CHAPTER 1

# Media, Society, and Us

Media literacy functions as a tangled web, intersecting and connecting nearly every aspect of our lives. This chapter invites you to begin to envision what that web looks like in your own life.

## Literacy as Social Practice

At one level, all learning is inherently individual. You didn't become literate just by watching someone else write or by listening to someone else read. At some point, you had to acquire these skills by doing them for yourself.

But whether or how well a particular child learns how to read or write isn't just about their own individual skills; it depends on a variety of *social* factors. Do their surroundings include an abundance of books in the language or languages they hear at home? How about skilled teachers and role models? Does their family or culture prioritize literacy? Do instruction techniques match the child's needs?

In places that emphasize empirical testing, it can be easy to lose sight of the fact that literacy isn't just about easy-to-measure, individual skills like phonics or fluency. Actual reading and writing are about sending and receiving communication using shared symbol systems. That makes traditional literacy an inherently social—and media!—practice.

Even comprehension and interpretation are dependent on social context. Our culture and community shape how we make meaning.

Perhaps the easiest way to illustrate the social nature of interpretation is to think of words that have changed meaning over time. Consider, for example, the famous Christmas carol, "Deck the Halls." In 1862, when Scottish musician Thomas Oliphant composed the song's lyrics, "don we now our *gay* apparel," he wasn't referencing a modern construction of sexual identity. One hundred years later, the word *gay* still meant happy, carefree, or celebratory, as in the Flintstones cartoon theme song, "we'll have a gay old time." Yet today, many children who hear those songs may be confused about the antiquated use of the word *gay*, especially if they have heard the word used as a slur. The phonics involved in reading the word *gay* haven't changed—the cultural context has.

To say that literacy is a social practice is another way of saying that we don't read or write in a vacuum. Consider how your interpretations are shaped:

- By the infrastructure and financial barriers that must be overcome to access information (including who controls the use of paywalls, which restrict access to paid subscribers)
- By which voices are present or omitted, marginalized or celebrated, privileged or intentionally silenced
- By whether you use or understand pop culture or literary references
- By your peers and role models
- By which tropes, genres, and vocabulary are deemed appropriate for particular audiences or circumstances (for example, when or whether it is okay to curse, use slang, or communicate by using abbreviations)

All these social variables are integral to making meaning and communicating with an alphabetic symbol system.

## Media Literacy as Social Practice

As renowned critical pedagogy theorists Paulo Freire and Donaldo Macedo wrote, we need to understand literacy as much more than a set of mechanical processes. We need "to view it as the relationship of learners to the world" (Freire & Macedo 1987). One of the great values of media literacy education is that it embodies this Freirean vision of reading the word *and* the world. Media literacy competencies not only enable people to analyze and evaluate discrete media texts, but they also enable people to examine the social aspects of those texts and the ways that media shape society.

Media literacy as *literacy* is about exploring our overlapping relationships to key aspects of life:

› Information—Where and how we get ideas about the world; how we make meaning from stories and symbol systems; how we learn; how our meaning making is both individual and social; whether our information sources facilitate or obfuscate reason, logic, and evidence

› Inspiration—How and where we find it; how we communicate through the arts; how we make choices to nurture or suppress creativity

› Labor—How we find and engage in meaningful work (both income generating and volunteer); what types of work exists as viable options; where work takes place

› Authority—What we accept as proper or credible societal authorities (government, law, religion, schools, media, family, and so on); how we teach children to trust *us* as authorities and to question media authorities at the same time (a key to success in a world in which misinformation and disinformation will be common)

› Physical sustenance—How we choose and obtain the things we need for physical survival; how we care for ourselves and the planet

› One another—How we engage in the various communities to which we belong (for example, online, our neighborhood, our workplace, our nation, the world); how we define the parameters of our broad social contract—the responsibilities, rules, and skills that we share in order to live together productively—in a world in which we may be in closer contact with someone on another continent than with people who live down the block; where we find common ground and how we respond to forces that intentionally try to divide us; how we establish and teach shared values like democracy, fairness, justice, and pluralism

Media literacy education is important because media play a central role in every one of these relationships.

To be sure, part of media literacy is learning to decode specific types of media texts. More on that in subsequent chapters. But helping children to become fluent *readers* and skilled *writers* in the multiple forms that are common to current media is about much more than simply teaching them to question advertising claims or to learn how to stay safe online. It's about opening up the world—and all its possibilities—to them. When we say that media literacy is an essential life skill, this is what we mean.

PAUSE TO **REFLECT**

Consider the role that media play (or have played) in each of the areas described above. Give one example of a way that media have improved that facet of your life and one way that they have been an obstacle. Can you identify any ways in which your use of media links multiple areas of your life?

When we conceptualize media literacy as *literacy,* we focus on opportunities. In thirty years of education workshops and conferences, I never *ever* heard anyone justify teaching kids to read in order to protect them from dangerous or deceptive print materials. It's not that problematic print materials don't exist. You have probably seen at least one children's book that repeats damaging stereotypes. And in our online lives, we are likely to come across text-based messages that are intended to mislead. Dangers exist, and we address them. But we rightfully choose not to make them the center of our literacy practice. That's because we understand that the primary challenge we are addressing is illiteracy, not bad books.

To be sure, we select books carefully and urge publishers to step up their game, but in our time with children, we offer strategies like daily read-alouds, print-rich environments, and exposure to the delight and discovery that await those who learn to decipher and communicate with alphabetic symbol systems. We emphasize connections, encouraging families to read to children as a way to strengthen bonds and enjoy time together.

Because image-based communication is accessible to young children in ways that print is not, media literacy education will use strategies that are a bit different from those we use to encourage print literacy. For example, rather than encouraging the creation of a screen media parallel to a print-rich environment, we'll focus on creating an inquiry-rich environment. But if we accept that media literacy is literacy for the multimedia world we actually live in, then we should approach it like print literacy. We don't ignore potential hazards, but we also don't fixate on them. We open up possibilities.

## Source

Freire, P., & D. Macedo. 1987. *Literacy: Reading the Word and the World.* South Hadley, MA: Bergin & Garvey.

CHAPTER 2

# Visual Literacy

In order to help children confidently navigate the forms of communication that are most common today, teachers need the ability to "read" images as well as print. But you can't teach what you don't know, and most of us have never been offered any formal training in visual literacy. This chapter addresses that gap, explaining how images communicate messages.

## Reading Images

What does the image in Figure 2.1 communicate to you?

Figure 2.1

Did you assume it was a word? Why? What clues suggest that it is something that someone might say or text?

If you can read Russian, you'll immediately recognize it as the word *zdravstvuyte*, which means *hello*. But if you never learned the Cyrillic alphabet, the contents inside the bubble are just a bunch of squiggles. Print is gibberish until we learn to decode it.

In contrast, people with functional eyesight can make sense of most visual information without any formal instruction at all. Did you recognize the image as a conversation bubble and then use that as a clue that the squiggles inside it were a word? Probably. Is that because a teacher included a unit on the meaning of callout bubbles in some distant-past language arts class? Probably not.

People with eyesight fluently process enormous amounts of visual information every day without anyone ever needing to supply direct instruction. Because of this, some scholars have argued that there is no such thing as visual *literacy* akin to the symbol system that is alphabetic literacy (Messaris 1994; Meyrowitz 1985). What these scholars miss is that there is, indeed, much image-based information that we do learn how to interpret, even if we aren't always conscious of having learned it. We do "read" images. Conscious awareness of that process is essential to understanding how we make meaning of media.

### Visual Homonyms

One of the simplest ways to demonstrate that visual communication uses symbol systems that are learned is to look at examples of identical images that have different meanings in different cultures. One recent example is the pinched fingers (or "finger purse") emoji introduced in 2020 (Figure 2.2).

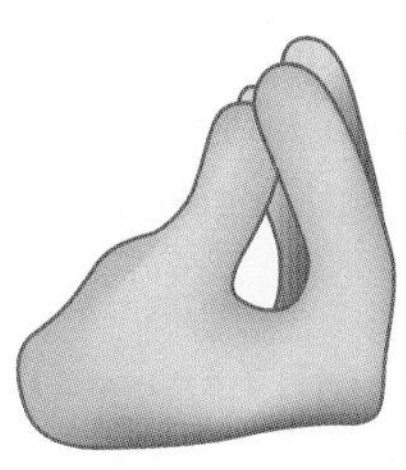

Figure 2.2

Its meaning changes drastically from country to country. In Italy, it can be a shorthand way of asking impatiently "What do you want from me?!?" while in other places it's the "chef's kiss" (a compliment for something that is delicious or perfect), an invitation to "show me the money," or in some subcultures, a suggestive reference to a sex act. In Israel, it can signal disdain or "wait a minute," and in Korea, a pop star popularized the gesture as a way to indicate affection (with the hand shaped to represent a dumpling).

Given all the possibilities, if someone sent you a text containing this emoji, how would you know what they meant? The most obvious answer is context. The sender's culture, your relationship with them, and surrounding text all provide clues.

## Visual Literacy Formula

There is a simple formula that expresses the way we make meaning from visuals:

**IMAGE + CONTEXT = Message**

To understand how the formula operates, let's start by examining a basic building block of visual symbolism: color. Think for a moment about all the different meanings you have learned for the color green. It can denote something that is mint-flavored, Irish, or environmentally beneficial. It can also mean "go," "open," or affinity for a professional or school athletic team.

Now, imagine that you are on a highway approaching a row of toll booths, each with a lighted signal above it. The signal is either red or green. Which lane do you choose? Despite the signal being similar to a traffic light, green can't mean "go" because what they want you to do is stop to pay the toll. But "this lane for minty freshness" doesn't make much sense. You select a lane with a green light because you know this:

**Green + Toll Booth Lane = Open**

A green dot by itself doesn't carry clear meaning, but put that green dot into the context of a light above a toll booth lane and the message is "open." Put that same green dot on a tube of toothpaste, and you change the message from "open" to "spearmint flavored." If you change the context, the meaning changes.

In *The Teacher's Guide to Media Literacy* (2012), Cyndy Scheibe and I explain that the formula is the first step of reading images. The actual process is more complex. If we continue with interpreting the color green, it's easy to see why.

Change the context from toll booths to lollipops. Green in the context of lollipops gives us some very important information: the flavor. Our own experience determines whether we think the flavor is lime, green apple, or something else. But no matter our personal conclusion, knowing the flavor of a lollipop is vital information, especially if you are three years old and choosing which lollipop you want! So, color in the context of lollipops is a salient variable, i.e., a variable we ignore at our own peril because it provides information that makes a difference.

But what if we change the context slightly. Put the color green in the context of a different type of candy—original M&Ms. What is the flavor? The flavor is, of course, chocolate. All M&Ms are chocolate inside their colored shells. So even though they are both types of candy, color is a salient variable in the context of lollipops and irrelevant (at least in terms of flavor) in the context of original M&Ms.

This tells us something important about how we learn to process visual information. Not only do we learn that context shapes message, we also learn *which* pieces of visual information are important in *each* context. We don't pay attention to everything all the time because we can't. To do so would quickly overwhelm our brain's capacity. Rather, we learn to pay attention to some things and ignore others, depending on the situation. We use selective attention.

To understand why selective attention matters, try this quick brainteaser. Which of the options below is numerically most different than the others? Note that it must be a *numerical* difference, so the fact that "thirty-one" is written with a hyphen doesn't qualify.

1) one

2) thirteen

3) thirty-one

Most people conclude that the answer is "one" because it is the only single digit option, but that's not accurate. Look again. It can't be the number "one" because there are two "ones" in the example:

"1" and "one," (three if you also count the "one" in "thirty-one"). And "2" and "3" are also single digits. The answer is "2." Not thirteen, but the number "2." It's the only even number in the example.

If you didn't say "2," you're in good company. In thirty years of presenting this brainteaser to thousands of people, only two have ever come up with the correct answer, and I'm fairly certain that one of them had previously read *The Teacher's Guide to Media Literacy*, where I originally wrote about it.

Why do so few people see the correct answer? Because Western models of education teach a visual language for multiple choice questions in which anything to the left of the parentheses is for organizational purposes only, and therefore not included in the options from which we might select an answer. As a result of that visual language, your brain eliminated half of the available information. An anonymous graffiti writer at Bard College (as transcribed and shared by Kenneth Stern, Director of the Bard Center for the Study of Hate) put it this way, "If I didn't believe it with my own mind I never would have seen it."

Because selective attention is, in part, learned, we can teach it. As we use visual media with young children, we can point out clues that are especially important to notice in order to understand media messages, like the direction of an arrow, where a character's eyes are looking, or lighting that indicates time of day. As we introduce more complex media, we can point out things that makers didn't want us to pay attention to but that we should get in the habit of noticing, like warning labels, the "fine print" (disclaimers), a business logo that indicates sponsorship, or people in the background reacting to bad behavior with laughter, approval, or indifference.

PAUSE TO **REFLECT**

How does the "selective attention" you have learned influence the image-based information you attend to or ignore in news or information sources? How about in the books you read with children?

## Shared Meaning

We can look to a tenet of child development—egocentrism—to add another layer of complexity to our understanding of visual language. Sometimes egocentrism is misconstrued as meaning that little ones are selfish, but that isn't quite accurate. It's that they don't yet have the capacity to understand the abstract, so they interpret the world through their own concrete experiences. Everything is, therefore, necessarily related to what *they* experience; they are the center around which everything else revolves. And they assume that everyone else experiences the world exactly the way that they do.

We slip into that same pattern when we look at media and assume that everyone shares our interpretation. Consider the traffic light. What does the yellow (amber) light mean? Most folks recall the explanation in the driver's manual and answer, "caution." But when you approach a yellow light, what do you actually do?

Some of us slow down, knowing that the light is about to turn red. Many of us do the opposite. We speed up so we can make it through the light before we get stuck having to wait for the red light to change back to green. When there's a mismatch of those interpretations—for example, a person making a turn assuming that everyone will slow down but drivers coming the opposite way actually speed up—there's likely to be a crash. We literally run into a problem when we assume we have shared meaning, but we don't.

In this case we have general agreement on the message of a yellow light, but our shared understanding isn't very meaningful. That's because, like print literacy, making meaning from images involves connecting to the world, not just discrete decoding techniques. In a media context, absence of shared meaning shows up most profoundly in disagreements about whether particular images are racist, antisemitic, sexist, homophobic, or some other form of hate speech.

The more different we are from someone else, the more likely it is that we will interpret what we see differently than them. Of all the factors that can lead to differences in interpretation (e.g., ethnic, national, racial, gender, or political identities) one of the most important for early childhood educators is age. We don't see the world the way that a toddler or preschooler sees it. That's because:

- Our greater experience in the world allows us to notice and understand context that a young child misses.
- We are able to understand abstract concepts (like off-screen action or motives) that very young children are not yet developmentally able to grasp.
- Everyone pays most attention to what's new to *them*.

As a vestige of our prehistoric ancestors' survival needs, our brains are hard-wired for a "flight or fight" response. Constant vigilance against attacks necessitated an ability to quickly assess whether something posed an immediate danger. Our brains learned to put aside familiar, safe things so we could direct our attention to things that were novel or in motion (and might come near enough to pose a threat). So, our attention is always drawn to what's new. Of course, what's new to a young child is rarely new to us.

That knowledge can improve our teaching. Without such awareness, it wouldn't be uncommon to read aloud a story like *The Three Little Pigs* and expect children to pay attention to the narrative. But the attention of children who have never before seen pigs or wolves may be drawn to the pictures instead. When they can't answer questions about basic parts of the story, you might mistakenly conclude that they must not have been paying attention. But if you had asked them to describe the characteristics of a pig or wolf, their responses might make it clear that they were paying attention, just not to the things that *you* assumed were most important or obvious.

Our brains process images so quickly that it is easy to forget just how much information we are taking in. A child seeing a pig for the first time, either in person or via an illustration, is learning its color and size, that it has four short legs (relative to its body size) and a short tail. Compared with humans, the pig has funny looking feet (split hooves), a snout rather than a nose, and pointed ears. They are learning its name and how to distinguish it from other four-legged animals (like the fact that it doesn't have fur like a dog or cat or wombat). Put aside for a moment that most illustrations of the *Three Little Pigs* also include things that are scientifically inaccurate (like pigs standing and walking on two hind legs or holding building materials in their "hands") and Eurocentric messaging about quality housing, that's a lot of new information to take in and process. It's no wonder

PAUSE TO **REFLECT**

This is an image from a set of alphabet cards. What letter do you think it illustrates? How do you know? Would children give the same answer? The original card said "I is for insect." Was that your answer? What are some of the other possibilities? As you look around at the illustrations of important letters, words, or concepts in your space, are you sure that you and the children have a shared understanding of each picture, or might you be making different meanings? How could you find out?

that pictures of something new draw children's focus and may temporarily crowd out memory of other parts of the media experience.

It is because we are so different from young children that it is essential to talk with them about media. Rather than assume we know what they understand, we invite them to share the meaning *they* are making. For examples of questions to start that conversation, see Chapter 6.

## Stereotyping and Implicit Bias

Visual language plays an outsized role in the prevalence of stereotypes and implicit bias. Professor Dolly Chugh offers a common word association to explain implicit bias, suggesting that if she said "peanut butter," many people would immediately name "jelly" as its seemingly natural pair. It's a learned association, but we experience it as automatic and without intention. In "Who Me? Biased?" (a series of video shorts by the New York Times Learning Network and American Documentary's POV, www.pbs.org/pov/watch/implicitbias), Chugh notes that every day we move in a virtual "fog" of such associations, and some of them link groups of people with certain traits. That's implicit bias.

Our implicit biases are often intertwined with stereotypes—an overgeneralized, explicit, illogical attribution of a set of characteristics to an entire group of people, often deployed to solidify the power of a dominant group. Young children might understand it as insisting that all people in a group are the same. Returning to the visual language formula, we can describe the process as seeing a particular trait (hair or clothing style, eye shape, religious symbol, skin color, and so forth) in the context of a person, and learning particular associations that accompany the trait.

So, for example, applying the visual literacy formula to the history of American racism, we can see that skin color in the context of people was attached to messages about White superiority and enslaved Africans being lazy, dumb, or prone to criminal behavior. The stereotype developed in order to defend slavery and shield Whites from seeing resistance to oppression in the work habits of the people they enslaved. Visual language didn't create the stereotype; it allowed for its widespread adoption, even by people who rejected a slave-based economy, as happened when some Vaudeville performers and early filmmakers relied on the stereotype for easy laughs in entertainment venues far beyond the boundaries of the slave states.

Interpretation of images also aided in the continuation of racist stereotypes long after the abolition of slavery. We see this process at work today in snap judgments made by police about the presumed threat posed by young Black men, comparatively high rates of Black boys being expelled from preschool, and the "adultification" of Black girls, where educators and authorities perceive them to be older and less in need of protection than children of other races (Epstein, Blake, & González 2017).

Once skin color was accepted as an important visual cue and attached to racist stereotypes, it was applied to many other groups. At various points in US history it became one of the factors used to declare a variety of groups, including Latin, Chinese, Southeast Asian, and even darker skinned immigrants from southern Europe as undesirable or ineligible for American citizenship. It even contributed to discrimination within groups, with lighter skinned people being favored over darker skinned kin.

Over the centuries we have become accustomed to using visual cues to distinguish one group of people from another. Military and religious institutions have used regalia to designate rank, monarchs have issued edicts reserving particular colors of clothing for royalty, and communities have donned tattoos, jewelry, or textile patterns to indicate tribal membership or ethnicity.

That history isn't inherently negative. In some circumstances, being able to make quick identifications can be helpful. But too often the characteristics we have learned to associate with particular groups lead to discrimination,

## PAUSE TO **REFLECT**

Years ago, in workshops I led as a PBS station education and outreach specialist, I would show a publicity still from the then new *Arthur* TV series and ask: "What race/ethnicity is Arthur? How do you know?" How would you answer those questions?

In one workshop, a teacher jokingly offered, "I don't know what Arthur is, but I know what he's not. He's not Black because no Black kid I know would wear a v-neck sweater and collar like that!" We all laughed, agreeing that this was probably true for our current time and place. From there we jumped into a discussion about what clues people used to try to determine an answer. Of course, Arthur is an aardvark, so technically he has no race. But he's also anthropomorphized, so he has human characteristics.

As people pondered the messages conveyed by those characteristics, some stuck to clues in the image, like the color of his skin or his mother's and sister's hairstyles. Others added knowledge from the show, like the way he spoke. And still others drew on their previous knowledge of author Marc Brown's books, noting that Brown is White and that Arthur seems to be his alter ego, which they suggested, would make Arthur White. In the end, there wasn't uniform agreement on Arthur's race. We did agree, however, that young children who related to the character probably saw themselves in Arthur, so they might conclude that he shared their race or ethnicity, whatever that was.

Then I asked, "What socioeconomic class does Arthur's family belong to? How do you know?" What would your answer be?

In one of the most memorable workshop moments of my career, one early childhood educator raised her hand and said, "the house is clean so I know they're not poor." As soon as she finished the sentence, the import of what she said hit her. Sometimes speaking thoughts aloud can produce powerful moments of insight.

She had been making a value judgment about families living in poverty by using visual cues that were often beyond an individual's control. She saw things like dirty clothes, a cluttered space, and broken fixtures as evidence of a character flaw rather than lack of access to a washing machine, inadequate storage for the number of people forced to share a small apartment, or an unresponsive landlord. And she realized it was these "messy" homes that she used to judge an entire group of people when, even in her own experience she had visited perfectly tidy homes of children whose families were financially insecure. She was mortified.

In fact, she had given the group an incredible gift. An amazing and deep discussion followed about the ways we use visual cues to make judgements about race and class, and that those judgments affect the children in our care. In the session's final reflections, many participants thanked her for the new awareness.

Children's media, including books, are filled with anthropomorphized animals, monsters, and objects come to life. What clues are you using to assign identities to these characters?

dehumanization, or a loss of dignity. The latter is what happens, for example, when visitors assume that a person of color is a secretary, orderly, or janitor instead of a professor, doctor, or CEO. Or when people see an individual who uses a wheelchair and speak to them as if they are hearing impaired or intellectually challenged.

Media have an unparalleled capacity to amplify stereotypes because they can repeat a message hundreds (or thousands) of times in the course of normal use. The repetition can make it seem like messages are broadly endorsed, even when they're not. Repeated enough times, messages gradually begin to seem normal. Our brain treats them as familiar, even when, intellectually, we know they are not true. Being media literate means we acknowledge this process and pay attention to the messages that our brain typically ignores or dismisses.

For example, we can improve our awareness of the stereotypes we have internalized by developing the habit of asking counterfactuals: "How would I interpret that behavior if it was done by someone of a different race, religion, or social class?" We can teach school-age children to ask counterfactual questions by starting with the phrase:

> *What do you think would happen if . . . ? What's your evidence?*

So, for example, we could ask this version:

> *What do you think would happen if a person of another gender [*fill in the blank—*wore that costume, posed that way, tried to do what the character in the story did]?*

Toddlers and preschoolers aren't developmentally ready to grasp the long-term effects of their media environment, but it is shaping them nonetheless. Much of what they see is beyond our control, but we can be mindful of the images and messages in the spaces for which we are responsible. These images are especially impactful because little ones know that we are in charge of certain places, and they assume we approve of the messages they encounter there. They trust us to act in their best interest. By ensuring exposure to diverse images, we take a small step toward counteracting negative stereotypes that children encounter outside our walls. In doing so, we lay a powerful foundation for an alternative vision of normal that is broadly inclusive and affirming.

## Evaluating the Media Environment You Create

As you look around at the space where children spend the most time, examine the environmental media (like posters, bulletin boards, product packaging, and logos) as well as media that children actively use (like books, apps, or videos), and ask yourself these general questions:

1. What are the media images that children see every day (or most often)?
2. What do you suppose children are learning from those images (and how do you know what they are learning)?
3. Do the images repeated most often give children an accurate view of the world?
4. Do the images I/we have selected convey the values I/we hope to instill?

To hone in on stereotyping, you might also ask questions like these:

- How do the images that children see depict life in other countries?
- Are those images realistic portrayals of daily life or are children learning to associate other places with folksy stereotypes? Would children be surprised to learn that Africa is a diverse continent with large cities and people who wear clothes just like theirs or do they believe that the entire continent looks like *The Lion King*? How many believe that Mexicans routinely walk around wearing sombreros, or that Japanese go to work or school wearing kimonos, or that every Arab owns a camel?

It's also important to take note of patterns in images of people that portray specific pursuits or jobs (e.g., athletes, nurturers, scientists, leaders, readers, helpers):

- Are all, or nearly all the images of any particular activity or profession of a single gender, race, ethnicity, or body type, (e.g., are leaders always White or male while people of color or females are included, but as followers or sidekicks)?
- Are there patterns you notice in body language (e.g., poses that suggest demur gestures are appropriate for some types of people but not for others), or hair styles (e.g., do the popular people all have straight hair)?

Stereotypes are never the result of a single media exposure. Their power comes from repetition, especially when the patterns that children see repeated by media are reinforced by things they experience in real life. Repetition can leave an impression, even if the message is never overtly championed in discrete slices of media. That's why being media literate requires that we extend analysis beyond individual media examples to include messages that are conveyed by a child's entire media ecosystem.

Media literate people are also mindful that what is omitted can be every bit as powerful as what's repeated. Children who lack role models that share key pieces of their identity—including

## PAUSE TO **REFLECT**

In 1991, the Florida Department of Citrus placed color versions of these two ads in a variety of popular magazines. Compare the body language in each. What do you notice? If you had to assign one adjective each to describe the body language in each picture, what words would you use? What messages are conveyed by stance, gaze (where eyes are looking), and hand position?

In addition to messages conveyed by body language, what messages are conveyed by choice of costume? How about framing (how much of the frame the child occupies)?

Overall, what's the main message about orange juice? How do these orange juice ads also convey messages about gender roles?

PAUSE TO **REFLECT**

Try this: Go to one of the stock photo websites and type in the word "scientist." What do you find? How many of the images are of people wearing white lab coats working indoors with test tubes and microscopes? Are there any images of scientists working outdoors or doing anything outside of a lab?

If you asked children to draw a scientist, what do you think they would draw? How do you think their ideas will affect their views of science or the possibility that they would want to be a scientist when they grow up?

physical attributes, culture, or temperament—can come to believe that certain jobs or pursuits are beyond their reach (Berry & Asamen 1993). If we're paying attention, we can use media to help fill in the gaps.

Early childhood educators intuitively understand the importance of images as communication. The books we share are filled with illustrations. Some don't even have printed words. Many of us adorn our childcare sites with image-based instruction signs.

Occasionally, in our enthusiasm to introduce young ones to the joys of reading alphabetic text, we fixate on teaching words and leave the pictures behind, as if image-based communication is inferior—something we use only until we learn how to read print. Countless filmmakers, photographers, actors, and artists would remind us that it isn't an either/or choice.

Images have intrinsic value as a form of communication, and from a practical standpoint, today's most common mass media intertwine text and image. It's not a competition. To be media literate, we still need to be fluent print readers and writers. But if we're only fluent in print, we aren't fully prepared to be literate in a digital world.

## Sources


Berry, G.L., & J.K. Asamen. 1993. *Children and Television: Images in a Changing Sociocultural World.* Newbury Park, CA: SAGE Publications.

Epstein, R., J.J. Blake, & T. González. 2017. *Girlhood Interrupted: The Erasure of Black Girls' Childhood.* Report. Washington, DC: Georgetown Law Center on Poverty and Inequality. www.law.georgetown.edu/poverty-inequality-center/wp-content/uploads/sites/14/2017/08/girlhood-interrupted.pdf.

Messaris, P. 1994. *Visual Literacy: Image, Mind, and Reality.* Boulder, CO: Westview Press.

Meyrowitz, J. 1985. *No Sense of Place: The Impact of Electronic Media on Social Behavior.* New York: Oxford University Press.

Scheibe, C., & F. Rogow. 2012. *The Teacher's Guide to Media Literacy: Critical Thinking in a Multimedia World.* Thousand Oaks, CA: Corwin.

CHAPTER 3

# How We Make Meaning

Great teachers are skilled at spotting teachable moments and knowing how to build on them. That ability rests on a thorough understanding of ourselves and the subject matter and skills we're hoping to pass along. The previous chapter began your preparation to be that great teacher by giving you an idea of how we make meaning from images. This chapter adds to your knowledge base by looking at the interactive nature of making meaning from media and how each person's individual experience influences interpretation.

## Our Interpretive Lens

The task of interpretation is sometimes presented as a search for intent—of a writer, poet, musician, film director, painter—as if there is a fixed meaning to every media artifact and all the meaning flows from media to us. And in some ways, that's true. There are techniques that media makers and platform designers use that increase the likelihood of particular reactions. (More on those in Part II.) But the interpretative exchange isn't controlled exclusively by the media maker.

Remembering that media literacy is a social practice helps us to understand that, in fact, making meaning isn't one-sided. Interpretation is always the product of the interaction between media makers and those they reach. To appreciate what *we* bring to the interaction, it is vital to know that we all interpret media through the lens of our own experience.

The core of our interpretive lens is universal, or at least it's shared by everyone in our culture. It's what allows us to agree that this icon 📶 indicates the signal strength of our wireless connection, or that a head nodding up and down is a way of saying yes. Without a core of shared meaning, communication would be impossible.

However, as we saw with the yellow traffic light and emoji examples in the previous chapter, we don't always have shared meaning. That's because, attached to our shared lens, we also each have a unique filter through which we view and process the world, including the media world.

## Our Filters

Take a look at Figure 3.1. In the picture, what do you notice about what this filter does?

Most people notice that the filter enlarges and sharpens the image, making the texture of the grass and sidewalk more clear. It also reverses them. If you looked only through the filter, you would think that the grass is on the left and the sidewalk on the right. This tells us something important about our own personal filters—sometimes they make things more clear, and sometimes they distort. And often, they do both at the same time, just like the filter in the picture.

Everyone's filter has two elements:

1. Our own personal knowledge, skills, beliefs, and experiences
2. The influence of aspects of our lives that are not universal, like where we live, our physical or mental health, or our religion

   These can lead us to consider certain people, things, or activities normal or central and others unusual or marginal. For example, a person in Missouri might see Moroccan food as exotic, but a person in Morocco sees the same food as unremarkable.

Figure 3.1 Photo by Matt Coatney. MattCoatney.com // Instagram: @m.coatney.

Media literacy education improves the quality of our personal filters in two ways:

1. By building on existing knowledge and skills

   This includes developing our awareness of media makers' techniques, purposes, and structures, and their consequences—the things that, in the moment of encounter, we cannot change.

2. By exploring the ways that our culture and identity influence the meanings that we (and others) make of media messages

   This includes self-awareness about the sources of our cultural values and how we approach differences.

Being media literate is a lifelong process of adding clarity to our filters and, as we do so, increasing our understanding of the ways that our perceptions shape our beliefs and choices.

To help you understand how your filter works, the rest of this chapter describes four common filter components. They aren't the only components, but each significantly shapes what you take away from the media you use.

PAUSE TO **REFLECT**

Anthropologist Wade Davis (2020) observed, "The world in which you were born is just one model of reality. Other cultures are not failed attempts at being you—they are unique manifestations of the human spirit." What do you think he is saying and how does it relate to being media literate?

## Expectations and Schemas

If you download a concert expecting a country music performance, but the star decides to devote half the concert to fusion jazz, you're likely to interpret the concert as disappointing, even if the performance is spectacular. Or imagine that you're doing a quick visual scan of thumbnails, looking for a news update. Are you likely to stop at something that looks like anime or a gothic horror thriller? Probably not, because you have expectations about what a news program looks like. Your expectations even influence your interpretation of the information in this book. Would you approach it the same way if it was in the form of, say, a comic book? Probably not, because our expectations influence how we engage with the media we use, and that influences our interpretations.

In the context of child development, expectations are what Piaget described as *schemas*. Schemas are internal scripts that children develop over time to explain how the world works. They include expectations about cause and effect—for example, when I dangle my spaghetti and let go, I know it will fall to the floor rather than float around the room, or when I make the video game monster gobble up the correct answers, I get to hear funny, entertaining sounds. They also include expectations about social patterns or conventions—for example, birthday parties include singing "Happy Birthday To You" as the celebrant is presented with a cake with candles that they blow out. If I attend a birthday party that doesn't include that moment, I'm going to be disappointed, even if I have a good time.

And, just like you, little ones develop schemas about media that influence their interpretations. They might expect that all the people online or on TV are as trustworthy as the grown-ups who care about them. Or they might think that all cartoons are made for kids. Of course, those expectations would be wrong and could lead to significant misinterpretations. So, we teach children that everyone sees things through a filter, and that learning about media can help them make their filter more accurate.

## Confirmation Bias

Schemas are important because in order to learn and remember things, we need to attach new information to something we already know. New information can lead us to change our schema going forward, or the schema can shape the new information so that it will conform to what we already believe to be true.

A version of the latter is a concept called *confirmation bias*. Everyone tends to seek, recall, and believe information that supports what we already believe and to dismiss credible information that challenges our existing beliefs.

There is no skill you can learn to prevent confirmation bias from occurring. It's the way our brain works. We're chemically hardwired to prefer what gives us pleasure (*Yes! I knew I was right!*) over messages that cause cognitive dissonance (*But I've always believed something different. I can't have been wrong all these years!*).

We mitigate the effect of confirmation bias by being aware that it is likely playing a role in shaping what we think and what we choose to share. That awareness is an important motivator for media literate people to routinely analyze *all* media messaging, not just messages with which we disagree.

PAUSE TO **REFLECT**

How does confirmation bias influence the conclusions you draw about children and media? Which headlines catch your attention and how carefully do you scrutinize them? Do you react differently when you see a toddler with a tablet than with a book?

## Trust

Another essential component of our filters are the clues we use to determine how seriously to take particular media claims. That process is more complicated than an on/off switch, with some sources being always trustworthy and others always suspicious. We develop a filter that considers information differently depending on where we encounter it, from whom, and what we want to know. We don't consult a dentist to diagnose a problem with our car and we don't go to an auto mechanic expecting help with a toothache. Expertise matters.

However, we don't rely on expertise in isolation. Media literate people distinguish between veracity and credibility. We never put trust in a source that isn't typically truthful. But we also know that a source can be entirely trustworthy and also wrong.

### PAUSE TO **REFLECT**

How do you determine trustworthiness, especially if you are evaluating claims from people you don't know personally? How do people in your peer group influence your assessment?

If you were looking for a trustworthy source of information about effective strategies for child care or early childhood education, how would each of these factors influence your judgement of someone who is presented as an expert? Consider this checklist.

| Factor | Less likely to trust | More likely to trust | It depends (fill in key variables) |
|---|---|---|---|
| Commercial sponsorship | | | |
| Religious beliefs or affiliation | | | |
| Political affiliation | | | |
| Previous publications in the field | | | |
| Advanced college degree | | | |
| Work experience as an early childhood educator | | | |
| More than 1,000 online followers | | | |
| Trusted by someone you trust | | | |
| Your own past encounters with this source | | | |

- Is there anything missing from this list that you look for?
- Would you give more weight to some factors than to others? What does that tell you about your filter?
- Under what circumstances are you comfortable seeking information from a single source?
- When do you think it is essential to consult multiple sources?
- If you are doing this as a class or as a professional development activity, how do your answers compare to others in the room, and what do you think accounts for any differences?

For example, if you're looking for movie recommendations, you could ask a close friend. But if you know they have very different preferences than yours, they may not be a reliable source, even though they love you and typically act in your best interest. In contrast, the algorithm that is used by your favorite streaming service to track your actual viewing might be a great source, even if it is profit-driven and steers you to choices that provide the company with revenue.

Figuring out which media sources to trust is always a dance of expertise, motive, and purpose. Sometimes the steps to that dance are very simple, and sometimes they are very complex. For media literate people, the dance always begins by asking, "Is this source credible *on this topic?* How do I know?" Understanding one's interpretive lens means also asking, "How is my filter influencing my assessment of the credibility of this source?"

## Desensitization

The previous chapter explained how repetition leads to perceiving certain things as normal. Another important effect that results from media repetition is desensitization. The first or even the second time we see a disturbing image, most of us are upset. Our bodies may even react physically, with a cringe or a queasy stomach. The twentieth time we see that same disturbing image, intellectually we still know that it's troubling, but it no longer upsets us in the way it did at first. We've become desensitized.

The process itself is neither good nor bad. We use it to our benefit when, for example, we train first responders to administer treatment to patients with grotesque injuries. Through repeated exposure, the responders' brains become desensitized to things that would make the rest of us turn away.

That same process can be harmful when, for example, we "witness" lots of media violence or, as gamers, we commit lots of violent acts. For most of us, it's not that we then seek those experiences in real life, but rather, gradually, a sort of numbness sets in that can lead to diminished empathy for victims.

In addition to violence, we can become desensitized to any number of things, including ideas that are embedded in language. For example, we stop noticing how often the culture centers men and marginalizes women when media routinely use gender qualifiers only for females, such as calling the US professional men's basketball league simply the NBA (National Basketball Association), but referring to the women's league as the WNBA (with the "W" for "Women's").

One place we see a pattern of desensitization at work is when there are several disasters clustered in time. The news provides graphic footage of the devastation, with heartbreaking tales of lost loved ones. And often there is an outpouring of financial support for the communities affected by the first event. But if, within a few weeks, there are three or four (or ten!) more events, good luck trying to raise funds for the victims of the last or latest disaster. The public just can't pay attention to the last event the same way that it did the first. Philosopher Sissela Bok (1998) called this form of desensitization *compassion fatigue*. There is only so much we can hold in our hearts at one time.

## Media Choices

Even though desensitization happens to everyone, it's part of our individual filters rather than group lenses, because what we become desensitized to depends on the media with which we interact. And we each choose different combinations of media.

Like literacy, our media interactions are influenced by social circumstances. People with disposable income sample from a very different media menu than those who rely exclusively on media that's available free over the air, who don't live in places with high-speed Internet access, or who can't afford unlimited data plans and the newest devices.

Our media choices also are influenced by our personality, our personal history (such as what feels nostalgic to us), and our peer group. If friends or colleagues are binge-watching a certain drama, playing a popular video game, or listening to particular music, you probably will, too, even if it's only so you can join in the conversation. At the same time, in any given group, there are also diverse media interests that aren't shared by peers. One friend might devote spare time to making TikTok videos, while another never misses a broadcast of their home team's games, and a third knows the lyrics to every song from their three-year-old's favorite video.

These differences contribute to differing filters, not only because it means we are exposed to differing content, but also because in the online world, our media choices are influenced by our media choices. Algorithms determine what we see or what we're offered, and those algorithms are designed to account for what we've already seen and done. So, we influence the algorithm, and it makes selections that, in turn, influence us. That means that what shows up on our screens is different than what others see, even when we are using the same search engine or social media.

The families you serve are part of this dynamic. The combination of individual media choices and each person's unique interpretive lens means that different families are taking in different narratives that shape their ideas about the world and their children. You can learn a lot about them—and possibly find ways to connect—by asking children and families to share their media interests.

PAUSE TO **REFLECT**

What are the central components of your current filter? How do they reflect influences like age, religion, education, race, ethnicity, geographic or national identity, gender identity, or personality type? What else colors your filter?

Can you think of a time when your filter distorted your perception of media or the world? What changed to make your filter more clear, so that now you recognize the distortion?

## Conclusion

The various components of our individual filters and our shared lenses work together to create each person's interpretive lens. Media literacy education helps us to recognize our existing interpretive lens and to construct one that is more sophisticated—more literate.

### Sources


Bok, S. 1998. *Mayhem: Violence as Public Entertainment.* Reading, MA: Perseus Books.

Davis, W. 2020. Wade David quotes. Retrieved 15 June 2020, from http://www.goodreads.com/author/quotes/4652058. Wade Davis.

CHAPTER 4

# Framing: How We Think About Our Work

Like everything we teach, media literacy education is a response to a perceived need. Disagreements over just what that need is have led to a diverse and sometimes contradictory array of practices (Huguet et al. 2019). Understanding the disagreements provides important context for understanding the practice of media literacy education. This chapter walks you through the key disputes among early childhood professionals, so you can be clear about your own approach and how it influences potential outcomes.

## The Power of Frames

If you paint or take a lot of photographs or video, you know that the way you frame your subject is important.

Take a look at Figure 4.1a.

Figure 4.1a Still images from Lindsey Stirling Shadows Video. (Used with permission of Lindsay Stirling.)

Describe what you think it is. Then, make a list of questions you have about the image.

In workshops, people often describe the image as a martial artist or warrior with a sword and shield. Questions typically range from "Where is this from?" to some version of "Who is this person, what are they doing, and why?" The conclusions and questions change when we expand the frame to include more information (Figure 4.1b).

Had you guessed that the shadow was a woman playing a violin? How did using a different frame change the way you understood the content? Now, what questions do you have?

Notice that our questions don't just reveal information about the image. They also reveal something about what *we* bring to the task of interpretation. Some people will still ask, "Where is this from?" and others now want to know who the woman is. But fans will already recognize the woman as performer Lindsey Stirling. They don't have to ask. They may even recognize the still as the beginning of her "Shadows" video. And we could change the frame again to confirm this interpretation (Figure 4.1c).

All media makers use framing to include and exclude information. That makes framing a powerful tool. It can change the way we see the world and the way that others see us.

### Pedagogy as Frame

The concept of framing also applies to thinking. The way we frame an issue or a task influences the way we think about it. When we apply that

Figure 4.1b Still images from Lindsey Stirling Shadows Video. (Used with permission of Lindsay Stirling.)

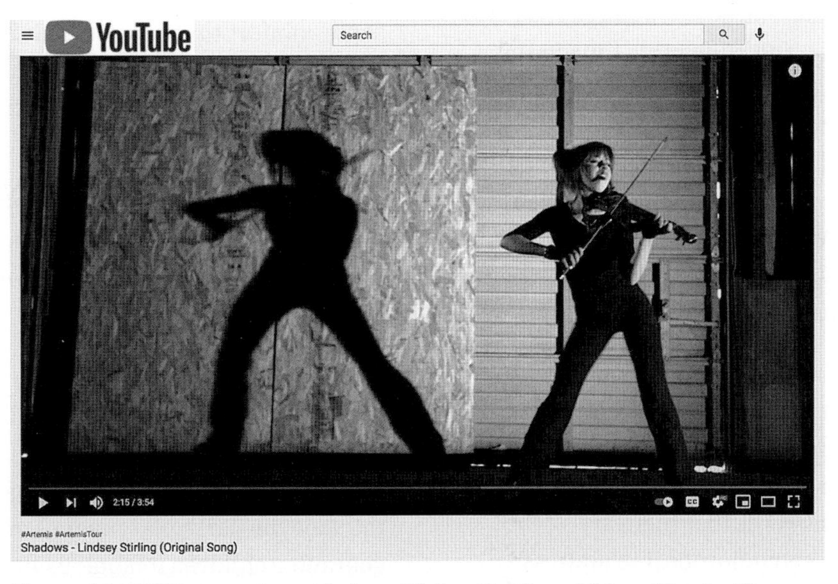


Figure 4.1c Still images from Lindsey Stirling Shadows Video. (Used with permission of Lindsay Stirling.)

process to education, we call it *pedagogy*. Our pedagogy is our approach to teaching—the set of actions that stems from and expresses our beliefs about these aspects of teaching:

- Children's capabilities and vulnerabilities
- The appropriate role of a teacher
- The learning process
- Cultural values
- Professional ethics
- Our general worldview (what we hope the world will be and how we envision children functioning in it when they are grown)

PAUSE TO **REFLECT**

1. Use the pedagogy bullets to create a description of your beliefs about children and good teaching.
2. Think about the way you use media with children. In what ways does your current practice reflect or contradict your pedagogy?
3. Are there any topics or subjects you teach for which your starting point is "first do no harm?"

Like all early childhood education, media literacy pedagogy is grounded in the awareness that "early childhood (birth through age 8) is a uniquely valuable and vulnerable time in the human life cycle. The early childhood years lay the foundation and create trajectories for all later learning and development" (NAEYC 2019, 13). As the Annie E. Casey Foundation (2013) aptly explains, "What happens to children during those critical first years will determine whether their maturing brain has a sturdy foundation or a fragile one" (1).

So if everyone agrees that the early years are vital, why are there wildly differing visions for developmentally appropriate media literacy education? The answer is that there are conflicting beliefs about how best to address the growing presence of media technologies in our lives.

Divergent approaches to media aren't new. Debates about media harms have accompanied the introduction of every form of mass media throughout recorded history. As British researcher Amy Orben (2020) describes in an insightful overview, there is a recurring panic cycle: A swift rise of a new media form is followed by concerns about the inordinate amount of time youth spend with that new media. This provokes attention from people in power, who fund research into the problem. The research concludes that, whereas the media that adults prefer to use is fine, the new media leads to physical, mental, and/or moral harm.

Orben begins her article with a 1941 study of radio effects from the *Journal of Pediatrics*. After surveying hundreds of youths aged 6–16, it concluded that half were "addicted" to radio dramas, and that frequent listening caused sleep disturbances and other poor health outcomes and attitude problems. Others noted that radio robbed children of needed quiet time, and that there was no way to keep children from listening. Such complaints are eerily similar to earlier objections to popular novels and newspapers and later objections to comic books. It isn't surprising to see the cycle repeat for television, video games, and social media.

Knowing that previous predictions of doomed generations were wrong should provide some comfort to those who fear the effects of today's digital media technologies. The most sensational claims will almost certainly prove to be unfounded.

That said, we need not abandon legitimate concerns in order to learn from history. As Orben suggests, we can refine research methods to avoid past mistakes (Orben 2020).

Current claims about media technologies range from complete moral panic (media will destroy children's brains and the fabric of society) to media as salvation (there is no harm and, by the way, the particular media I'm selling will guarantee children a fabulous future). Not surprisingly, reality is more complex than either of these extremes. More on what research reveals in Chapter 10. This chapter's purpose is not to settle the debate, but rather, to explore how our approach to media influences our practice.

## Choosing a Frame for Media Literacy

In a 2019 TED Talk, eminent researcher Sonia Livingstone (2019) observed that digital technologies have "become the terrain on which we are negotiating who we are, our identities, our relationships, our values, and our children's life chances." She was speaking about parenting, but her observation applies equally well to teachers and childcare providers.

The stakes are incredibly high, encompassing every aspect of who we are and who we hope our children will be. Our media decisions aren't just about media, they are an expression of our deepest anxieties and hopes. So, our choice of pedagogy for media literacy education isn't trivial.

It is interesting, then, that historically, when it comes to dealing with media, early childhood education has focused on media effects rather than pedagogy. This section looks at where we've been and suggests that we need to reframe. We won't—and shouldn't—abandon concerns about media in our lives. But in order for media literacy education to be effective, we need to transition from an effects-centered model to one that is centered around teaching and learning.

## Our History: A Public Health Paradigm

The pedagogy that has historically dominated early childhood education's approach to media and children is based in a medical, public health paradigm. In this framing, the paramount need is to keep children safe and healthy, and the essential question is how best to do that. Because health and safety are the goals, a public health prism naturally directs educators' attention to the ways that media pose a threat to children's well-being.

Concerns are broad and substantive: materialism, a weakening of democracy, and environmental sustainability, along with an array of conditions that are typically the domain of health professionals. Susan Linn, founder of Fairplay (formerly the Coalition Campaign for a Commercial Free Childhood), cites media use as a cause of childhood obesity, eating disorders, sexualization, youth violence, family stress, depression, low self-esteem, underage drinking, and tobacco use, and more (Linn 2010). Proponents see media use as displacing vital activities like physical movement, interacting with real people, and handling three-dimensional objects. In keeping with a medical framing, some pathologize such displacement with labels like "play deficit disorder" (Levin 2013, 35) or "nature deficit disorder" (Louv 2005).

Like most public health initiatives, the public health paradigm is concerned with prevention. Young children need to be protected *now*, in the crucial years that their brains, bodies, and foundational relationships are developing or, advocates argue, the negative effects of too much media will follow children their entire lives.

For guidance on strategies, educators acting from a public health paradigm primarily turn to medical sources. One familiar example is *Caring for Our Children* (CFOC), the National Health and Safety Performance Standards Guidelines for Early Care and Education Programs developed by the American Academy of Pediatrics (AAP), together with the American Public Health Association (APHA) and the University of Colorado College of Nursing's National Resource Center for Health and Safety in Child Care and Early Education (NRC) (AAP, APHA, & NRC 2019). Its 2019 standards and guidelines—specifically, "Standard 2.2.0.3: Screen Time/Digital Media Use"—recommend that digital media should not be used at all with children younger than 2 and should be used for no more than one hour total (including time at home) with children ages 2 to 5. That single hour must be "high quality programming," which the standard defines as free of ads, violence, and "sounds that tempt children to overuse the product." And this "high quality" fare must be "viewed with an adult who can help children apply what they are learning to the world around them."

The standard adds several restrictions for which there is broad consensus and substantial supporting research. No digital media during snacks, meals, and nap time. And no media on in the background (that is, when it's not the focus of the activity), because "media can be distracting, and reduce social engagement and learning." The standards go further with their recommendations:

> For children ages 5 and older, digital media can be used to complete homework if necessary, but entertainment media time should not displace healthy activities, such as exercise, refreshing sleep, and family time, including meals.
>
> Caregivers/teachers should communicate with parents/guardians about their guidelines for home media use.
>
> Programs should prioritize physical activity and increased personal social interactions and engagement during the program day. Media use can distract children (and adults), limit conversations and play, and reduce healthy physical activity, increasing the risk for overweight and obesity.
>
> Overuse of media can also be associated with problems with behavior, limit-setting, and emotional and behavioral self-regulation; therefore, caregivers/teachers should avoid using media to calm a child down.

The standards also include this explanatory note:

> *Please note: For the purposes of this standard "screen time/digital media" refers to media content viewed on cell/mobile phone, tablet, computer, television (TV), video, film, and DVD. It does not include video-chatting with family.*

Although the intent of these suggestions is to support the health of young children as they engage with media, some points don't ring true. For example, the suggestion that entertainment media not replace "healthy activities" implies that using media for fun can't be part of a healthy life. Certainly, we all need exercise, sleep, and family time. But we also need entertainment and fun. For many children, that fun comes from engaging with media. Media use and health are not inherently mutually exclusive.

Also, did you notice that the public health paradigm narrows the discussion to digital and screen media, and then further limits it to noninteractive viewing (specifically exempting video chatting, for example)? The CFOC standards do not address use of voice assistants, digital play, cameras, audio recorders, or other screen-based media- or art-making tools. And they don't mention "media literacy," even though they encourage use of media like books and puzzles, and they recognize that media such as classroom posters can convey stereotypes (CFOC Standard 2.1.1.8). This gap is mirrored in other popular guidelines. For example, neither the widely used Early Childhood Environment Rating Scale (ECERS) rating scales nor recent Head Start guidelines address media literacy at all.

When use of screen media and well-being are positioned as mutually exclusive, the resulting risk assessment is obvious: the risks posed by screen media greatly outweigh any potential benefits. The logical strategy, then, is to limit "exposure," as if screen time is akin to toxic radiation (Wohlwend 2011). It's a pedagogy of avoidance.

In some versions of the paradigm, this means a total ban. Others, like the CFOC standards, approach screen media more like a drug. Children can benefit from using a proper dose, but too much is dangerous, so adults impose significant limits. And on the infrequent occasions when media are used, adults are always included. Children are never permitted to use media by themselves.

To find "high quality programming," those who act from a public health paradigm rely on children's media researchers to determine the efficacy of the media "drug." Well-respected researchers, mostly from the field of psychology (Daniel Anderson, Deborah Linebarger, Valeria Lovelace, Shelley Pasnik, and Ellen Wartella to name just a few), test a range of educational claims for selected series, apps, or games. Those that demonstrate positive results are differentiated from potentially problematic entertainment fare, which is to be avoided. This limits acceptable children's media choices to those that are noncommercial and researcher-approved. In a moment we'll explore why that's a problem.

In a public health paradigm, if there are media literacy lessons at all, they typically are designed to inform children about media dangers, usually via direct instruction. The consistent message to children is that there are always better ways to spend their time than to use screens.

## The Education Paradigm

Because the public health approach to media in early childhood has been so common for so long, you may have found yourself nodding in agreement with some of its strategies, or even thinking, "I do that." Adopting an education framing won't force you to give up everything you do now. In fact, you'll likely find that the strategies for teaching several core media literacy competencies are quite familiar.

The challenge of the public health paradigm for media literacy educators is not its concerns about media effects. Rather, the challenge is that counting screen minutes isn't an *education* strategy. It doesn't help children develop media literacy skills, knowledge, or habits.

Everyone agrees that keeping children safe and healthy is a basic, nonnegotiable responsibility, even when we disagree about the exact nature of the risks or about how much risk is acceptable. The two paradigms are not stand-ins for opposing sides of the debates over media effects. Actually, most media literacy educators and advocates are involved in media literacy because we believe it is important to pay significant attention to the role of media in our lives. Given the prevalence of media, it would be foolhardy to do otherwise.

In the United States, nearly all children 8 and under live in a home with at least one television and mobile device. Prior to the COVID-19 pandemic, screen time estimates for this age group averaged about two-and-a-half hours per day (Rideout & Robb 2020). Similar reports of high exposure and high usage rates are common in developed nations. In the United Kingdom, for example, 76 percent of preschoolers regularly use tablets, smartphones, or computers (Childwise 2019).

In the public health paradigm, these observations manifest as the argument that kids are already spending too much time in front of screens, so let's not add to the problem by using screen media in childcare settings or primary school. In an education paradigm, the ubiquity of screens (and other media) is exactly what makes the integration of media essential.

Given the reality that media are integral to our culture, it seems odd to expect educators to respond by intentionally excluding media from our work. Just as it would be absurd to suggest that we could help children become print literate by keeping them away from books, it is counterproductive to suggest that we can help them become media literate by keeping them away from media. That's why an education lens shifts the discussion from *if* we should use media (or for how many minutes) to curriculum-based decisions about *how, what, when,* and *why.* It's what the NAEYC and Fred Rogers Center position statement on technology calls "intentional use" (2012, 5).

This shift also changes how we evaluate our work. In a public health approach, success is measured by how well *adults* keep children away from screens. An education approach measures *children's* progress. It starts with the goal of creating a media literate society and asks what skills and knowledge are needed to reach that goal. Success is determined by children's acquisition of the knowledge and skills that we identify as appropriate for their developmental level.

The education frame accepts that no matter the choices we might wish families and care providers would make about screens, nearly all children are using media technologies, and they will continue to use them with or without us. From an education vantage point, it is better for children to use devices *with* us. Otherwise, their technology habits are likely to come from marketers, peers, or others who may not share our expertise or our concern for children's well-being. So, while a health frame says brains develop better if we wait to introduce screen media until children are older, the education paradigm says that media, used appropriately, can open up new worlds and nurture healthy brain development. Besides, if we want to help children establish healthy habits, it doesn't make sense to wait until behavior patterns are entrenched. Asking children to unlearn bad habits is harder than helping them establish good routines in the first place.

The paradigms also view children's essential nature differently. A public health frame casts children as vulnerable to harmful influences, including media, so little ones are given no independent opportunities to use media the way they might independently play with blocks or dolls.

The education frame agrees that young children are uniquely vulnerable but responds by asking educators to help children gradually build the skills and knowledge they need to make them less so—just like teaching children how to cross a street safely so that eventually they can walk around their neighborhood without holding our hands. The foundational assumption of the teaching–learning process assumes that children are essentially capable and that educators help children gain a sense of independence and control by providing opportunities to apply what they have learned. It's impossible to provide those opportunities if your primary goal is to keep children away from media. Our views of children's nature always translate into practice.

The education paradigm relies on a constructivist model in which adults build on the skills and knowledge that children already possess. In contrast, the job of a public health educator is to transmit information, so lessons often are grounded in a "sage-on-the-stage" or "banking" model, with adults telling children (who are assumed to know little or nothing about media) what to think.

For example, in one common lesson using a health frame, an adult explains to children that advertisers are fooling them. The activity positions adults as the media interpreters and children as fools. Children learn that they can't trust their own judgment (because they've been fooled) and that they can't ever trust advertisers. On the surface, that might seem like an important message, but it turns out to be a problem when children encounter public service announcements that we want them to trust (like following rules about masks and social distancing during a pandemic).

Educators avoid those outcomes by changing the language. They let kids in on advertisers' "secret code" by teaching clues that children can look for to find out what an ad might really be saying. This positions children as capable of analyzing ads for themselves and begins to give them the skills to do so. A small shift in the way we frame a lesson can make a huge difference in what children learn, not only about the topic, but also about themselves. It's not that we don't teach about advertising or explain that advertisers are more likely to be serving their own rather than children's best interests. It's that when we use an education frame, we do it differently. *How* we teach is as important as *what* we teach.

One of the most striking differences between the paradigms is what they mean by the word "media." In a public health frame, media nearly always refers to electronic screens. In an education frame, the task is literacy the way that Paulo Freire conceived it—reading and writing the word *and* the world. In a child's world, media aren't restricted to screens.

PAUSE TO **REFLECT**

Take a walk around your site, both indoors and outside. Identify all the media children routinely encounter. Don't forget to include non-screen media. How many do you routinely discuss with children? How many do you think the children would identify as media?

The education paradigm's approach to screen use flows from there. It includes providing children with opportunities to think more deeply about the media they routinely encounter—including screen media that wouldn't qualify as "high quality" or "educational." If it's part of their world, it's important to create spaces where we can help them grapple with it.

This is particularly true for little ones, who don't automatically apply information learned about one thing to another. If all we ever model is analyzing books, then we make it seem like thinking deeply about other media is unimportant. If we exclude screens, we send exactly the opposite of our intended message that it is important to question all media, perhaps especially screen media.

Increasingly there is also a concern that the term "screen time" isn't meaningful anymore (for example, see Daugherty et al. 2014; Reeves et al. 2019; Strauss 2019; Whitlock & Masur 2019). Because we now do so many different things with screen technologies, the phrase is too broad to be scientifically or practically helpful. Media scholars Sonia Livingstone and Alicia Blum-Ross add that measuring time spent "may work in the field of health, where less sugar or more exercise is generally useful advice. But in relation to digital technologies, where neither less nor more is the obvious answer in a thoroughly digitally mediated age, a different approach is needed" (Livingstone & Blum-Ross 2020, 44).

As the NAEYC and Fred Rogers Center position statement on technology puts it, "Not all screens are created equal" (2012, 3). What children are actually doing with media technologies is a much more salient variable than time spent. Effective education is not about counting screen minutes; it's about making screen minutes count. Even the media policy of the AAP (2016), often cited to justify limits on media use, calls for media literacy education for children ages 5 and older, recommending that pediatricians "advocate for and promote information and training in media literacy."

PAUSE TO **REFLECT**

Consider common recommendations for quality early childhood education practices:

- You can't just tell kids what not to do; you need to also tell them what they *can* do.
- Children are most engaged by things that sprout from their own interests.
- Children learn through play, especially free play.

Which paradigm seems like the best match for each practice and why? Which of the practices could fit either frame (and what would that look like)?

## Who Are We in This Moment? Who Do We Want to Be?

Finally, just as our questions about the pictures at the beginning of this chapter reveal something about *us*, the frame we choose influences which parts of ourselves we bring to the task of teaching media literacy. (See Appendix: Am I Using a Media Literacy Education Paradigm? at the end of this chapter.) As Akiea Gross, educator and founder of Woke Kindergarten, reminds us, "the way that we show up, the way that we enter spaces . . . [is] part of the curriculum" (Washington 2020).

We can enter the relationship from a place of anxiety about media, but that means taking the risk that our guilt and apprehensions seep into the design of teaching practices, even unintentionally. We need to be sure that the person we are when we walk into the room with children is the person we want to be. Children pick up on our emotional state. If we're anxious, they know.

It is exhausting to be in a constant state of alertness, thinking that we must police media use because we worry that every minute of screen time puts children in greater peril. Play is out of the question because in the dualism of a public health paradigm, authentic play—which is healthy—happens only separate from screens—which are unhealthy. When our practice is infused with anxiety, media literacy education isn't much fun, and neither are we.

PAUSE TO **REFLECT**

What if we saw children's media use as a strength rather than a deficit? What could we do to help them build on the skills they already possess?

An education frame asks us to approach the task differently. It requires us to bring the parts of ourselves that are creative and hopeful, even playful, as we craft activities that empower children through skill-building. In an education paradigm, media literacy activities invite a sense of wonder and exploration, and we share in children's amazement and delight as they master new skills or understand important ideas for the first time. It's easy for our joy to overshadow whatever anxiety we might feel.

Effective early childhood education is based on cultivating a positive relationship with each individual child. Barriers that prevent children from sharing with us significant aspects of their daily life and culture—including media—can sabotage that process.

The child who comes into our care with a favorite TV character emblazoned on their backpack or t-shirt is sharing with us an important part of their identity. Likewise, a child who bonds with a parent—especially a noncustodial parent—by playing a video game or watching sports or movies on TV may be eager to tell stories about that media experience as a way to share a significant aspect of their life with us. Same thing with a child whose immigrant family uses digital technologies to provide hard-to-find daily lessons that strengthen family ties by teaching native language, religion, or cultural traditions (Livingstone & Blum-Ross 2020). If we respond to these screen-based activities with disapproval instead of curiosity, we make it harder to develop a trusting relationship.

Television shows, songs, movies, and games function as cohort markers. In later years, they serve as common ground, allowing strangers to bond over shared memories of favorite characters or music. When childcare providers or teachers signal that discussions of media are off-limits, we risk shutting out conversations that can be an important conduit for connection.

This isn't about staying silent in the presence of danger or surrendering our professional judgment. We have a responsibility to challenge media that make it harder to raise healthy, ethical, engaged children. But we also have a responsibility to make sure that we aren't just imposing *our* tastes or preferences on those who don't share them.

As media scholar David Buckingham (2011) has pointed out, often objections to particular media are more about asserting a moral authority based in class privilege—and I'd add racial and religious privilege—than any real proof of harm. Before we act on our instinct to protect children against media that *we* find troubling, we need to pause and be clear that we aren't simply replicating the power dynamics of existing social structures or imposing our own cultural preferences on families whose culture differs from our own.

PAUSE TO **REFLECT**

In her thoughtful review of the history of literacy, Kathleen Tyner (1998) writes, "Once a literacy shift is set in motion, it gathers its own momentum. Questions about whether the changes in literacy practices are for the better or for the worse depend on the loyalties and vantage point of the questioner" (17). So, what are the "loyalties and vantage points" of those who resist media literacy education in early childhood? Of supporters?

# Conclusion

Media literacy education invites us to bring our best selves to the table. It provides a way to act on our concerns about media by engaging as a guide rather than in the role of compliance officer or judge. Being a guide allows us to strengthen relationships by welcoming and cultivating children's media-related questions and conversations, and it grows children's skills in the process. The rest of this book provides examples of what that looks like in practice.

## Am I Using a Media Literacy Education Paradigm?

For decades, our work with children has been grounded in certain truths. We use inquiry to connect media literacy education practice to these essential concepts. For each concept below, circle the question you are most likely to ask, or pose your own question. Then consider what the question reveals about your approach to teaching media literacy.

› **Free play is essential to the development of children's cognitive and social-emotional capacities.**

- **a.** *How do screens interfere with play?*
- **b.** *How can I help children integrate a device like a tablet or camera into their free play without it becoming a distraction?*
- **c.** *How can children gain the benefits of free play in a world that includes all sorts of media?*

*My question is* ______________________________
______________________________________________.

› **Stories are central to children's exploration of values, relationships, and the mysteries of the world.**

- **a.** *How much screen time is okay before it displaces better storytellers, like books or people?*
- **b.** *How do I integrate digital storytelling into my teaching?*
- **c.** *What forms do narratives take in the digital world and how do we help children explore all of them?*

*My question is* ______________________________
______________________________________________.

› **Having frequent opportunities to engage in meaningful conversations is important for language and social-emotional development.**

- **a.** *How do we limit tech time so we can provide more time for authentic conversations?*
- **b.** *Can we use Alexa, Siri, Echo, or other voice assistants to help children practice language skills? How about conversations with robots or stuffed animals with AI enhancements?*
- **c.** *How do people engage in meaningful conversations in the digital world and how do we best prepare children to engage in those conversations?*

*My question is* ______________________________
______________________________________________.

› **Developing meaningful, nurturing, stable relationships with caring adults is vital to healthy development.**

- **a.** *How do we limit screen time, so children participate in more interactions with real people?*
- **b.** *How might I use digital devices to help children keep in touch with loved ones who are far away?*
- **c.** *How do people establish and maintain caring relationships in the digital world and how can we make sure that children are included in those opportunities?*

*My question is* ______________________________
______________________________________________.

If you are working with a staff, you might invite people to complete this reflection independently, and then compare answers to identify the sources of variations in practice. Then, as a group, try to answer all the "c" questions, as well as any questions generated by staff members.

Note: The "a" questions reflect a public health paradigm. The "b" questions are typical of someone who teaches with technology or who is focused on digital literacy, but not necessarily media literacy. The "c" questions reflect a media literacy education approach.

## Sources


AAP (American Academy of Pediatrics) Council on Communications and Media. 2016. "Media Use in School-Aged Children and Adolescents." *Pediatrics* 138 (5): e20162592.

AAP (American Academy of Pediatrics), APHA (American Public Health Association), & NRC (National Resource Center for Health and Safety in Child Care and Early Education). 2019. *Caring for Our Children: National Health and Safety Performance Standards; Guidelines for Early Care and Education Programs*. 4th ed. Itasca, IL: AAP. https://nrckids.org/files/CFOC4%20pdf-%20FINAL.pdf.

Annie E. Casey Foundation. 2013. *The First Eight Years: Giving Kids a Foundation for Lifetime Success*. Policy report. Baltimore: Annie E. Casey Foundation. www.aecf.org/resources/the-first-eight-years-giving-kids-a-foundation-for-lifetime-success.

Buckingham, D. 2011. *The Material Child: Growing Up in Consumer Culture*. Malden, MA: Polity.

Childwise. 2019. *The Monitor Preschool Report 2019: Key Behaviour Patterns Among 0–4 Year Olds*. Report. Norwich, UK: Childwise.

Daugherty, L., R. Dossani, E.-E. Johnson, & C. Wright. 2014. "Moving Beyond Screen Time: Redefining Developmentally Appropriate Technology Use in Early Childhood Education." Policy brief. Santa Monica, CA: RAND. www.rand.org/pubs/research_reports/RR673z2.html.

Huguet, A., J. Kavanagh, G. Baker, & M.S. Blumenthal. 2019. *Exploring Media Literacy Education as a Tool for Mitigating Truth Decay*. Report. Santa Monica, CA: RAND. www.rand.org/pubs/research_reports/RR3050.html.

Levin, D.E. 2013. *Beyond Remote-Controlled Childhood: Teaching Young Children in the Media Age*. Washington, DC: NAEYC.

Linn, S. 2010. "The Commercialization of Childhood and Children's Well-Being: What Is the Role of Health Care Providers?" *Paediatrics & Child Health* 15 (4): 195–7.

Livingstone, S. 2019. "Parenting in the Digital Age." Talk presented at TEDSummit 2019 in Edinburgh, Scotland. www.ted.com/talks/sonia_livingstone_parenting_in_the_digital_age.

Livingstone, S., & A. Blum-Ross. 2020. *Parenting for a Digital Future: How Hopes and Fears About Technology Shape Children's Lives*. New York: Oxford University Press.

Louv, R. 2005. *Last Child in the Woods: Saving Our Children from Nature-Deficit Disorder*. Chapel Hill, NC: Algonquin Books.

NAEYC. 2019. "Advancing Equity in Early Childhood Education." Position statement. Washington, DC: NAEYC. www.naeyc.org/resources/position-statements/equity.

NAEYC & Fred Rogers Center for Early Learning and Children's Media. 2012. "Technology and Interactive Media as Tools in Early Childhood Programs Serving Children from Birth Through Age 8." Joint position statement. Washington, DC: NAEYC. www.naeyc.org/sites/default/files/globally-shared/downloads/PDFs/resources/position-statements/ps_technology.pdf.

Orben, A. 2020. "The Sisyphean Cycle of Technology Panics." *Perspectives on Psychological Science* 15 (5): 1143–57.

Reeves, B., N. Ram, T.N. Robinson, J.J. Cummings, C.L. Giles, J. Pan, A. Chiatti, M. Cho, K. Roehrick, X. Yang, A. Gagneja, M. Brinberg, D. Muise, Y. Lu, M. Luo, A. Fitzgerald, & L. Yeykelis. 2019. "*Screenomics:* A Framework to Capture and Analyze Personal Life Experiences and the Ways that Technology Shapes Them." *Human–Computer Interaction* 36 (2): 150–201.

Rideout, V., & M.B. Robb. 2020. *The Common Sense Census: Media Use by Kids Age Zero to Eight, 2020*. Report. San Francisco: Common Sense Media. www.commonsensemedia.org/sites/default/files/uploads/research/2020_zero_to_eight_census_final_web.pdf.

Strauss, E. 2019. "Why We Should Stop Calling It 'Screen Time' to Our Kids." *CNN Health,* November 14. www.cnn.com/2019/11/14/health/screen-time-rename-parenting-house-wellness-strauss/index.html.

Tyner, K. 1998. *Literacy in a Digital World: Teaching and Learning in the Age of Information*. Mahwah, NJ: Lawrence Erlbaum Associates.

Washington, A. 2020. "How Do You Teach Antiracism to the Youngest Students?" *The Hechinger Report,* August 27. https://hechingerreport.org/how-do-you-teach-antiracism-to-the-youngest-students.

Whitlock, J., & P.K. Masur. 2019. "Disentangling the Association of Screen Time with Developmental Outcomes and Well-Being: Problems, Challenges, and Opportunities." *JAMA Pediatrics* 173 (11): 1021–2.

Wohlwend, K.E. 2011. "Constructing the Child at Play: From the Schooled Child to Technotoddler and Back Again." Paper presented at the National Council of Teachers of English Annual Convention, in Chicago, IL.

PART I

# Getting Ready Wrap-Up

## PAUSE TO **REVIEW**

How would you explain these terms or concepts to a colleague or friend?

- confirmation bias
- desensitization
- implicit bias
- interpretive lens
- inquiry-rich environment
- "reading" images
- the difference between veracity and credibility
- the power of repetition
- visual homonym
- pedagogy of avoidance

What does it mean to say that literacy, including media literacy, is a social practice?

In no more than 280 characters, how would you describe the major differences between a public health and an education approach to media literacy?

______________________________

______________________________

______________________________

## PAUSE TO **REFLECT**

One thing I learned was ______________________________

One "hmmm moment," I had was ______________________________

(A "hmmm moment" is something that made you pause and say, "Hmmm. I'm not sure about that. I need to think more about it.")

One sentence from Part I that I want to remember is:

______________________________

______________________________

PART II

# Defining the Task

**Imagine that someone handed you a hammer and a hacksaw and said, "Okay, start." You'd likely look at them quizzically and answer, "Start what?" Because we never start projects with tools. We start by defining the task. Then we choose (or design) the tools we need to successfully meet the needs of that task. And those tools might be different for different people, depending on their experience, skills, and values.**

In education, activities and teaching strategies are tools. A review of media literacy lessons won't make sense unless it is situated in the context of our goals. Once we have a clear picture of our task and our own skill set and approach, we're ready to determine specific strategies to engage children. As you prepare to examine the goals of media literacy education, ask yourself:

*What are my goals for media literacy education? How has my interpretive lens influenced the way I answer that question?*

CHAPTER 5

# What Is This "Media Literacy Education" of Which You Speak?

More than two decades have passed since we entered the 21st century, so it's a little weird that some educators still talk about 21st-century skills as if they are part of some future vision. Media literacy education provides an immediate way to address 21st-century skills and also gear up for what comes next. It combines literacy with critical thinking and reflection skills in 10 core competencies that prepare people to tackle the challenges of life in a media-driven society. You might think of it as literacy for the real world. This chapter outlines the competencies and explores their intertwined nature.

## Starting with a Question

As we consider how to teach media literacy, we are immediately faced with the challenge of trying to plan for a future with capabilities that we don't yet fully fathom. We are just beginning to grapple with the societal impacts of artificial intelligence, digital surveillance, 3D imaging, voice-controlled interfaces, and the prospects of quantum computing. It's a good time to shift our questions to account for the possibilities.

We will continue to ask, "What do we do about problems that media create?" But in the context of ever-expanding functions offered by digital devices, it's time to de-center debates about screens. It isn't enough to simply add "opportunities" to our question, as in "What do we do about the problems *and opportunities* that media create?" The point isn't to achieve balance; it is about shifting the question entirely. We now must ask,

> How have digital communication technologies changed what it means to be literate, and what do the changes in literacy mean for our practice as educators?

## Media Literacy Education Goals

To address the literacy question in ways that are meaningful for educational practice, we begin with our endpoint, our "big picture" goal:

**The purpose of media literacy education**

**is to develop the**

***habits of inquiry***

**and**

***skills of expression***

**people need to be**

**lifelong learners,**

**critical and creative thinkers,**

**effective communicators, and**

**engaged, ethical community members and citizens.**

**(Adapted from NAMLE 2007)**

In other words, being a learner, thinker, communicator, and citizen inevitably involves media, and we want that involvement to be thoughtful, ethical, effective, and creative. To reach that future, we focus on the development of *habits* and *skills*.

*Habits of inquiry* means routinely asking relevant, analytical questions and knowing how to find credible answers. In a media literate society, inquiry would be every person's default mode.

*Skills of expression* means being able to effectively share ideas using the wide range of communication tools available. It includes writing and image making, artistic expression, and also knowing how to engage and collaborate in a world where media communication isn't just occurring in a one-way direction.

When you create media literacy activities, these two things—*habits of inquiry* and *skills of expression*—will serve as touchstones. Outcomes will fall into one or both categories.

We also want to encourage specific dispositions. After all, it doesn't help to have media literacy skills if one isn't also inclined to use them. So, we immerse children in a celebratory culture of inquiry that values reason and evidence, curiosity and creativity, ethics and responsibility, self-awareness and agency, respect and justice, diversity and community.

PAUSE TO **REFLECT**

Look carefully at the purpose statement for media literacy education. Why do you think the author chose to present it this way instead of as a standard paragraph? How did that choice influence the way you read the statement and made meaning from it? What's the link between this reflection exercise and media literacy?

## Core Competencies

To transform goals into achievements, we move from the general to the specific. The first step is to understand key media literacy skills, knowledge, and dispositions. Media literate people can do these things well and are motivated to want to do them:

**Access:** facilitate equitable availability and effective use of media

**Attend:** notice media, media structures, and media messages

**Comprehend:** accurately identify types of media and understand basic media messages

**Inquire:** use relevant, probative questions to analyze media messages and find credible answers

**Reflect:** ask how media or media messages affect me or others

**Evaluate:** ask if this media is right for me or my task

**Communicate & Create:** express oneself using multiple types of media

**Engage & Explore:** use media actively for purpose and enjoyment

**Connect & Collaborate:** use media to work and communicate with others

**Act:** take meaningful individual and community-minded steps based on what one knows about media and media messages

Combined, the competencies give children the essential foundations for a media literate life. Envisioning the competencies as gears illustrates the importance of the word *combined*. Each of the competencies exists independently, but their power comes from being interconnected. As children develop their media literacy competencies, the size of the gears increases. The larger the gears, the more power the system generates (Figure 5.1).

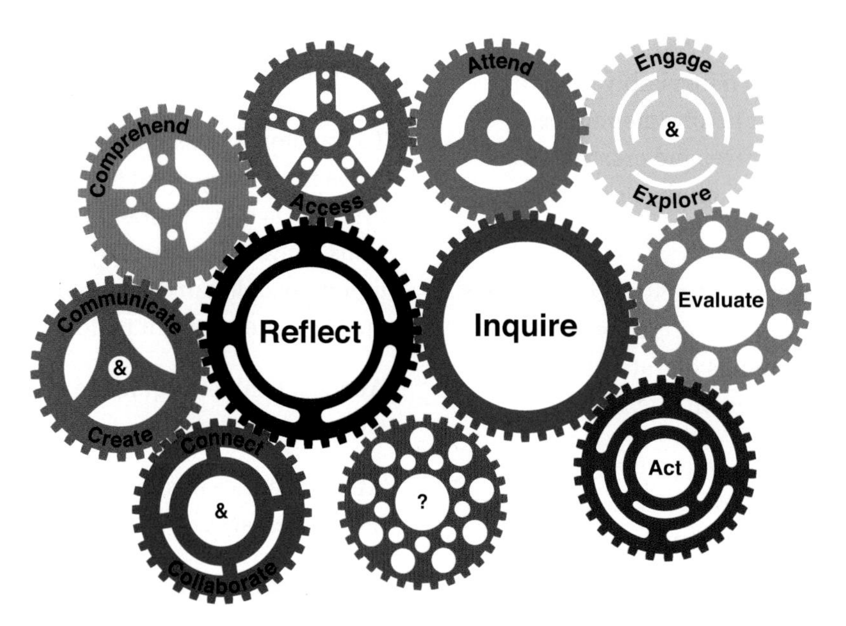


Figure 5.1 Media Literacy Competencies.

If you look carefully, you'll see that Inquire and Reflect are in the center and slightly larger than the other competencies. That's because they are the core of media literacy practice. All of the other competencies will incorporate Inquiry or Reflection (or both) in some way.

The interdependence is a bit like reading print. It is important to know how to sound out words, but if you never learn the meaning of the words, the ability to correlate letters with sounds isn't very useful. Similarly, knowing how to use digital media technologies but without inquiry or reflection, doesn't ignite the benefits of being media literate.

In media literacy education, it is important for children to develop *all* the competencies. We even include a gear with a question mark because as technologies and society continue to change, it is possible that new competencies will emerge.

When you are just starting out, trying to teach so many competencies can sound like an impossibly complex and time-consuming task. Ten competencies are a lot. What makes it manageable is that the competencies are interconnected and overlapping.

To see how this works, let's take a closer look at each competency. We'll examine the end goal—that is, the ways that an adult might demonstrate the competency's skills, knowledge, and dispositions. We'll also take a quick peek into how early childhood educators might begin to lay the foundations needed to reach each goal.

## Access: facilitate equitable availability and effective use of media

To maintain a media literate society, communities, homes, schools, and child care sites, regardless of wealth or location, must be equipped with vital media tools, including affordable high-speed, high-capacity Internet access. Advocating for or providing that type of universal access, on par with other essential public utilities (like potable water and electricity) are key to the *Access* competency, at least for adults.

Young children aren't in a position to be decision makers about the availability of media, so the focus of the *Access* competency in early childhood education (ECE) is primarily on helping children learn how to use media tools in thoughtful, ethical ways. Media literate people who excel at *Access* are eager to learn and are able to:

- Take advantage of the full range of tools offered by common communication technologies

- Understand enough of the "grammar" and functions shared by digital tools to easily figure out how to use new or unfamiliar devices, apps, or platforms
- Understand the features of online sites and digital tools well enough to keep themselves safe and make informed decisions about use
- Follow the rules and etiquette of media activities that make the experience more productive and rewarding

*Access* does not require mastery of every available device, platform, or program. Given the array of options and constant change, that would be an impossible standard.

### *Access* in ECE

Early childhood educators who help children learn how books work (how we read English left to right, turn pages in sequence, find the names of authors and illustrators) already teach *Access*. To expand that concept to other types of media, some early childhood professionals become "media mentors" who introduce children and families to cameras, computers, coding, apps, and the like (for example, Donohue 2017; Haines, Campbell, & ALSC 2016). They show them how to use media technologies to achieve their goals (wanting to play a video game with their friend or take and send a picture to a relative in another country, for example) and also allow for open-ended exploration. According to the Erikson Institute's TEC Center, educators should

> Create a low-risk environment for children to learn how to use and select technologies such as makerspaces, STEM activities, or a technology "petting zoo." Allow children to explore these spaces and materials without requiring a specific product as an outcome. (Herdzina & Lauricella 2020, 16)

Media literacy educators also make sure to pair technical coaching with habits of *Inquiry* and *Reflection*, interweaving the competencies. So, for example, we show children how to use tablets to take, save, edit, and share photos. As part of that instruction, we help them think through when and why they might want to take a picture. We make sure they know that it is disrespectful to take someone's picture and share it without the subject's permission. We teach not only the *how*, but also the *why* and the *what if* (considering the possible outcomes of the photographer's choices and the parameters of ethical behavior).

Making sure that all children have access to media technologies is an obvious equity issue. Equally important is helping children learn to effectively use media tools. Research indicates that children from well- and under-resourced families and communities use devices differently (Neuman & Celano 2012). Children who benefit from high-speed wireless access, unlimited data plans, the latest devices and content, readily available adult coaching, and free time to experiment are likely to engage in a wider range of tasks than those who don't. So, we advocate for equitable access to hardware and infrastructure, and also help bridge existing gaps by showing children what's possible and providing hands-on opportunities for them to explore.

Another aspect of the *Access* competency is the ability to use media safely, so media literacy educators provide guidance on things like cyber safety, privacy, targeted marketing, and in-app purchases. Eventually children will be able to balance for themselves the risks and rewards of using specific media. In the meantime, adults have a responsibility to serve as gatekeepers. We decide which devices and content young children are able to *Access*. We accompany that control with media literacy education so that children won't always need us to make decisions for them.

## **Attend:** notice media, media structures, and media messages

Like the proverbial fish who doesn't see the water in which they swim, many of us are so accustomed to the omnipresence of media, we ignore much of what's there. Media literacy requires that noticing becomes routine.

We use the label *Attend* rather than *notice* because the goal is more than simple perception. A scientist might use the term *observe*. We look carefully and with purpose.

People who have fully grasped the *Attend* competency are aware of obvious media via screens and speakers, and also media in the form of branded clothing, maps, product packaging, bumper stickers, store displays, surveillance cameras, and the like. They recognize that their social network profiles, pages, posts, and platforms are media.

They are also aware of media structures and features. They understand the ways that these influence messages and users' experiences. So, for example, when they use YouTube, they pay attention to the video and also to all of the things on screen around the video and whether or not "Autoplay" is on or off. They also recognize that

- "Free" apps or platforms may not require cash, but instead require trades, like giving up privacy or personal data, or taking time to view ads.
- Apps and platforms use subtle, and sometimes deceptive, design (dark patterns) to influence behavior (e.g., making purchasing buttons big, bright, and hard to avoid, or requiring the user to opt out rather than opt in to automatic subscription renewals).
- Recommendations, ads, or search results on social media and search engines are based on what the platform's owner already knows about you.
- Comments don't always reflect the opinions of actual people, but rather are sometimes bots or paid endorsements.
- "Convenience" technologies like video doorbells, voice assistants, and "smart" appliances (the Internet of Things), as well as interactive toys, may be listening in or tracking people and reporting data back to the company that made or sold the device, which may then share the data with others, including law enforcement or other government agencies.

Attention matters because we can't think analytically about media we don't notice. The media literate response we're ultimately looking for isn't just "Oh, look, there's some media!" It's "There's some media. It's time for my brain to kick in and use all those great analysis and reflection skills I have learned!"

### *Attend* in ECE

For the youngest children, we nurture the *Attend* competency by simple routines such as pointing out and naming the media we use, see, or hear: *Did anyone notice the new sign outside our center today?* or *I'm going to add this flyer about the farmers' market to the media on the refrigerator. Which magnets should we use to make sure it stays put? The magnets are media, too. The fridge has become a media gallery!*

It isn't realistic to think that we're going to provide this level of narration all the time. Instead, we narrate just often enough that little ones begin to internalize the habit of *Attending*. Gradually, they'll come to understand that paying attention to the various media in their environment is important to do, even if they don't yet fully understand why.

## **Comprehend:** accurately identify types of media and understand basic media messages

Imagine being asked to determine which physicist's explanation of the world is most convincing: the one arguing for string theory, a second who supports emergent gravity, or a third advocating for loop quantum gravity. You recognize the individual numbers in their mathematical proofs, and you can define words like *loop* and *gravity*, but chances are, you can barely follow their reasoning. And because you can't comprehend their presentations, you can't analyze or draw conclusions. It's not because you lack intelligence; it's because you don't have a deep background in physics (unless, of course, you do; in which case, just ignore this example!).

Media *Comprehension* similarly requires more than simple identification of discrete parts of a message. It's about making meaning from those parts. For example, most children could point to a movie screen and identify a shoe, a girl, a prince, and a pumpkin. That does not mean they understand the story of Cinderella. In a media literacy context, *Comprehension* means having the requisite knowledge to understand the sum of what you're looking at or hearing, not just individual parts. Media literate people who *Comprehend* do the following:

- understand the surface level messages of a story, video, song, infographic, and similar types of media
- differentiate between types of media, especially when the differences influence our understanding of the core message (e.g., a fictional story versus a documentary, or a sponsorship banner featuring a pet food company compared with a PSA for the local animal shelter)
- distinguish between things that are real and that are fantasy (this isn't as straightforward as it might seem, even for adults, so we'll examine the issue in more detail on pp. 121–122)

### *Comprehend* in ECE

Most teachers already check for comprehension when they give instructions or read aloud. Media literacy educators extend that practice to all sorts of media.

For the youngest children, comprehension might be as simple as naming things they see on a screen or in a book and then pointing out those same things in their environment: "Look, there is a car in this picture [pointing to the car]. And look through the window. There are automobiles parked outside, including a red one, like the one in the book!" Toddlers can begin to help name similarities and differences of objects in media and in their off-screen lives:

> *The horses in the cartoon are blue and purple. But you've seen people riding real horses. What colors were those horses?*
>
> [Child answers, "Brown . . . and white spots."]
>
> *Yes. And remember, we saw a black horse, too? And some horses are gray or chestnut. But real horses in nature are never blue or green. That's one of the fun things about cartoons. They can help us imagine pretend worlds, so the people who make the cartoon can make horses any color they want. If you made this cartoon, what color would you make the horses?*

We can also check for *Comprehension* while nurturing the habit of thinking about media messages by inviting children to notice and retell the stories they see in videos, movies, and even video games.

## **Inquire:** use relevant, probative questions to analyze media messages and find credible answers

*Inquire* is the competency that people most closely associate with critical thinking. In fact, critical thinking is so central to being media literate that Chapter 6 is devoted entirely to *Inquiry* and how to teach it.

In media literacy, thinking critically and being critical aren't the same thing. *Critical* doesn't mean "finding fault with." It means interrogating media deeply enough to uncover multilayered messages, embedded power dynamics, and strengths and weaknesses of claims or techniques. It also means recognizing the actual or potential impact of media messages, media structures (like ownership or platform design), and form or genre.

In addition to asking relevant questions (i.e., questions that have a chance of leading to effective analysis of the specific issues under examination), *Inquiry* requires that we understand how to find answers and how to judge the veracity of the answers we find. People who excel at *Inquiry* are intellectually curious, open minded, and logical. They

- Know how to ask analytical questions about the media they encounter and have the disposition to do so
- Connect their conclusions to specific evidence
- Are interested in epistemology—exploring how they know what they know or think what they think
- Employ a full "toolbox" of strategies to judge the credibility of information, including routinely verifying what multiple sources say about the source of a claim (lateral reading), as well as about the claim, itself
- Understand that a source which is credible on one topic might not be credible on all topics

### *Inquire* in ECE

Young children don't need much encouragement to ask questions. Inquiry comes naturally when so much of what you encounter is new to you! The challenge for media literacy education is helping children learn to ask the types of questions that empower them to think critically about the media they encounter.

To illustrate, let's return to our Cinderella example from the *Comprehend* competency. In a traditional discussion, a teacher would check for comprehension and draw attention to the moral of the story. Depending on your interpretation, the moral might be that being mean isn't rewarded so it's better to be nice, or that we shouldn't judge people by their wealth, or perhaps the Horatio Alger–type message that even a poor orphan can become a princess if she is good, humble, and hard working.

A media literacy approach extends the discussion:

- School-age children might be invited to carefully examine the way the artist drew Cinderella and the other women in the story. The teacher might ask, *What do you think they are saying about what makes a person beautiful or ugly? Who is helped or hurt by those ideas?*
- Or they could use the story to explore language choices: *What's a "cinder"? What does Cinderella's name tell you about her? What other names do we know that tell us something important about a character or a person? What does your name say about you?*
- Or the teacher could introduce versions of the Cinderella story that are told in other cultures, such as Yeh-Shen (China), Nyasha (Zimbabwe), Rough-Face Girl (Algonquin), or Rhodopis (Egypt). Invite children to compare and contrast. They could explore what each version reveals about the values of the culture it comes from.
- Or perhaps the group could invent a version of the story in which Cinderella saves the prince and think about why the original storytellers didn't write it that way.

What would you ask? Even for a relatively simple story like Cinderella, the possible questions are numerous and diverse.

## **Reflect:** ask how media or media messages affect me or others

In media literacy education, *Reflection* is both simple and profound. It is the conduit through which we introduce ethics. It is also the only competency that calls for us to pay specific attention to our physical well-being.

Media literate people who practice *Reflection* are thoughtful and self-aware. They do three major things:

1. When they make media, they pause to ask how their message(s) might affect others. They do so from an ethical foundation, knowing that media makers have power and that the power comes with a responsibility to consider the well-being of audiences and our planet.
2. When they consume media, they pay attention to their emotions and what they learn about themselves from their reactions. Metacognitive awareness of their interpretive lens helps them understand why particular media messages or experiences evoke particular emotions and why other people may not share their feelings.
3. When they use media, they regularly pause to assess their physical reactions. They are aware of why and how media can trigger physical responses, like muscles tensing while watching a suspense-filled movie or suddenly craving chocolate after seeing an ad for brownies (sorry for the trigger here—tell your body to ignore your brain's signal that you want a brownie now). They also maintain an awareness of time on device and respond when their body sends signals that they need to take a break.

### *Reflect* in ECE

To help little ones develop the capacity to *Reflect*, we face two challenges. The first is to help young children make sense of their body's signals when, developmentally, they are just figuring out what their bodies can do. For them, therefore, we model pausing to check in when they have been using media, helping them name what they feel, both emotionally and physically.

For toddlers, we can also point out what we observe: *I've noticed that after you play that game, you seem to be in a bad mood, like you want to hit someone.* or *We started today with a video that reminded us to be kind, and I have seen lots of people smiling today. I think those things are connected.*

With a bit of prompting, preschoolers can describe what they feel. And older children can extend that naming to engage in basic conversations about the sorts of techniques media makers use to elicit particular feelings.

We also make pausing for check-ins a part of our regular routine whenever we've asked children to be sedentary for a while—story time, circle time, a table activity, and the like. That way, the problem is properly identified as being too sedentary, not using media per se. We model taking mini-breaks to stretch or wiggle or run in place, observing that, for those who are able, staying active and using all of our muscles help us feel good.

The second challenge is to help little ones learn to think about the perspective of others when they are, themselves, at an egocentric developmental stage. For them, we nurture the habit of asking questions, even before they are fully capable of asking and answering for themselves.

When children are making media, we introduce questions like *What could you include in the video that would make your uncle proud?* or *If your friends heard your song, do you think it would make them feel happy or would it hurt their feelings?* We walk them through the clues they know that might provide answers, and we remind them that they have feelings when they encounter media and other people do, too. As an added benefit, helping children to make this empathetic aspect of *Reflection* a habit provides a strong foundation for cyberbullying prevention.

## **Evaluate:** ask if this media is right for me or my task

Every day we make judgments about media: What's the best way to share important information with parents? What can I listen to on my commute home that would help me relax? Should I block the person who keeps sharing misleading posts? Should my child-care center invest in whiteboards or tablets?

People who are highly skilled at *Evaluation* can easily answer such questions. They value the process of reasoning and they

- Are familiar with the strengths and weaknesses of major media tools

- Are clear about their communication goals and choose the tool(s) best suited for each task (e.g., understanding that the abbreviations that work well in a tweet aren't appropriate for a grant application cover letter, or that viewing a video might be a better way to learn to play the banjo than following written instructions)
- Find and select media that are age appropriate, free of demands for information they shouldn't be sharing, and supportive of their values
- Can discern the credibility of information sources
- Can curate appropriate resources for particular audiences (e.g., a librarian basing purchasing decisions on the needs of local families)

### *Evaluate* in ECE

One of the most effective things we can do to help children develop the *Evaluate* competency is to share our *Evaluation* thought processes out loud. Here's one very simple example:

> Yesterday we learned that fries are potatoes and that they start as plants. We wondered what potato plants look like. I know that plants change as they grow (just like people!), so I went online to find a video. I was surprised at how many there were! I chose this video to show you because it was made by a professional farmer who grows potatoes right here in our state, and because it has really clear pictures of real plants during the entire growth process, from planting to harvest.

In approximately 30 seconds, this comment lets children know that:

- We can use media to find information about things that interest us.
- We choose the type of media that best matches our task (and video is useful if we want to see things that change over time).
- We use specific criteria to select media resources.
- Our selection criteria are shaped by our purpose.

In this case, answering the question about potato plants leads the child-care provider to value information that is from a local professional with firsthand knowledge, and also that, in this circumstance, clear pictures of real plants are better than animation or drawings. When we frequently share the thinking process behind our media choices, children come to expect *Evaluation* as the norm.

For the youngest children, we share in order to model. When children are developmentally ready, we begin to draw attention to specific criteria that they might also use. The next step is to help children practice asking *Evaluation* questions themselves: *Is the new superhero movie too scary for kids like me? Should I believe this? Instead of a thank you note, can I just send a text with a smiley emoji?* Then we walk them through possible criteria they might use to answer their questions. At the end of that process, as long as no danger is involved, we let *them* make the decisions.

Helping young children learn to discern credibility and trust their own judgment is one of the greatest challenges for media literacy educators working in early childhood. After all, at this life stage kids are just beginning to figure out when their older sibling is kidding or telling the truth, or whether the Easter Bunny is real.

Little ones clearly need our guidance and expertise; they benefit from being around trusted authorities. At the same time, we need to begin teaching them to question the authority of information sources, including us.

There is no easy answer to this conundrum, but it is not dissimilar to the challenge of allowing children to take reasonable physical risks while also protecting them from harm. We nurture their ability to trust their own judgment by

- teaching skills and offering opportunities to practice (like how to "read" a food package—see pp. 106–107)
- allowing for mistakes (e.g., letting them try a snack endorsed by a favorite character even though we know they won't like the flavor)
- stepping in when necessary (e.g., no snacks with dangerous allergens)

Experience is a great teacher. Gradually, children learn to distinguish between the sibling's serious advice and their teasing. Or that the Easter Bunny is imaginary, that real bunnies don't lay eggs, and that for practicing Christians, Easter celebrates something substantially more momentous than a bunny with chocolate. In the meantime, the clearer we are about the tools that *we* use to assess credibility, the better we can be about taking advantage of teachable moments to demonstrate how to use those tools.

## Communicate & Create: express oneself using multiple types of media

Do you think of yourself as a media creator? If you've made a social media profile, sent a text, designed a flyer or bulletin board, shared a selfie, or created a slide deck for a presentation, then you've created media. In the digital world, it's not just professional media makers who create media. User-generated content is the life blood of platforms like Instagram, Pinterest, TikTok, Twitter, YouTube, and Facebook.

Media literacy education prepares people for the "writing" side of literacy in our digital culture. That means knowing how to express oneself effectively in varying media forms and, importantly, how to do so ethically.

People who are proficient media *Creators* in a converged world

- Can effectively use print, image, and audio to convey ideas for specific target audiences and purposes (e.g., persuasion, explanation, storytelling, art, collaboration, instruction)
- Can create and effectively use basic graphics (e.g., infographics, headers, sketch notes, charts and graphs, GIFs, memes, graphic art)
- Know how to use online tools to share their work
- Use media as an outlet for their creativity

They don't weaponize their media skills by trolling, spreading misinformation, or promoting hate-based ideologies.

### *Communicate & Create* in ECE

The hands-on nature of making media will consistently provide one of the best, developmentally appropriate ways for children to learn media analysis. It will be a staple, or even a centerpiece, of your media literacy education efforts.

One obvious place to include media making is in literacy instruction. Alongside traditional print activities, create opportunities for children to express themselves using images and audio. So, for example, children can illustrate their stories, record interviews with each other during which they tell stories and answer questions, or use a digital storytelling app to make a comic strip or simple animation. Provide opportunities to make both simple and complex media (e.g., single photos and also complete books, podcasts, or videos). Sometimes this will require direct instruction in how to use and care for a piece of equipment and other times children will benefit by having the freedom to explore media tools, so they teach each other or discover for themselves the possibilities.

Media literacy educators also talk with children about the media they make—their choices and intentions, what they included or excluded, target audience, and the like. And we provide opportunities to add to or edit their media if the conversations provide new insights or ideas.

## Engage & Explore: use media actively for purpose and enjoyment

People who are proficient *Engagers & Explorers* are open to learning from media and from other people. They

- View, play, or listen to media actively and with purpose, often engaging in follow-up conversations and activities based on what they've seen, heard, or done
- Use media in open-ended exploration that feeds their curiosity
- Incorporate favorite media characters into their play or art in ways that do more than merely repeat what they've seen on screen
- Create play experiences and stories that extend across multiple media—also sometimes referred to as "transmedia play" (Alper & Herr-Stephenson 2013)
- Notice and appreciate the aesthetic aspects of media
- Are willing to experiment (i.e., engage in a pattern of planning, failing, and trying again) and embrace taking reasonable risks while using media
- Can identify existing risks and weigh them against possible rewards
- Use media as inspiration

### *Engage & Explore* in ECE

Sometimes when early childhood educators think about integrating media, they limit their options to very formal educational purposes, like apps that rehearse math skills or educational videos on a relevant topic. But children also need time to play with media in multifaceted ways. After all, for young children, play is more than educational; it is central to learning.

As with free play generally, we help children develop agency and learn about themselves by allowing them to explore media with supervision but without interference. When we think of the task as providing opportunities that encourage playfulness and discovery, we jumpstart children's (and our own) creativity. Here are just a few possibilities:

- Provide time to play with media devices that feature open-ended functions, like cameras, voice recorders, or art-making apps.
- Make devices available in play areas so children can organically incorporate them into their free play.
- Allow children to take apart old technology tools or destroyed books as a sensory play experience (Herdzina & Lauricella 2020, 19).
- Accept children's invitations to play media-based games together (board games, video games, world-building apps, and the like), prompting them to wonder about messages conveyed by the game as you go.
- Provide opportunities for children to *lead* conversations about media they have seen or played—not an adult-directed Q & A, but children talking about what interests them.
- Actively encourage children to use media as a way to explore things that pique their curiosity (and, when needed, show them how).

## Connect & Collaborate: use media to work and communicate with others

Before digital media, there was no easy way for viewers, readers, or listeners to "talk back" to their media or talk with each other. In contrast, consider these incredibly diverse ways that people now use media to work together:

- Teach or take a course online
- Tweet to crowdsource an answer to a question

- Use a Facebook group to organize a family reunion or political protest
- Play a multiplayer online game
- Participate in the Audubon Society's Great Backyard Bird Count
- Engage in a cultural exchange by videoconferencing with a class in another country
- Transform a book club into a group that writes and shares fan fiction online
- Co-edit a document posted in Google Drive or convene a parent meeting via Zoom
- Swap ideas with other teachers via a lesson plan exchange website
- Use Wikipedia to update information on important topics

These are just a few of the activities we enable by including *Connect & Collaborate* as a media literacy competency.

People who excel at *Connecting & Collaborating* practice what education veterans Art Costa and Bena Kallick (2014) have called "thinking interdependently," that is, they are able to work productively with others, aware of their own unique abilities to contribute, and welcoming of diverse points of views. They

- Are effective, ethical users of social media
- Use media for individual and social play (e.g., playing video or online games)
- Understand the capacities of media technologies and use what they know to make sound judgments about whether particular tasks are well suited for online *Collaboration*
- Readily share their knowledge to help others learn things that make *Connecting*, group work, or play more effective, like game strategy or tips on effective use of software
- Are mindful of the possibility that they may be engaging with people who don't share their cultural "filter," and have the cultural competence to act accordingly

## *Connect & Collaborate* in ECE

With school-age children, there are dozens of ways to introduce and practice working together using media tools. It can be as simple as showing children how to save their work on a shared tablet without deleting someone else's work or as complex as involving an entire class in making a documentary film about a class project. With careful scaffolding, we can use video or online games for educational purposes and encourage peer-to-peer coaching about how to play. Or we can use collaborative digital storytelling apps (e.g., Puppet Pals 2, Sock Puppet, or Toontastic 3D) or discussion tools (e.g., VoiceThread) to engage groups of children in dialogue. Voice recording programs are ideal for those whose reading and writing skills are still emerging.

For younger children, the challenge is a bit different. Toddlers and preschoolers are just beginning to experience the shift from individual play, to side-by-side play, to paired play, and eventually, to group play. They aren't developmentally ready to work together on complex media projects.

They can, however, contribute to parts of group projects. For example, they can suggest ideas or emojis for a text message to families that summarizes the day's activities. Or they can help choose pictures for a Center's web page.

Occasionally, you can call children's attention to the *Connection & Collaboration* that you or the people around you already do. Do you use an app like ClassDojo or Seesaw to keep in touch with families? Does the school administrator use software for scheduling? It's not that we expect young children to learn to use the secretary's spreadsheets; it's that we want them to see the available tools and all the different ways that people use them to work together (just like we encourage traditional print literacy by pointing to ways that grown-ups use print media).

And, of course, we can build children's *Connection & Collaboration* skills with hands-on media making, like creating a collage of images representing what they've learned about caring for pets, or a "PSA" mural that shows the importance of washing our hands so that everyone stays healthy. With mixed-age groups, older children can identify the PSA's target audience and specific details of the message, and younger children can help create the art.

## Act: take meaningful individual and community-minded steps based on what one knows about media and media messages

*Act* is the way we assert agency in the face of powerful media influences. It's what we do to connect what we know with the world and with social justice. For students who are discovering for the first time that media can be unfair or misleading, it's the way we channel their frustration, anger, and cynicism into something more useful. Ultimately, it's what makes learning powerful.

Like literacy and learning, there are individual and also societal aspects to *Act*. On the individual side, the *Act* competency means that once you've acquired a skill, you do the work to apply it. For example, a person who learns that their favorite social media platform has committed privacy violations might decide to update their privacy settings to keep apps, sites, and devices from collecting and sharing their information. Their decision doesn't challenge the system but does make a difference for them personally.

*Act* is also what we do to reach beyond the personal to encompass the greater community. We use what we know to step back and look at the big picture. To follow up on the previous example, we wouldn't just ask if a particular site is tracking *us*; we'd also explore what we can do to protest an increasingly intrusive, profit-based surveillance culture and then join with others to take action.

People who excel at the *Act* competency care about being part of a community, want to make the world a better place, and believe that they can make a difference. They

- Connect what they learn about media to what they do
- See beyond the individual and work to make systemic improvements
- Work to ensure that media serve (or at least avoid undermining) the public interest
- See the connections between various types of injustice (intersectionality) and understand the role that media play in perpetuating or ending those injustices
- Have a sense of which actions are possible and make sound judgments about which would be most effective
- Choose to act without anyone telling them or forcing them to do so
- Make media that address injustice or otherwise improve community life

### *Act* in ECE

Young children often have an impressive sense of what's fair. When we prompt them to bring that sense to the things they notice in media we can help them link what they are learning to what is happening in their communities and the broader world. We can engage them in problem solving, and invite them to *Act* without telling them what to do.

This last part—not telling them what to do—is the hard part, at least for the grown-ups. In early childhood settings, it is likely that at some point in the process we'll need to narrow children's choices. But if *Action* is merely following the instructions of an authority figure, we rob children of a chance to develop a sense of agency, and they don't really develop the competency. So, we let them decide what *they* think is the best strategy to pursue.

To help you envision how this can work with young children, here's an example from award-winning early childhood educator, Vivian Vasquez (2014, ch. 5):

> One of Vasquez's young students arrived at school talking excitedly about local reports of whales endangered by pollution in a nearby waterway. To help the children connect what they were hearing to what they already knew, Vasquez chose to read-aloud a book based on the "Baby Beluga" Raffi song that children loved. Then she led the group to analyze the two portrayals (news and book) by creating and comparing lists of the words that each source used to describe the whales.
>
> Examining the differences, one child asked, "Which one is real?" (by which he meant "Which is accurate?"). Vasquez explained that different types of media texts offer different perspectives. That's important modeling for media literacy educators. It wasn't that the song was false and the news was real. Both sources offered valuable, though different information.
>
> Children liked the song but observed that Raffi didn't say anything about the whales being in danger, so they rewrote the song to come up with a more comprehensive representation. They also decided that they wanted to help the whales. Again, this is important modeling. The suggestion for action came from the children, not the teacher.
>
> One girl continued to investigate the issue with her mom, and they discovered the World Wildlife Fund's research on whales. They brought their findings to the group, which then decided to raise money to donate to WWF by selling special snacks at the class store.

That's where Vasquez ends her account, but it's not hard to imagine that the store created even more opportunities for integrating media literacy, making signs, creating ads, and the like. What makes this flow of activities so compelling is that it started from children's interests rather than a teacher-imposed agenda, and then evolved organically.

The teacher was not without influence. Vasquez had the power to stop and redirect an activity at any point. And she certainly guided the children toward inquiry. But because she used her power to create space for children to discover for themselves, they learned significant media literacy concepts:

- Language choices influence interpretation.
- Different types of sources emphasize different types of information.
- One source doesn't tell the whole story.

They also combined media analysis with science, language arts (writing song lyrics), and taking action that connected them to their community.

This multilayered set of activities, where one reinforces the next, is common when teachers are skilled at media literacy "improvisation," that is, being comfortable and knowledgeable enough about media to respond to teachable moments. Great media literacy educators have age-appropriate engagement strategies at their fingertips (like using a word comparison to help children learn to analyze different media), so they can serve as guide to little ones as they explore and learn.

One interesting note about this activity: Vasquez never labels it "media literacy." This isn't uncommon. Lots of educators are teaching media literacy without using that label. Look around. You might be surprised by how many examples you find.

## Pulling It All Together

Covering all 10 competencies is less daunting than it might initially seem because their acquisition isn't a straight-line sequential process. As the Vasquez example illustrates, often classroom experiences address multiple competencies simultaneously. To clarify, we'll look at a different example to sketch out the ways that specific competencies show up in a common activity.

Consider a lesson in which 4- and 5-year-olds have been taught to use the cameras on their tablets. They are escorted on a neighborhood walk and asked to find and photograph an important sign. They start by agreeing on what a sign is and generating a list of what sorts of signs might be important. This includes the teacher observing that different people can think different things are important, so everyone doesn't have to take the same picture.

During the walk, the grown-ups help with reading, as needed. This could also be an opportunity to help children think about the richness of multilingual neighborhoods. If there are lots of signs in Spanish, for example, a chaperone who didn't speak Spanish could sound out the sign and ask the children what the words meant. Or if there's a sign that uses an unfamiliar alphabet, perhaps a worker in the business that displayed the sign could be asked to help. Everyone might discuss why some signs are only in English and others include different languages.

After the walk, as attention allows, some children show their pictures, explaining what they photographed and why. An aide helps each child print a copy of their picture, explaining what she's doing as she works.

They assemble their pictures in a display with the title "Important Signs in Our Neighborhood." They show their display to other groups and also share a picture of the display on their website and in their newsletter. The teacher introduces the group to the word *caption* and asks for suggestions, which she writes down. She guides them to a consensus on a sentence that explains their display.

Here are competencies involved in this lesson:

› *Access*—Children are practicing using tablets to take photos, save, and print them. A follow-up discussion could even note instances where the photo didn't quite capture what was intended and children could coach each other about how to get a better shot.

› *Attend*—Children are noticing signs in their neighborhood.

› *Comprehend*—Children learn what a sign is and what the basic messages are on signs in their neighborhood.

› *Inquire*—Children are thinking about the purposes of the signs in their neighborhood.

› *Reflect*—As they make decisions about their display and their picture caption, they consider who will see their work and whether their audience will understand what they are trying to say.

› *Evaluate*—Children are making a decision about which signs are important.

› *Communicate & Create*—Children are taking photos, creating a display, contributing to a website and newsletter, and writing a caption.

› *Connect & Collaborate*—Children work together to create their display and write a caption. The display and the newsletter are ways connect with others in their building, community, and families.

Now imagine possible follow-ups. Children might consider whether there are signs that the neighborhood should have, but doesn't. They might *Act* to create those signs and then work to get them posted. Or they might take a second walk, this time taking a picture of something about which they have a question. When they return, their search for answers takes them into *Engage & Explore* territory. This single project could easily incorporate all 10 media literacy competencies and much more.

As you consider how you will help children acquire the media literacy competencies, there are things you may already be doing that are related but may need some modification. Two of the most valuable are "media management" and "teaching with technology."

PAUSE TO **REFLECT**

Which competencies could you cover in each of these activities?

- Children have been learning about trees and you are helping them make a video to show their families what they have learned and where they found credible information.
- Children are using tablets equipped with artmaking and alphabet apps to create their own individualized set of alphabet cards.

## Media Management

"Media management" refers to the rules that adults set to govern time, place, and content on media devices. Early childhood educators do "media management" when we select classroom media, make technology purchasing decisions, or set rules about using or sharing media or taking care of devices (e.g., no cameras in the bathroom). Media management doesn't completely dovetail with the goals of media literacy education because if children are not directly involved in rule making or choosing media, then it doesn't give *children* skills.

Rule setting for media use in early childhood education settings will never be a one-set-fits-all practice. There are some things you might consider as you integrate media literacy into your teaching:

- Approach media technology the way you would any other tool, toy, or engaging activity: Use your regular transition routines to end screen time and start new activities. Be sure that children have the skills they need to wrap up their media time (e.g., teach children how to save their projects or games and safely shut off their device). Include reminders in your transition announcement (e.g., *Time to save your story now. We are going to put our coats on and head outside in two minutes.*).
- Use common-sense prevention strategies to avoid conflicts before they happen:
  - Don't offer engaging video games before nap time.
  - Approach longer videos like a chapter book—don't view it all at once. Practice splitting viewing into multiple sessions and tell children what you're doing (e.g., *We're going to watch part today and part tomorrow.*).
  - Anticipate that, like rereading favorite books, children will want to view favorite videos more than once. Schedule times when a video would be available to watch again.
  - Choose apps, games, and videos that include natural pause points.
- Discuss the use of assistive technologies and apply the discussion to everyone (e.g., *What do you need the technology to help you do? Is it something you need help with all the time, or do you only need it to do a specific task?*) Use the discussion to explain why some children will need to have a tablet or laptop with them all the time while other children will need to follow rules about when to put away media devices.
- Acknowledge the fun of using media technologies so that children know you understand their desire to keep playing or viewing, and, because you know that, you only ask them to stop using screens when it's important that they stop.
- Introduce the word *obligations* and invite children to help you make a list. What are their obligations and how can they make sure that media technologies don't interfere with fulfilling them? Are there ways that media technologies could help them meet their obligations?

- When possible, model what you want children to do. For example, if you want them to put away media devices during meals or snacks, the grown-ups need to do so, too. If there are times when children are prohibited from using a device, but you need one, explain why.
- Whenever possible, involve children in rule making:
    - If transitions are a problem, engage children in creating their own transition routines. They're more likely to follow rules that they have a hand in crafting.
    - Discuss where/when it makes sense to take a break (e.g., *When you have completed two levels, it's time save your game and let someone else have a turn.*).
    - Let children help declare times or places to be designated as screen-free zones. These might be based on caring for devices (e.g., no cameras near the water table), or perhaps creating special quiet zones that are places we go when we need to calm down or when we need to rest our brains and bodies (e.g., no tablets during nap time).

## Teaching with Technology

"Teaching with technology" is what educators do when they address core curriculum needs by using technology. This would include things like showing a PBS program to teach a science concept, filling a classroom with QR codes that children access with tablets, offering dual language learners software that helps them learn their second language, or sparking children's interest with an augmented reality version of a favorite book character.

Used well, these can be wonderful tools, offering experiences that aren't possible with analog alternatives (e.g., being able to see what your body looks like inside, or being able to point a camera at a bird and switch to macro-mode so it's easy to see the details without disturbing it). Decades of research show that well-designed videos, especially if viewed actively and followed up by off-screen practice, can be very effective at introducing and reinforcing important content (e.g., Huston et al. 2007; Linebarger 2009; Pasnik 2019; Rasmussen et al. 2016; Schmidt & Anderson 2007). Though the body of research for well-designed digital resources is not yet as robust, and though hundreds (or perhaps thousands) of apps that bear the "education" label are of dubious value, there are ample indications that well-designed apps and software are effective educational tools (e.g., Aladé et al. 2016; McCarthy, Tiu, & Li 2014; Papadakis, Kalogiannakis, & Zaranis 2018; Pasnik 2019).

As exciting and innovative as these tools can be, and as important as it is for media literate people to know how to use digital technologies, we must be mindful that children don't acquire media literacy's critical thinking, reflection, or expression skills merely by using digital media. Their use must intentionally incorporate opportunities to acquire or practice media literacy competencies, including analyzing the media used for teaching. In media literacy education, media technologies are tools, not learning outcomes.

## Teaching for Lifelong Learning

Media literacy isn't a cover-it-once, test-it-and-forget it topic. It's a complex skill set and lifelong pursuit. In the early years, we introduce the competencies as an archway into a media literate future. Each of the competencies is a necessary brick in that arch, with *Inquire* and *Reflect* as conjoined keystones.

As I wrote a few years ago, media literacy education "is about helping children develop the life skills they need to become thinkers and makers in the multimedia environment that is their reality" (Rogow 2015, 91). Today I'd add "and their future."

## Sources


Aladé, F., A.R. Lauricella, L. Beaudoin-Ryan, & E. Wartella. 2016. "Measuring with Murray: Touchscreen Technology and Preschoolers' STEM Learning." *Computers in Human Behavior* 62: 433–41.

Alper, M., & R. Herr-Stephenson. 2013. "Transmedia Play: Literacy Across Media." *Journal of Media Literacy Education* 5 (2): 366–9.

Costa, A.L., & B. Kallick. 2014. "Describing 16 Habits of Mind." Online handout. https://habitsofmind.org/sites/default/files/16HOM2.pdf.

Donohue, C., ed. 2017. *Family Engagement in the Digital Age: Early Childhood Educators as Media Mentors*. New York: Routledge.

Haines, C., C. Campbell, & ALSC (Association for Library Service to Children). 2016. *Becoming a Media Mentor: A Guide for Working with Children and Families*. Chicago: ALA Editions.

Herdzina, J., & A.R. Lauricella. 2020. *Media Literacy in Early Childhood Report: Framework, Child Development Guidelines, and Tips for Implementation*. Report. Chicago: Technology in Early Childhood (TEC) Center, Erikson Institute. http://teccenter.erikson.edu/wp-content/uploads/2020/06/TEC-MediaLiteracy-Report.pdf.

Huston, A.C., D.S. Bickham, J.H. Lee, & J.C. Wright. 2007. "From Attention to Comprehension: How Children Watch and Learn from Television." In *Children and Television: Fifty Years of Research*, ed. N. Pecora, J.P. Murray, & E.A. Wartella, 41–64. Mahwah, NJ: Lawrence Erlbaum Associates.

Linebarger, D. 2009. *Evaluation of the* Between the Lions *Mississippi Literacy Initiative: 2007–2008*. Report. Philadelphia: University of Pennsylvania, Children's Media Lab.

McCarthy, B., M. Tiu, & L. Li. 2014. *Learning Math with* Curious George: *PBS KIDS Transmedia and Digital Learning Games in the Preschool Classroom*. Report. San Francisco: WestEd. www.wested.org/wp-content/uploads/2016/11/1456767519resourcelearningmathwithcuriousgeorge-3.pdf.

NAMLE (National Association for Media Literacy Education). 2007. *Core Principles of Media Literacy Education in the United States*. New York: NAMLE. https://namle.net/wp-content/uploads/2020/09/Namle-Core-Principles-of-MLE-in-the-United-States.pdf.

Neuman, S.B., & D.C. Celano. 2012. *Giving Our Children a Fighting Chance: Poverty, Literacy, and the Development of Information Capital*. New York: Teacher's College Press.

Papadakis, S., M. Kalogiannakis, & N. Zaranis. 2018. "The Effectiveness of Computer and Tablet Assisted Intervention in Early Childhood Students' Understanding of Numbers: An Empirical Study Conducted in Greece." *Education and Information Technologies* 23: 1849–71.

Pasnik, S., ed. 2019. *Getting Ready to Learn: Creating Effective, Educational Children's Media*. New York: Routledge.

Rasmussen, E.E., A. Shafer, M.J. Colwell, S. White, N. Punyanunt-Carter, R.L. Densley, & H. Wright. 2016. "Relation Between Active Mediation, Exposure to *Daniel Tiger's Neighborhood,* and US Preschoolers' Social and Emotional Development." *Journal of Children and Media* 10 (4): 443–61.

Rogow, F. 2015. "Media Literacy in Early Childhood Education: Inquiry-Based Technology Integration." In *Technology and Digital Media in the Early Years: Tools for Teaching and Learning,* ed. C. Donohue, 91–103. New York: Routledge; Washington, DC: NAEYC.

Schmidt, M.E., & D.R. Anderson. 2007. "The Impact of Television on Cognitive Development and Educational Achievement." In *Children and Television: Fifty Years of Research*, ed. N. Pecora, J.P. Murray, & E. Wartella, 65–84. Mahwah, NJ: Lawrence Erlbaum Associates.

Vasquez, V.M. 2014. *Negotiating Critical Literacies with Young Children*. 10th anniversary ed. New York: Routledge.

CHAPTER 6

# Engaging Through Inquiry

We take extra time to explore the Inquire competency because it is embedded in every one of the other competencies; it's impossible to teach media literacy or become media literate without it. More than simply asking a question and soliciting an answer, media literacy inquiry is a repeating cycle of questioning, exploring, reasoning and reflection—a process that wraps children in a security blanket of confidence as they build their knowledge and skills, especially when *they*, and not just *we*, ask the questions. And when it goes well, you can feel the energy of discovery filling the room.

## Creating a Culture of Inquiry

It's a truism of human nature that when things are made easy, more of us are likely to do them. And so it is with media literacy inquiry. Children are more likely to embrace the habit in an environment where inquiry is easy and routine. So, part of teaching media literacy is creating a culture that allows the following to occur:

- Questions are welcome.
- There is often more than one "right" answer.
- Everyone is expected to ask as well as answer questions.
- Everyone expects answers to be linked to evidence.
- We ask questions of all media, including media we like and media we create.
- It's common to adapt opinions (change our minds) to accommodate new information.

As a pedagogy, media literacy education asks early childhood professionals to see ourselves as leaders of a community of knowledge seekers. We treasure imagination along with reason, and reach beyond simple cognitive queries to intentionally pose questions that lead to more questions. Rather than asking questions like "If I have three power tokens and I capture one more, how many will I have?" we might ask, *"I wonder why a game wouldn't just let us ask our opponent to share or trade the tokens? Why would someone want to make it hard to win? What lessons do you think the game designers are trying to teach?"*

In their compelling work on reflective practice, *From Teaching to Thinking: A Pedagogy for Reimagining Our Work*, veteran educators Ann Pelo and Margie Carter (2018) further explain,

> A culture of inquiry values complexity. . . . [It] holds as its project the shared construction of knowledge and understanding, rather than the transmission of information and topical knowledge. (52)

They reference human rights luminary Elie Wiesel, who once observed that the word *question* contains the word *quest*. When we engage in inquiry, we're partners with children in a quest (Wiesel 2000). We do it *with* children, not to or for them. We open up places for children to share their questions and honor their existing expertise.

This model of teaching is essential to developing children's media literacy skills, because traditional pedagogies, in which the adult is the expert with all the answers and the child is rarely required to do any intellectual seeking of their own, are more likely to instill obedience than critical thinking. In such systems, children learn to trust authorities *instead* of developing, and ultimately trusting, their own skills and judgment. It's a trap that can appear to be successful as long as everyone follows authorities that merit our approval, but as children grow and increasingly go online independently, that circle of approval is likely to be fleeting.

There have always been, and will continue to be, "snake oil salesmen" competing for our attention. And right now, social media algorithms that favor extremes are likely to push people to encounters with skilled marketers, hate group recruiters, cult leaders, propagandists for foreign powers, financial cons, conspiracy theorists—all sorts of commercial, religious, and political "authorities." Some are specifically dedicated to spreading disinformation. And any of them can appear to be at least as convincing as you are, if not more so.

In that context, the last thing that early childhood educators want to do is to accustom children to rely on others to interpret media for them. If all we offer is a version of "believe my narrative, not theirs," we leave people—young and grown—vulnerable to malign actors. Nor do we want to do the opposite, teaching children to disbelieve everything and trust no one. That approach yields cynical, nonthinking adults instead of people who are skeptical and engaged. So, we don't teach children to doubt, we teach them to investigate. And as you'll see below, we teach particular categories of questions that can help them investigate media and media messages.

If we're successful, analytical questions about media become an intrinsic part of children's interpretive lens. In the same way that once you know how to read print, your (healthy) brain can never look at a page with text and not see words and sentences, once you are media literate, questioning media is unavoidable and automatic. It's what the brain does to make sense of what it is encountering.

In practice, teaching media literacy is not a competition between "inquiry" (asking) and "instruction" (telling). Instruction in traditional subject area content is essential to media literacy because background knowledge is essential for effective media analysis. A broad knowledge base enables sophisticated readings. Without it, people miss or misinterpret references to history, literature, music, pop culture, current events, and the like. So, inquiry doesn't replace teaching the core curriculum; it provides a different pathway to get there.

PAUSE TO **REFLECT**

As you consider how you will create a culture of inquiry, what experiences with inquiry do you draw from? In your own life, when was inquiry rewarded or discouraged? How do your past experiences influence your approach to engaging children in inquiry?

## Media Literacy Questions

It's almost instinctual to want to shout and wave big red warning flags when we see media that strike us as problematic. Mainstream media has no shortage of troubling messages that we rightfully feel compelled to counteract. We want little ones to know that put-downs hurt people's feelings, even if a laugh track makes it sound like people think they're funny. Or that ads can make it seem like junk foods are fun and delicious, even though they aren't actually healthy for us or the planet. Or that apps requiring players to buy things are really more like stores than games. Or that Asian cultures are much richer than the depictions in B-grade martial arts films.

But in media literacy education, analysis isn't about showing children what they missed by pointing out what *we* notice. Instead, we invite children to tell us what they notice and then help them to notice more. We don't tell children what the messages are; we guide an inquiry

DEVELOPING HABITS OF INQUIRY & REFLECTION IN EARLY CHILDHOOD

## KEY CATEGORIES OF MEDIA LITERACY ANALYSIS & SAMPLE QUESTIONS

**I wonder...**

### AUTHORSHIP
- Who is telling this story?
- Who made this? or Who made up this story?

### PURPOSES
- Why was this made?
- Who is this for (target audience)? or Who are they talking to?
- What does this want me to do?
- What do they want me to think (or think about)?
- Why would they want me to do or think that?

### CONTENT
- What is this?
- Who are they talking to?
- What is this about? or What is this saying?
- What does this tell me about __________?
- Who are the leaders/followers? Who gets helped/who are the helpers?

### TECHNIQUES
- What do I notice about ________?
- What do I notice first?
- What do they want me to notice first?
- How do they get me to notice what they want?
- How did they make that? Where was the camera?

### CONTEXT
- Does this fit into any patterns I've seen before?
- How is this like what I already know?
- Where did this come from?
- When was this made?
- Is this from a long time ago or now?

### CREDIBILITY
- Is this telling the truth? or Should I believe this?
- Why should I believe this?
- How do they know what they are saying is true?
- Is this a face or opinion?

### ECONOMICS
- Who paid for this?
- Who might make money from this?
- Am I trading something valuable to watch/play/read/listen to this?
- What does "free" mean?

### EFFECTS
- Who might be sad/happy because of this?
- Who might this help/hurt?

### INTERPRETATIONS
- What does this mean?
- What do they think is important?
- What would _______ think about this? (insert name, group, profession, etc.)
- How does this compare/contrast to what I already know?

### RESPONSES
- How does this make me feel?
- Now that I know this, what do I want to do?
- What can we do to change the story?
- What else do I want to know?

### FOLLOW UP
How do I know? What makes me think that?
What's my evidence? How could I find out?

Figure 6.1 Key Categories of Media Literacy Analysis and Sample Questions. Adapted from NAMLE's 2007 Core Principles of Media Literacy Education by Faith Rogow with input from Project Look Sharp. Used under terms of 2020 Creative Commons Attribution Non-Commercial, No-Derivatives License.

PAUSE TO **REFLECT**

Take a moment to look at the media literacy questions.

Which of these do you already ask when you use media? How about when you use media with children? Which hadn't occurred to you before reading this book?

Which do you think will be easy to teach children to use? Which will be harder?

process that helps them discover messages for themselves and then ponder what they discover. We model how to use evidence to reach conclusions and, when necessary, explain things that are unfamiliar or confusing. But mostly we pose questions and listen. It's not a particularly efficient process, especially compared to direct, didactic instruction. It is, however, the way we teach children to think.

There's no need to start from scratch to figure out what sorts of questions to teach. The media literacy prompts we use for analysis and reflection fall into 10 categories plus follow-up. These are listed in Figure 6.1, along with sample questions.

## A Deeper Dive into Media Literacy Analysis Questions

Rather than separating us into those who already have the answers and those who need to learn, the best questions expand our thinking and deepen our connection. They arise from things that are already happening in children's lives both in and out of our care. So, the questions in Figure 6.1 aren't prescriptive, they're samples. The questions you actually use will vary depending on what you're analyzing and why you're engaging children around a particular media text.

In contrast to memorizing a specific list of questions, working with categories offers educators flexibility to respond to teachable moments and integrate media literacy analysis into a wide variety of circumstances. So, for example, imagine you've discovered that a group of children in your first grade class have been watching vintage cartoons that include stereotypes of Mexicans. They laugh at the characters who are the butt of the subtly racist jokes and begin imitating accents of English speakers whose first language is Spanish, clearly making fun of them.

You could find a clip of the cartoon and analyze it together, using some of the sample media literacy questions, like "Who made this?" or "How does this compare/contrast to what I already know [about Mexico or Mexicans]?" Or, knowing that the kids love the head of the afterschool program, Freddy, who is Latino, you could start a discussion of the cartoon by asking, "I wonder if Freddy would think this is funny?" In this case, asking a question about Freddy is a media literacy question (specifically, an *effects* or *interpretations* category question). It is likely to be a more powerful provocation for deep thought than any pre-scripted media literacy question.

Leaving options open so that we can find the most effective wording to meet the immediate need is the most important reason to use question categories. They provide a way to connect media literacy to children's experiences and to topics you are already teaching. Understanding their purposes will help you adapt or invent wording that meets your needs.

Keep Figure 6.1 nearby as you read the rest of this section and stop before each category to look at the sample questions. Then read the explanation to connect the questions with their functions. Take note of the ways that the categories are interdependent and how they relate to the 10 media literacy competencies outlined in Chapter 5.

### *I wonder . . .*

We often begin questions with "I wonder . . ." because we pose questions as an invitation to investigation and insight, rather than as a quiz. It is also a great way to frame questions as a way to instill habits of inquiry for children too young to ask for themselves. Even before they fully understand, we model the Inquire competency by introducing wonder as a first step of analysis.

### Authorship

We ask questions about *authorship* not just to uncover a name, but because knowing that name is key to our ability to take additional steps to Comprehend, check *credibility* (Evaluate), or *interpret* messages (Inquire).

To talk about media makers, early childhood educators often use the familiar language of "story" and "storyteller." That makes it easier for little ones to understand and learn the concept, especially in cases where media makers are organizations or never seen. And it reminds everyone that there are narratives in all sorts of media: ads, games, films, athletic competitions, songs, and so forth.

Before moving on to the other categories, it's also worth noting that when educators ask children media literacy questions, it's reasonable to expect different answers from children of different ages. The youngest will respond with things that are most immediate and concrete. As they develop, you can expect children to be able to handle greater abstraction.

For example, if you are reading aloud, the youngest children may identify *you* as the storyteller because you are right there with them. Or they might name an obvious narrator within the story, itself. As little ones become accustomed to hearing us begin read-alouds by identifying the author and illustrator, they'll begin to understand that media creators—even those we can't see—tell the story, and that media stories can be told by a team of people. Eventually, school-age children can also understand that the publisher is part of that team, because out of all the possible stories in the world, the company decided to spend money to print this one, and they made choices about what it would look like (its size, what's on the cover, whether it's a board book, paperback, hardcover, digital, or some other format).

### Purposes

We ask *purpose* questions to understand the reasons (note the plural) that a media message was created and who it was made for (target audience). We use intention to evaluate *credibility* and consider our *response*.

To address young children in developmentally appropriate ways, we ask in concrete, personal terms: *What does this want me to do or think? Why are they talking to me?* We don't always ask questions in the first person, but modeling "I" language on occasion is useful because it intrinsically puts children in the role of questioner.

Expect that answers will be based on what's easily viewable:

> [discussing a toy ad]
>
> Child Care Provider (CCP): "I wonder what they want you to do?"
>
> Child 1: "They want me to have fun."
>
> CCP: "To have the fun they show, what would you need?"
>
> Child 1: "My friend."
>
> CCP: "Anything else?"
>
> Child 2: "The toy."
>
> CCP: "And how could you get the toy?"
>
> Child 2: "You could get it."
>
> CCP: "For me to get the toy, I'd have to buy it. So, I guess this ad wants us to buy the toy."
>
> Child 1: "Yeah."
>
> CCP: "Do we ever have fun without the toy? What could we do today to have fun even though we don't have the toy?" . . .

Note that you don't have to teach everything in every conversation. If you routinely engage in these sorts of exchanges, there will be plenty of opportunities for children to start noticing patterns. They will begin to mimic what you model. Their answer will acknowledge that the ad wants them to buy the toy (or ask an adult to buy them the toy). And there will be opportunities to expand the investigation, perhaps inviting slightly older children to share a time when they got a toy they wanted that didn't meet the expectations they inferred from an ad. They might even reflect on the reasons that they do or don't still play with that toy.

By the time children are school age, they can begin to examine ideas and not just concrete actions, adding *techniques* and *interpretations* questions to the discussion of *purposes*. It may start with a shift in the way they consider the concrete. Continuing with the previous example, they may say something like, "This wants me to think the toy is fun. If it's fun I'll ask papa to buy it for me." They are also developmentally ready to start looking a little deeper. For example, perhaps the ad featured pink and purple and showed girls playing with the toy. The discussion might continue:

> Teacher: "Did they include any other clues about what they want you to think?"
>
> Child 1: "There are girls playing with the toy"
>
> T: "What do you think that evidence tells you?"
>
> C1: "That girls will like the toy."
>
> C2: "Yeah, it's a girl toy."
>
> T: "Can you tell us what you mean by that?
>
> C2: "It's for girls."
>
> T: "Do you mean that it's *only* for girls?"
>
> C2: "Yeah, it's all pink."
>
> T: "Who else thinks that the pink means the toy is only for girls?"
>
> [lots of hands go up]
>
> "What color would they have used if they wanted to show that the toy was for boys?"
>
> [a chorus of "Blue" ensues]
>
> T: "That's interesting. Are you saying that only boys like blue and only girls like pink? Is that true?"

The rest of the discussion will depend on their answer. If they say yes, the teacher can suggest examples that counter the stereotype, focusing as much as possible on things in children's own lives (e.g., a girl who loves her blue coat or a boy who is attached to his hot pink flamingo sunglasses). If they say no, the conversation could continue about who should get to decide whether a girl or boy thinks a toy is fun. We can explain that toy makers and stores use color to influence (limit) our choices (*techniques*), and because they believe we'll buy a toy that we think matches who we are (in adult terms, we'll make a purchase as an expression of our identity). So, a box is blue or pink not because it makes the toy more fun, but because they think we're more likely to buy it if we can use it to show other people that we're a boy or a girl.

The teacher could even highlight that toy makers and marketers have other possible choices by posing a gender-inclusive question like "What color(s) could they have used if they wanted to show that the toy was for everyone?" Target audience (*purposes*) questions can lead to deep thinking about differing needs and desires: Why isn't everything for everyone? How do they know what I need?

At this stage of development, it is enough to understand that marketers sometimes present things that aren't accurate reflections of real life. Deep explanations of why marketers do what they do can wait until children are older.

### Content

Teaching children how to ask *content* questions is an excellent way to help them practice the Comprehend competency and notice salient details (clues) that aid *interpretation.*

Using familiar concepts, we help children share what they know. So, for example, we ask about what something is "saying" to help little ones understand that media are communicating with them, just like people communicate with each other by talking or signing. It can be instructive for us to hear children describe the main message of a media text. Are they seeing the same main message(s) that we would? Do children understand the story well enough to re-tell it? Do they understand key words or phrases?

Beyond comprehension checks, the specific questions we model depend on our goals. *Content* questions can be used to help children to

- Connect the media they're analyzing to other things they've been learning
- Differentiate between types of media (so, for example, they can make choices about whether to believe the information or whether it would be okay to *respond* to a post or share a picture)
- Explore social issues and the possible *effects* of media messages

## Techniques

Media makers use specific techniques to convey messages and attract and hold our attention. Noticing those techniques is part of our *interpretation* toolbox. It reinforces the key concept that all media are constructed and offers opportunities to improve the Attend as well as the Inquire competencies. So, we ask questions that help older children to

- Learn specific things to look for (e.g., pauses that create suspense, what's big or tiny)
- Connect techniques to *purposes*
- Apply what they've learned to their own media making (part of the Communicate & Create competency)
- Use what they've learned from their own media making to analyze media made by others (Inquire).

For the youngest children, it's enough that they know that techniques exist.

## Context

*Context* questions (e.g., when something was created or where it was shared) are connected to several competencies, including Inquire, Evaluate, Comprehend, Attend, and sometimes Reflect. They help children to

- Attach what they are learning to what they already know (including their own personal experience)
- Spot patterns (e.g., In movies, are some places always friendly and others always scary? In the video game, do all the things we capture or avoid have anything in common?). Do some sources always use the "weasel words" *technique* (e.g., "You *could* save *up to* 50%!" instead of the more straightforward "You will get 50% off")?
- Pay attention to where they are encountering media and how that influences *interpretation* and *response* ("I heard it in a cartoon" is different from "I saw it on a poster at the doctor's office")
- Notice information that is essential for *interpretation* and Evaluating relevance (e.g., deciding whether a reference was too out of date to be helpful, or understanding why a character lost in the wilderness wouldn't just call for help on their mobile phone by looking at the date that the story was written or the time period it depicts)

## Economics

To young children, nearly all media seem to be free. But, of course, nothing is actually free, so we ask *economics* questions to help children understand:

- What they're trading for the media they use
- Who benefits from those trades and in what ways

- How the need or desire to make money influences content and structure (see Chapter 7)

Unless someone else has paid the bill for us (like a foundation that provides free resources), we gain access to media by paying taxes, purchasing tickets or a subscription, spending time to view or listen to ads, or granting permission to collect and sell our personal data. Understanding the nature of the transaction helps us to Inquire, Evaluate, and Comprehend, and is often a precursor to the Act competency.

### Credibility

Some media share explicit, straightforward messages, but all media convey ideas. So attentive media use is always an exercise in discernment. That's why we ask *credibility* questions. They're integral to the Evaluate competency.

If we only asked, "Should I believe . . . ?" children would learn to expect that there would always be a simple yes or no answer. But often that's not the case. So, we teach them to ask, "Why should I believe?" and then help them learn situation-specific criteria for judging credibility.

Most young children don't have enough life experience to judge whether a media message is true, but asking helps acclimate them to the idea that there are certain types of expertise we value, that the choice of people who are interviewed or cited matters, and that people shouldn't be considered authorities on a topic just because they have an opinion or are an expert in something unrelated.

This can be more confusing to children than we might expect. If I say that I like Upstate New York, that's an opinion. But when I say I live in Upstate New York, that's a fact. That can be a tough distinction for young ones because both are true. We want children to begin to understand that media sometimes show things, and people sometimes say things that aren't facts, even when they make it seem true or real. But in the early years, rather than strive for a detailed understanding, the goal is to instill an intuitive sense of the difference between fact and opinion.

### Effects

When we teach children to ask *effects* questions, we are helping them understand that media have consequences and that the impact of particular media can help some people and hurt others. It's an especially important category of questions for children to ask themselves when they are making their own media (Create).

*Effects* questions can prime children to consider that others might react differently from them. They can also spark a desire for kids to Act on effects that they think are harmful or unfair.

### Interpretations

*Interpretation* is often what people think of when they think about media analysis. It is the essence of making meaning from media and understanding our part in that process. In addition to thinking about media messages (Inquire), when children learn to ask *interpretation* questions, they

- Gain awareness of their existing interpretive lens (Reflect)
- Gain critical distance, which helps them separate themselves from media makers, so they can choose to accept or reject media priorities or messages

### Responses

*Response* questions address two different things: What do I feel? and What do I want to do? The latter provides a gateway to transform insight into action and connect with communities to make the world better (the Act competency). The former increases children's self-awareness, which can be especially helpful in learning to self-regulate media use (the Reflect competency) and improve the ability to select media that meet their needs (the Evaluate competency).

### Follow-Ups

Just as we typically begin with "I wonder," we nearly always ask media literacy analysis questions in conjunction with follow-ups. This is how we link conclusions to evidence and help children understand the implications of their analysis and see answers as the beginning rather than the end of an investigation. Tone of voice matters. We ask, "How do you know that?" not as an accusation, but in the spirit of "That's interesting, tell me more."

## Tips for Using Media Literacy Questions

- Questions don't need to be asked in any particular order, nor will every category apply to every media example.
- Often, you'll need only one prompt to kick off a discussion that will cover many categories. Overlap is common.
- Apply questions to making media, as well as existing media. Just shift the words a bit, for example, "What do *I* want people to do?" instead of "What does this want me to do?"
- Wording that leaves open the possibility of more than one answer is preferable to questions that imply a single, correct response.

  For example, asking Why was this made? instead of What is the purpose? encourages complex thinking and the possibility that a media maker might have many simultaneous goals (e.g., artistic, political, educational, financial), or in team efforts, that team members may have different purposes.
- With the youngest children, especially at first, the specific answers are less important than the habit of questioning.

  Reliance on evidence-based reasoning can be tricky when dealing with little ones, which is why we keep the focus on establishing the habit of linking conclusions to evidence without worrying too much if the actual conclusions drift a bit from what we might expect. Think of it more as an opportunity to practice a skill than a test of mastery, like a child learning to kick a ball. We can set the ball in front of them and make sure there aren't any breakables nearby. If they connect foot to ball, we don't worry too much about whether or not the ball actually goes into the goal. That will come with time and practice.
- Take advantage of one-on-one opportunities to model questioning, but also be sure to engage in group analysis.

  Exchanging thoughts in a group exposes children to novel ideas, helps them experience a diversity of ideas as normal, and underscores the idea that inquiry includes listening as well as speaking (taking turns). It also reinforces the part of the Act competency that is about community. Analysis isn't just about understanding personal preferences or opinions; it's about identifying the ways that media affect everyone.
- Approach questions as strings rather than singles.

  It can be the second or third question in a string that brings real insight to the inquiry. We use strings to expand analysis, link questions to children's lives, or build on simple comprehension checks. So, for example, we might start with "What do you notice about . . . ?" and follow up with "Why does that matter?"

  Or consider this analysis of a fast-food restaurant:

  - Just to make sure everyone knows the vocabulary, we could ask, "What color is her uniform?" But that's not a very interesting question, so we'd quickly move to
  - "Why do you think her uniform is yellow?" "What else do you notice that's yellow?" The second question provides a hint that helps children discover the answer to the first.
  - If they notice that the colors of the uniforms match the colors of the chain's logo, we can move on to deeper questions

about branding: "The company actually calls this color 'gold.' Why would they say 'golden arches' instead of 'yellow arches'?"

Veteran educators Kristin Ziemke and Katie Muhtaris (2020) illustrate how questions relate and build with this awesome string they co-created with elementary-age students:

- *What do I already know about this author?*
- *What does the author know about this topic?*
- *How do we think the author feels about this topic?*
- *What can we learn about this topic from the author? (117)*

Note that they start with a question about *authorship*, then move to a question about sources and *credibility*, followed by a question about *techniques* and *interpretation*, and wrapping up with a *responses* question.

› In terms of skill development, the media you analyze matter.

As you select which media to spend time analyzing, keep these factors in mind:

- The goal is literacy. We want children to be able to read *all* media, so provide opportunities to show what media do well, not just what they do wrong.
- When children are just starting out, it will be easier to analyze a still image than videos, games, or apps, where images are moving, fleeting, and accompanied by sound.
- The vast majority of media examples should come directly from children's lives—things already in the classroom, videos you know they have seen at home, signs that children pass on the way to your center, and so forth. This provides a direct connection to children's lives, so skills are applicable in a concrete and immediate way.

It will also help you avoid a common error. There is a media literacy practice that goes something like this: A teacher identifies a media-related concern. For example, she notices that children are favoring sugary snacks over fresh fruit. So, she finds a misleading ad for a sugary snack and plans a group analysis. The children view the ad, and because everyone always pays most attention to what's new, the kids focus on the ad's upbeat music, bright colors, and apparently delicious snack. They have now been introduced to a snack they'd never encountered before, and their first exposure is via a carefully crafted, slick advertisement shown by a trusted authority. It's a marketer's dream.

Even children who fully understand the nutrition lessons that the teacher uses to frame the ad are likely to be curious about the new food. The outcome is exactly the opposite of what the teacher was trying to achieve. In general, we don't want to introduce new media that exposes kids to things they've never encountered, especially if they are things that we want children to avoid.

There are important exceptions to this rule. You might, for example, want children to grapple with issues in ways that they won't take personally. If you analyze an ad for their favorite snack (because that would be following the guideline to use a media example that children have already seen), the discussion could quickly devolve into defensive justifications rather than analysis. To get around that problem, you can use old ads that are parallel, but for products that aren't sold anymore. Then you can ask how they might apply what they've learned to media they know.

› If you are analyzing a narrative, limit the questioning the first time through.

To ensure comprehension, children need to take in a story in its entirety before we ask them to start dissecting it. And if you disrupt an engaging story with lots of digressions, they'll be rightfully annoyed. Fortunately, children often enjoy repeated viewings or readings. That's when you'll get the best results from introducing analysis questions.

- Limit the "like."

  Note that the sample questions don't include "What did you like?" or its twin, "What was your favorite?" ("What did you like best?"). These can be fine questions if the answers reveal something you need to know. If, for example, you are a librarian trying to figure out which book or video to recommend to a particular child, asking what they liked about the most recent selection could be a valuable, probative question.

  Too often, however, preference questions are asked without any real purpose. And when they become one of the questions that grown-ups ask most often, they can become a problem. Here's why:

1. Preference questions aren't great critical thinking questions.

   If part of what we want to instill is the habit of linking answers to evidence, then we don't want the questions we ask most often to be unanswerable using logic and reasoning. For example, if you ask me why I like vanilla ice cream, the best answer I can give is that I think it tastes good. There is no evidence you can bring to convince me that, logically, I should prefer chocolate. Instead of opening our conversation to ever more interesting possibilities, my answer ends the conversation.

2. Answers often require a vocabulary and awareness that young children lack.

   Children might be able to tell you that they liked a particular game because it was fun, but they won't be able to explain why. Or their answers won't really provide insight:

   "I liked it because it was funny."

   "Tell me more about what made it funny."

   "It made me laugh."

3. Choosing favorites limits options when there is no need to choose.

   If you watched a video series from your local zoo, and you were especially intrigued by three of the animals featured, whose interests would be served by forcing you to choose only one? The answer might just be marketers. They often ask us to "like" things or vote for "the best" because that helps them develop the profile that they will use to sell our eyeballs to advertisers, and it helps advertisers customize what they show us. Rather than present the world as a series of false choices, the critical inquiry version of "Which was your favorite?" is to engage in compare and contrast (e.g., "What was interesting or boring about _______?").

4. Asking about "favorites" or "likes" places the focus of interpretation exclusively on the personal.

   That can reinforce a thinking pattern that promotes self-centeredness, privilege, consumerism, and, eventually, obsession with earning "likes" from others. What if, instead, we helped children see that the world doesn't revolve around "likes" and there is value in examining what's good for everyone, not just an endless search for things *they* like?

5. Bottom line: For media literacy analysis, before you ask about favorites, ask yourself if there is a valid reason to force children to choose in this situation. Don't ask children which parts they liked or what was the "best" unless the answer is really what you need to know.

## Media Analysis in Action

As the leader of a community of learners, you can use media analysis questions to open discussions and guide explorations in ways that are surprisingly substantive. Consider, for example, the possibilities offered by analyzing Figure 6.2.

Posters like the one in Figure 6.2 hang in early childhood education settings all over the world. At first glance, it appears to be very simple with a clear purpose: to illustrate the four seasons. Analyzing it allows you to cover its science lesson and model inquiry at the same time, and that can open the door to deep conversations (Table 6.1).

**Figure 6.2 Poster of the seasons. Used with permission, Creative Teaching Press, creativeteaching.com.**

**Table 6.1 Integrating Media Literacy: Seasons Poster Analysis**

GOAL: Imagine that the children in this scenario are 4- and 5-year-olds. Your primary objective is to introduce a unit on the seasons in which children learn the name and associated weather of each season.

Your secondary goal is to model inquiry and observation and apply those skills to analyzing a media document. You don't expect that children will walk away from this lesson having mastered the inquiry skills, but the modeling will contribute to their eventually learning how to question media for themselves.

| | Question Category |
|---|---|
| You (Y): I've been wondering about this poster that has been hanging on our wall. Posters are a type of media. Let's look at it closely. What do you think this poster is trying to tell us? | *Content* |
| Child 1: Kids like being outside. | *(Not the observation you expected! But you stick with media analysis questions, trusting that if you continue to talk about the poster's messages, seasons will surely come up.)* |
| Y: What makes you think that? | *Follow-Up* |
| C1: The kids are smiling. | |
| Y: That's an important observation. Looking at people's faces can tell us how they are feeling, and a smile usually means they're happy. What clues do you see that they are outside? | *Techniques, Content, Interpretation* |
| C1: There's outside stuff. | |
| Y: Outside stuff? | |
| C1: A sun. | |
| C3: And leaves. | |
| C2: And they have hats. The rule is no hats inside. | |
| Y: Those are good pieces of evidence that they are outside. | |
| So one message of the poster is that kids like to be outside. Does anyone see any other messages? | *Follow-Up* |
| Children: Ummm | |
| Y: Do you think they are all in the same place? | *Interpretation* |
| C1: Yeah, it's all white. | |
| Y: That's true—every square has a white background. | |
| C3: But they are different. | |
| Y: Tell me more. What do you notice that's different? | *Follow-Up, Content* |
| C3: One has snowflakes and one has flowers. | |
| C4: And one has leaves . . . and that one (pointing) has bees. | |
| C5: And one doesn't have a hat. | |
| C6: What's she holding? | |

**Table 6.1 Integrating Media Literacy: Seasons Poster Analysis cont'd.**

| | Question Category |
|---|---|
| Y: You mean the one without the hat? [child nods, "Yes"] Who can answer C6's question? | *Content* |
| C2: Watermelon. I love watermelon. | |
| Y: Has anyone else ever eaten a watermelon slice like in the picture? [hands go up] What did it taste like? | *Context, Interpretation* |
| C4: Sweet. | |
| C5: Yummy. And drippy. | |
| Y: Watermelon is a sweet, juicy fruit. Maybe we can have it for snack sometime soon. I remember having watermelon on the Fourth of July. Do you remember when you had watermelon? Was it snowy or sunny? | |
| C2: Like the picture. Sunny. | |
| Y: So, if the word under the picture with the watermelon is the name of the season—the time of year—when we eat watermelon, what do you think the label says? | *Content* |

Once they know "summer," you can ask what the poster tells them about how many different seasons there are and how they know. That leads to everyone counting the boxes together, which you use as a segue to affirm that the year is divided into four seasons, the way the poster is divided into four boxes. You review the names of each of the seasons.

You might then ask what they think the title of the poster is and whether they can spot it. If they point to the word across the top, ask how they know that's the title (*techniques*) and note things like size and placement. As you read the title with them, perhaps sounding out the first letter together, continue the discussion by asking how the title relates to the poster's messages (*techniques, content*).

You follow up reading aloud all the words, introducing the words in other languages spoken by children in the group, asking which season we are in now, and inviting children to name some of the things that are unique to each season. You can even point out that the people on the poster might, indeed, all be in the same place (like Child 1 said in Table 6.1), but at different times of the year.

You could wrap up the analysis by asking if they think the poster does a good job of reminding children like them about the differences between the seasons (*interpretations* with a nod to target audience, which is related to *purposes*). Ask if there is anything the children would add to a square that would make the messages about the season even more clear to them (a version of the question "What's missing that might be important to know?"—a *content* question we often ask older students).

End by asking if there's anything else anyone notices that they want to talk about or any other questions they have about the poster. If they have questions, ask, "How could we find an answer?" (*follow-up*) and guide them in the process. Or if you need to move on, write down their questions and come back to them later.

This particular dialogue was guided toward teaching the names and distinguishing characteristics of the four seasons. There are lots of other ways that the leader could have steered the conversation to cover different topics.

At the moment the child asked about watermelon in Table 6.1, the exploration could have shifted to types of fruit, where they're grown, when they are harvested (and why we call that being "in season").

Or when a child asked, "What's *she* holding?" the teacher might have asked, "What makes you say *she*?" That could spark a lesson examining the validity of the clues that people use to distinguish between boys and girls (e.g., hair length). Note that the poster itself does not preclude more fluid gender interpretations, so it could provide an opportunity to talk about how different people express their gender identity or that some people reject dualistic gender identity.

Or you could link the discussion to both science and geography by asking children to think about whether the poster's pictures are accurate representations of what happens where they live. That question might be accompanied by time outdoors, with questions to ponder like "Is it only sunny in summer?" "Is it never winter in places that rarely or never get snow (e.g., Miami, Phoenix, San Antonio)?"

After considering the climate patterns where they live, the teacher could ask children what they want to do (*response*). Perhaps they could create their own media depicting the seasons (and, of course, have conversations about their target audience and what they choose to include). Or maybe they'd choose to communicate with the people who made the poster to find out why they show the seasons the way that they do.

Or the discussion could become a compare and contrast using other seasons posters. Do they all include the same clues to the seasons? Do they all have the same seasons in the same positions (i.e., is winter always top left with the other seasons in order going clockwise)? Noticing these sorts of details reinforces the key media literacy concept that all media are constructed. For each poster, media makers had to make choices about where to put the picture for each season and what would be included in each picture.

The oldest children might go on to explore how the months that we think of for each season are different in other parts of the world (e.g., December–February is winter in North America and summer in Australia). Talk about how that might influence the images on holiday cards.

Or the teacher could begin with a completely open-ended query: "What do you notice?" That could lead to children's questions like "Why don't they have noses?" and a discussion of the function of noses or styles of drawing ("How did we know they are people even though they don't have noses?"). Or maybe children notice the variations in skin tone that they compare to themselves, or bees and a butterfly that leads to an investigation of pollinators and their relationship to flowers. Perhaps they make up stories that might happen in each square, and then make lists of what would need to be added to each picture to illustrate the story. They might even practice making inferences from images by exploring the messages about temperature or weather that are conveyed by people's clothing.

Without a media literacy education approach, a poster depicting the seasons would likely hang on the bulletin board and, if referenced at all, would only be pointed to briefly as an illustration while the teacher explained the seasons. But what looks like a very simple, common poster turns out to be a rich source of discussion and discovery when we treat it as media worthy of analysis.

## Refining Your Analysis Skills

Of course, the analysis doesn't always go quite as smoothly as described here. Kids' attention will wander. They'll bring up things that seem to be totally off topic or interrupt each other. Conversations can be winding and messy.

Like any skill, analysis takes practice. The more you do it, the better everyone will get (including you). Just keep in mind that media literacy analysis is not a test and you're not a proctor. Once children get the hang of it, you'll find that they love talking about media because it is an important part of their lives, and because even those who struggle with other skills often have valuable contributions to make.

To get to that comfortable point, where discussions of media are natural and the analysis is rich, there are some important things to notice about how the analysis of the poster was structured:

- Most of what the adult leader says is in the form of a question. The leader even uses questions to move the analysis in certain directions (e.g., asking if all the people on the poster are in the same place as a way to help children take a close look at the differences in the four squares).
- Vocabulary that will enable future analysis is introduced naturally, as part of the dialogue (message, label, background, poster, observation, evidence, clue, notice). The context of the conversation supplies the meaning without having to stop to memorize definitions.
- The exchange is relatively short. With young children, you aren't going to spend half an hour discussing a media document. Instead, plan to come back to it several times as needed to respond to children's interests or meet your curriculum requirements.
- At least part of the conversation flows from children's interests. Children often tell us with their questions what they're ready to learn. How deep you go will depend on what children are ready for and what you want/need to address. In this instance, the leader allows for a short digression about watermelon, and then uses the topic to return the focus to seasons.
- Rather than asking little ones to focus on everything all at once, we steer the discussion to focus on one thing at a time. Technology integration specialist Gail Lovely does this literally, by covering parts of an image in order to draw attention to a specific part of the picture and then gradually revealing additional sections. You can see her describe the process here (starting at 3:15): https://www.youtube.com/watch?v=Tfvn2g50PNw.

## Tip for Working with ELLs/DLLs

Analyzing media can also provide rich opportunities to involve English or dual language learners. Images have the advantage of being understood by children who speak various languages in a way that text is not. Children can point to what they mean, and even if they are speaking in their first language, others will understand, at least in general terms. Also, consider ahead of time key phrases that everyone needs to know so they can follow the discussion (e.g., What do you notice? How do you know? Show me.). Be sure there are translations available for these phrases.

## Developmentally Appropriate Expectations for Analysis

"There's no way my children could do that. They're too young!" Sound familiar? Some early childhood professionals believe that young children aren't capable of media literacy inquiry—that is, until they try it.

Media literacy education pioneer Cary Bazalgette (2010) reminds us that young children routinely watch much more complex and sophisticated narratives than they are being offered as beginning print readers. They are often capable of much deeper thinking than we give them credit for, as the work of many media literacy educators demonstrates (e.g., Vivian Vasquez, Vítor Tomé, Cyndy Scheibe, Akiea Gross). There are many more who offer developmentally appropriate examples of general critical thinking (e.g., Ann Pelo, Margie Carter, Janis Strasser, Lisa Mufson Bresson).

Based on what we know about children's development (and remembering that individual children develop in spurts, at different rates, and don't magically change on their birthdays), here's a rough outline of what you might expect from neurotypical children at varying ages:

0–2

Model asking media literacy questions but don't expect answers.

2–3

Ask media literacy questions and expect some answers, but not necessarily answers based on logic or reason.

3–4

- Ask media literacy questions and expect children to understand *what* exists without necessarily understanding *why*.
- Expect that they can learn to spot a few concrete analytical clues (things you can easily see or hear in a media example) and understand overt message(s), but don't expect explanations of the reasons for including such clues.

4–5

- Ask media literacy questions and expect that children can link answers to specific evidence that is document based or from personal experience.
- Ask media literacy questions in ways that introduce analytical *concepts* (e.g., people make media; who we are influences how we interpret media messages) and social issues (e.g., representation; the impact of consumer culture). Expect children to understand that media makers make choices, but don't expect them to be able to consistently identify the reasons for those choices or their consequences.

5–7

- Ask media literacy questions and expect that children can provide evidence-based answers that explain messages, including who might benefit or be harmed by certain messages, and also why media makers might have included particular messages (i.e., they understand intent). Note that the ability to identify media makers' choices and link messages to potential consequences means that children are ready to engage in discussions of social justice issues and actions they might take. Also expect that answers might include simple inferences.
- Expect children to start asking their own media literacy questions and have ideas about how to find credible, evidence-based answers.
- Expect children to begin to ask and answer basic media literacy questions about the media they make.

Perhaps the most convincing evidence that media literacy conversations are both possible and important, even with very young children, is found in research-based education standards.

The "Professional Standards and Competencies for Early Childhood Educators" position statement from NAEYC (2020) expects professionals to engage "in genuine, reciprocal conversations with children; eliciting and exploring children's ideas; asking questions that probe and stimulate children's thinking, understanding, theory-building, and shared construction of meaning" (19).

The 2016 Ontario, Canada, Kindergarten Program extends such skills specifically to media. These standards from the Ontario Ministry of Education (2016) embrace a critical literacy approach to enable kindergartners "to navigate a text- and media-saturated world in order to meet the challenges of an ever-more-complex society." The recommendations involve "looking beyond the literal meaning of a text in order to analyse and evaluate the text's complete meaning and the author's intent . . . to construct, understand, and express our world." The explanation continues,

> For this to happen, children must see their classroom as a place where they can safely ask questions, examine their own and others' viewpoints, clarify their thinking, and take a stand on the issues and relationships that are important to them and their future. A learning

environment that is respectful and that is co-created with the children promotes the development of skills such as risk taking and inquiry that are fundamental to critical literacy and critical thinking.

Keeping all these considerations in mind, educators can provide multiple opportunities for children to develop critical literacy skills by:

- Providing entry points for discussion of the children's questions and wonderings
- Reading aloud with the children and asking questions to stimulate discussion . . . For example, after reading about a social issue that is important to the children, the educators may ask questions to focus and scaffold discussion, such as, "Someone wrote this story. Who do you think it's written for?"; "Let's look at it from the point of view of J. . . ."; "Whose voice is missing?"; "How could the story be told differently?" (Ontario Ministry of Education 2016, 70–1)

Writing in general terms about education for all ages, the NCTE Task Force on Critical Media Literacy (2021) echoes Ontario's Ministry of Education, describing critical literacy as a pedagogy focused on disrupting structural inequities and injustices. When we use that pedagogy to tie inquiry to action, they write, we "help learners see themselves as empowered change agents, able to imagine and build a better and more just world" (6).

You'll find additional standards in the Appendix C: Resources. All of them are based on multiyear efforts by teams of professionals who consider published research and collect evidence from practicing educators, and all assume that inquiry and analysis are well within the developmental abilities of young children.

# Synthesis

In a 2012 convocation address to the Harvard Graduate School of Education, Professor Eleanor Duckworth summarized her constructivist approach to education saying, "Learners thrive when a teacher is interested in their questions and thoughts, and is helping them take these thoughts deeply into a subject matter through their own explorations" (Duckworth 2012). To put it another way, if you want *children* to be interested in their thinking, *you* need to demonstrate an interest in their thinking.

When the media texts we share are accessible, and the analysis process grows out of curiosity and appreciation that little ones' perspectives are valuable, we're likely to be surprised not just by what they learn, but also by what *we* learn.

PAUSE TO **REFLECT**

Choose any media example you have shared (or intend to share) with children. What's one question you could ask that would help them think more deeply about its messages? What might you plan to ask as a follow-up?

## Sources

Bazalgette, C., ed. 2010. *Teaching Media in Primary Schools.* London, UK: SAGE & Media Education Association.

Duckworth, E. 2012. "Faculty Convocation Speech." Presented at the Harvard Graduate School of Education 2012 Commencement in Cambridge, MA. www.gse.harvard.edu/news/12/05/commencement-2012-professor-eleanor-duckworths-convocation-speech.

NAEYC. 2020. "Professional Standards and Competencies for Early Childhood Educators." Position statement. Washington, DC: NAEYC. www.naeyc.org/resources/position-statements/professional-standards-competencies

NCTE (National Council of Teachers of English) Task Force on Critical Media Literacy. 2021. *Report of the Task Force on Critical Media Literacy.* Report. Urbana, IL: NCTE. https://ncte.org/critical-media-literacy.

Ontario Ministry of Education. 2016. *The Kindergarten Program, 2016.* Toronto: Queen's Printer for Ontario. www.edu.gov.on.ca/eng/curriculum/elementary/kindergarten.html.

Pelo, A., & M. Carter. 2018. *From Teaching to Thinking: A Pedagogy for Reimagining Our Work.* Lincoln, NE: Exchange Press.

Wiesel, E. 2000. "Oprah Talks to Elie Wiesel," interview by Oprah. *O, The Oprah Magazine,* November. www.oprah.com/omagazine/oprah-interviews-elie-wiesel/all.

Ziemke, K., & K. Muhtaris. 2020. *Read the World: Rethinking Literacy for Empathy and Action in a Digital Age.* Portsmouth, NH: Heinemann.

CHAPTER 7

# Building Media Knowledge: Key Concepts

As the previous chapter explored, one of the ways that we teach children to think critically about media is by introducing particular categories of questions they can ask. To build the background knowledge that makes sophisticated analysis possible, there are also important media concepts that they, and their grown-ups, should learn—many more than are possible to cover in this book. Fortunately, just three key concepts unlock nearly everything else:

1. All media are constructed.
2. People use their individual skills, beliefs, and experiences to construct meanings from media messages.
3. Media shape and are shaped by us.

These concepts are the bedrock on which media analysis is built. This chapter explains them and explores their implications for teaching, learning, and analyzing media.

## 1. All Media Are Constructed

Len Masterman, one of media literacy education's earliest advocates, tells the story of art teacher Fred Bazler. Mr. Bazler held up a painting of a horse and asked his class of eight-year-olds what it was. When the kids answered, "A horse," their teacher insisted it wasn't. Confusion reigned until the class realized that it wasn't a horse; it was a picture of a horse (Masterman 1985).

What Mr. Bazler's students learned that day is that all media are re-presentations (representations). We are never just looking at media through our own eyes; we're also looking through the eyes of media creators. When we say that all media are "constructed," we are acknowledging that media are made by people, and everyone who makes media has particular purposes and perspectives that influence the media they create. Understanding the constructed nature of media helps us see and understand the links between media makers' choices and the messages they convey.

Here's how to explain the concept of "constructedness" to young children:

- *People* make media.
- The people who make media (including us!) make choices about what to include and leave out, and how to tell their "stories."
- Those choices matter because they affect what audiences think and feel.

The point isn't to teach a definition, or even the word *constructed*. Instead, the goal in early childhood is to instill an intuitive sense of the concept.

### People Make Media

To adults, the idea that media are made by people seems obvious. We understand that even "automatic" algorithms and bots are designed by people. But for very young children, media appear out of nowhere and media makers are invisible. A child taps on a screen and Poof! there is a video.

Disembodied voices come out of a box. For little ones, it's a major insight to realize that media makers exist.

So, media literacy educators help children develop a habit of awareness—they make the invisible visible. One way to do that is to sprinkle comments into regular routines. If you play music for transitions, you can announce the artist at the start of the song (just like you name the author and illustrator when you begin a read-aloud). If you see a flyer tacked to a telephone pole you can ask, "I wonder who designed that?" as you walk by. Is there a painting in the hallway? Point out the artist's signature and the next time you ask children to put their names on their drawings, make the link. These are each passing moments. No need to dwell in order to achieve this particular media literacy outcome.

When you routinely take note of media makers, eventually children will follow your lead. As they develop language and cognitive skills, they're likely to start asking for themselves, "I wonder who made that?"

## People Who Make Media Make Choices

Sometimes early childhood educators refer to media as providing a "window on the world." They mean that media can introduce children to new ideas, people, places, and things. Media can, indeed, be phenomenally good at showing worlds beyond the boundaries of personal experience. When we label that portal as providing a "window," however, it's easy to forget that media are never neutral.

From live-streamed concerts or on-the-scene news reports to Zoom meetings and webinars, it can feel like you're experiencing media events for yourself, but the very definition of media is that there's always something (made by someone) between you and the things you see and hear. That means media are never "windows on the world" in the sense of looking at something directly. Even windows have frames that restrict your view.

You may have heard this idea expressed as "all media are biased." In media literacy, to label something as "biased" is just another way of saying that it was made by people. Bias isn't necessarily bad—it's human. And unavoidable. In media literacy, *bias* isn't a synonym for *unfair*. It's not even always intentional or conscious.

Biases might include a maker's explicit or implicit beliefs about politics, religion, or identity. They also might reflect the fact that at any given moment a media maker is interested in some topics and not others, or that they've internalized messages about

- Using particular words in certain situations—for example, whether there is pressure to "code switch," reserving native language patterns for private communication while adopting dominant speech patterns in order to be taken seriously in public, especially at school or work
- Media conventions—the production techniques people learn that make certain shots, actors, or design choices seem "right" in specific situations
- What counts as expertise—how people determine whom to believe when there are conflicting claims or which people should be interviewed or consulted when discussing certain topics

Because media always reflect their makers' biases, NAMLE's *Core Principles of Media Literacy Education* (2007, 1.6) advises that "teachers do not train students to ask IF there is a bias in a particular message (since all media messages are biased), but rather, WHAT the substance, source, and significance of a bias might be."

## Media Makers' Choices Matter

Teaching the concept of constructedness helps children understand that media are complex, and if they learn to look beyond the surface, they'll find all sorts of intriguing things. But because little ones are at a developmental stage when they aren't yet able to fully understand the motives of off-screen media creators, the concept of media makers making choices can be difficult to understand. Media literacy educators use hands-on media-making activities to bridge that gap between the abstract and the concrete. But not just any media making. A media literacy version of media making engages kids in making production decisions and explaining their choices.

Imagine, for example, giving children the opportunity to make digital or hard copy cards for a beloved intern who is graduating and moving away. Invite each child to talk about how they want the intern—their "target audience"—to feel when they open their card and how what they include on their card will help them communicate that message. Take a moment to marvel at each child's power to make the aide feel happy or appreciated by the specific content they choose to include (e.g., *"She's going to love that you drew your shoes with bunny ears because you remembered the trick she taught that helped you learn to tie them"*). For more examples of making media with children, see Chapters 9 and 10.

Once children see themselves as media makers and are aware of their own choices and the potential effect of those choices, they are ready to understand that all media makers make choices. At that point, you can help them begin to link what they know about their own media making to the media they use. Depending on their developmental stage, it would be appropriate to expect that:

- Very young children can understand that the media they see and hear are made by people.
- Young children can also understand that those media makers make choices.
- Older children can understand the first two and also that media makers' choices influence messages. They can ask basic media literacy questions for themselves and begin to learn how to find answers.

Children who understand all three aspects of constructedness are primed to understand the concept of "motive," which means, among other things, that they can begin to grasp the concept of "selling intent," that some media are more about selling them stuff than entertaining or informing them. They will also begin to develop a sense of themselves as media makers, with all the responsibilities, power, and potential that entails.

## 2. People Use Their Individual Skills, Beliefs, and Experiences to Construct Meanings from Media Messages

Children's television icon Fred Rogers sometimes shared stories about unusual instances when a child was disturbed or frightened by something they saw on the stereotypically wholesome *Mister Rogers' Neighborhood* (Rogers 1996). What Fred discovered was that no matter how mindfully the production team designed scenes to mitigate anxiety, children viewed the show through their individual interpretive lenses. He described them as children's "inner dramas" (Rogers & Head 1983, 167). The divergent reactions remind us that, no matter their age, children are already making meaning from media and that meaning is influencing how they interact with the world.

We began to explore this concept in Chapter 3. Our shared cultural lens allows for many common, widely held interpretations—what scholars refer to as "dominant" readings. But, as the *Mister Rogers* team realized, our personal filters sometimes lead to alternative interpretations. These are typically less common, but they are no less valid. Recognizing this interpretive lens helps us to understand some of our differences and so to be better teachers.

## Effects Aren't Automatic

One very important consequence of people making meaning through the filter of their own experience is that interpretations, and therefore media effects, are never automatic. Let's explore this for a moment.

When you aren't aware of a child's "inner drama," their reactions to certain media can be puzzling. But when you take the time to get to know a child, things are often clear and predictable. For example, the story of a windy day that most people see as delightful or fun might trigger trauma for a child who has lived through a recent hurricane or upset a child whose birthday balloon was carried away by the breeze.

Or consider this example. Like many early childhood advocates, I've never been a fan of the *Mighty Morphin Power Rangers*. I appreciate the entertainment value of the show's campy humor, but its repetitive plot line suggests that violence is an effective way to resolve disputes and is justified when perpetrated by the "good guys." For years, scattered research and anecdotal reports told stories of children (especially boys) who copied the Power Rangers' fighting moves and hurt their playmates (Boyatzis, Matillo, & Nesbitt 1995; Levin & Carlsson-Paige 1995). But some children copied the Rangers' moves without ever hurting another child. And still others watched the show and never acted it out at all. We won't take the time to explore the many factors that determine how each child's unique interpretive lens influenced their response to the show's messages. The point here is that variations in children's filters exist and our teaching practices must account for those variations.

Early childhood educators Matthew Lawrence and Deb Curtis provide a good example. Instead of forbidding the rough-and-tumble superhero Power Rangers play they observed, invited children to tell them about the Rangers. Because they opened up space for conversation, they discovered that children liked the Rangers primarily because the Rangers help people. That insight led them to a role that staff could play: They offered to be people in need of help. And once they were part of the game, they could reinforce the message that helping is a good thing and that children can play physically without being violent (Lawrence, with Curtis 2020). We are more effective as teachers when we prioritize understanding how individual filters affect the ways that children see media rather than judging their media preferences or framing their preferences as a clash of cultures that pits our values against the media that they love.

Critical literacy educator Vivian Vasquez provides evidence that opening up nonjudgmental spaces for children to talk about media can lead to the very critiques of media that address our most pressing concerns. She writes that opportunities to engage with critical literacies "arise as we create opportunities for children to first make visible what is on their minds" (Vasquez 2014, 6). In Vasquez's junior kindergarten class, children led and set the agenda for regular class meetings. In one of those meetings, two children included a topic that for them was immediate and important. They were frustrated that the *Power Rangers* show kept changing the characters. Through discussion, they linked what was happening on the show to an insight from a prior meeting when they discovered that McDonald's changes the giveaways in Happy Meals® so kids will keep coming back to get the new toys. They reasoned that the people who make *Power Rangers* did the same thing. In other words, they were beginning to understand how market forces shape media.

Had talk about *Power Rangers* been discouraged, the class never would have gained this important insight. They reached their conclusion with some guidance to be sure, but without an adult lecturing at them about the manipulations used by corporate media. And though Vasquez doesn't explicitly say so, I'd guess that because the children discovered the information on their own, the learning was likely more powerful and "sticky" than if a grown-up had just told them about the ways that marketers use novelty to encourage viewing or purchasing.

Engaging with rather than judging children's media preferences doesn't mean we give up our own media evaluation. The success of these interventions doesn't change my mind about *Power Rangers*. I still think there are far better superhero role models, including those with magical powers that children can only pretend to copy rather than the easily mimicked punches and kicks used by the Rangers. But the examples from these educators remind me that divergent interpretive lenses are part of being human. They help me appreciate the habit of asking children about the meaning they are making rather than assuming I already know or that they should share my views.

It doesn't do any good to tell a child not to like what they like. The job of an educator can't be to condemn media that give children pleasure. Instead, we use a media literacy inquiry approach to add new information and perspectives that can help children think in more complex ways about the media they enjoy.

PAUSE TO **REFLECT**

What shows or video games from your childhood gave you pleasure? How do you think they affected your ideas about the world?

What did the important grown-ups in your life think about your viewing or playing choices?

How did they communicate their opinions to you? Do you think they understood why you liked the media you chose?

What lessons does your own childhood experience offer about how you could talk with children about their media choices today?

## Accepting Multiple Interpretations

Understanding that everyone interprets through their own filters is an exceptionally important concept for teaching because it means that different people can interpret the same things differently without anyone being wrong. If multiple conclusions are possible, then our goal in teaching media analysis can't be to guide children to a single "correct" interpretation (even if that interpretation is ours and we are sure that we are right!).

Instead, we work to help children develop the habit of linking conclusions to evidence and, as they are developmentally able, we help them to notice their unique interpretive lens. In other words, media literacy is about teaching children *how* to think, not *what* to think. Making that shift can profoundly transform our teaching.

At a media literacy conference many years ago I had an "aha" moment that clarified for me just how important it is for teachers to be open to multiple interpretations. A morning workshop leader well known for media interpretation showed and critiqued a popular beer ad in which a celebrity treated his date poorly. He concluded that the ad's message was sexist, and therefore damaging.

At lunch I found myself at a table with several high school students. Curious about their opinions of the mostly adult conference, I asked what had stood out for them so far. They responded by deriding a "clueless" session leader who had, in their view, completely misinterpreted a beer ad. They agreed that the man's behavior in the ad was obnoxious, but argued that the message was actually anti-sexist. They explained that the man in the ad was a comedian well known for playing a buffoon. For them the message was, "Do the opposite of whatever this dude does. Never treat women this way."

The problem wasn't that the students disagreed with the workshop leader. The problem was that the leader prioritized demonstrating his own skills rather than inviting the group into an inquiry process. He left the students feeling shut down and invisible. As a result, they disengaged and their interpretation remained at a surface level. They missed an opportunity to examine deeper issues about how humor that relies on stereotypes might unintentionally reinforce them. And the instructor missed an opportunity to broaden his own analysis and learn from more diverse perspectives.

If everyone in that room had started by acknowledging that there were likely to be multiple valid interpretations, the session might have focused on what we learn about each other from the process of analyzing the ad. That discussion might have given everyone new insights and we all would have left the room feeling eager to explore more media together. Instead, a teacher who was invested in everyone endorsing his expert conclusions ended up alienating the very students he hoped to empower.

Early childhood educators need to exercise a bit of finesse to apply this lesson to our own work because we often need to provide explanations in order to ensure basic understanding. From there, it's easy to slip into telling children what to think (i.e., interpreting for them). As much we need to address comprehension, we also need to use questions that prompt children to figure things out for themselves. So, as often as possible, we need to step back from the role of "expert" in order to open up space for rich, multifaceted meaning making.

### PAUSE TO **REFLECT**

Using media to teach requires us to anticipate differences in interpretation. Imagine that you are crafting a lesson on neighborhood "helpers" and plan to use a video about first responders. The video shows children how to spot the people who can provide aid so they know whom to approach if they are ever in trouble and need help. It includes police officers. What questions would you ask yourself in order to prepare for the ways that children might respond to the video?

If you're having trouble thinking of questions, try these:

- Who might be frightened or upset by the video and why? How will I respond to them?
- How might race influence the ways that children react to the video?
- Might some families object to their children being taught that police are safe and trustworthy, and if they do, how will I respond?
- How could I design a lesson that addresses concerns and also helps *all* children learn to identify people in their community who will help them?

## Not Every Interpretation Is Valid

Recognition that everyone interprets through their own filter does not mean that "anything goes." We can't point to a rectangle and insist that it is a sphere. No one gets to invent their own reality devoid of history, facts, or common cultural understanding. As media literacy educators, we are always open to learning more about how others think. What allows for that openness is a reliance on everyone to use reason and evidence as a common ground.

The establishment of that common ground increases our capacity to negotiate controversies. For example, imagine that the leadership and staff of a child-care center has decided to institute a new rule banning display of the Confederate flag. The director must now respond to a few resistant families.

But this is a media literate community in which everyone acknowledges that people's interpretations will vary. So, the director has no problem acknowledging that while some people display the Confederate flag as an intentional provocation to assert racist power, others interpret the flag as a symbol of pride in aspects of their Southern heritage that they don't associate with support for slavery or hate.

Acknowledging that varying interpretations exist isn't the same as accepting them all as equally valid. In this case, the "heritage" interpretation, even when well intended or the result of a knowledge gap, can't erase the reality of the flag's origins.

The Confederate flag was created to signify affinity with a group of citizens who chose to wage a war to dissolve the United States in order to preserve states' legal authority to enslave Black people. The fact that for some families the flag's meaning has grown beyond those origins doesn't change the reality that other families will reasonably see it as a symbol of racism and oppression. For them, the symbol will unavoidably trigger the pain and outrage that flow from recalling its historical association with brutality and injustice. They can't choose to "un-know" the history they know.

Understanding the concept that people interpret media through the filter of their own lives means that we treat interpretation as a dialogue, not a debate. It's about learning, not winning. So, the director doesn't have to convince the families that the Confederate flag is racist and the families don't have to convince the center staff that it's not. If everyone understands that people interpret through the lens of their own experiences, then they can agree on the reality that both interpretations exist. In fact, the acknowledgment of multiple interpretations underscores the possibility that the display of the flag at the child-care center could be easily misinterpreted, and misinterpretation could inflict harm on the center and the community it serves. Hence the decision to implement the ban.

Media literacy enables us to acknowledge, name, and respect the diversity of interpretations that exist in our community. Doing so makes people feel "seen" and respected and ready to shift away from an argument about whose interpretation is correct to a more helpful and substantive conversation. In this situation, people might move forward by using a different type of media literacy question: Instead of the Confederate flag, what symbols could the center include that wouldn't evoke a history of racism and pain but would celebrate the great parts of Southern heritage?

Understanding the interpretive lens is foundational work for culturally responsive and anti-racist teaching. It makes obvious the flawed thinking behind "I don't see color" approaches because it reveals the impossibility of sameness and requires us to see the whole child. As distinguished education scholar Lisa Delpit wrote about the importance of understanding who you were teaching, especially if you were teaching "other people's children" who don't share important aspects of your background, "Knowing students is a prerequisite for teaching them well" (Delpit 2012, 87). She wasn't intending to directly address media literacy issues, but it applies.

In order to treat every child fairly and with respect, we have to be willing to see and understand the entirety of who they are, including their unique filters. In our society, people with power have historically chosen to designate race as a significant difference and have implemented policies based on that difference. The effects can last for generations, even after systems have undertaken efforts to purge themselves of the original discriminatory laws and practices. As a result, racial identity will be a part of *every* child's filter.

It's not a choice to accept the legacy of White supremacy or not; it is inextricably part of our cultural fabric, even for recent immigrants who played no part in forging the nation's early years. Just as we can't draw a rectangle and insist that it is a sphere, we can't teach in a culture that has been constructed from racism and pretend that we are untouched by it, even as we work to end its injustices. Acknowledging and teaching about our interpretive lenses begins the process of equipping children to address the legacies of imposed inequities.

## Teaching the Concept of Interpretative Filters

Young children aren't developmentally ready to fully understand that their experiences—and the media interpretations that flow from them—aren't shared by everyone else in the world. But they encounter differences every day. You can lay a strong foundation for media literacy by taking advantage of those opportunities.

For example, a child may already know that their older sister doesn't enjoy the same games or videos that they enjoy. You can remind them that what their sister likes doesn't make their own preferences wrong, or vice versa. They are each interpreting through the filters of their own experience.

Or perhaps you overhear children disagreeing about a popular movie featuring cats. You could join the conversation saying something like, "All of you are right. People can think different things about the same movie. I wonder why you each reacted differently?" Invite them to share recent interactions with real cats. Was one of them recently scratched by a neighbor's calico while another loves their family's new kitten? Helping children to connect the dots between their own lived experiences and their reactions to what they see on screen grows their capacity for empathy as well as media analysis skills.

Or maybe you're reading aloud a book that includes illustrations of the way something looks from the perspective of different characters. (e.g., Anansi the Spider and the people he encounters, or Clifford the Big Red Dog and Emily Ann). Help children notice how the illustrations change depending on whose eyes we're looking through. Follow up with a hands-on demonstration by inviting children to use the camera on a tablet or phone. Help them hold it up high and then close to the ground so they can see the difference between what something looks like from above and from below. Or pose a drawing challenge: If a seagull in the sky and a fish in the water were both looking at the same boat, what would each see? Any way you teach it, the lesson is that sometimes different interpretations are rooted in our physical differences or the point of view from where we're standing.

Or you could explore different views that come from differences in knowledge. You might show and talk about a video like "The Biggest Rainbow" episode of *Curious George* in which George reads a book about pots of gold at the end of rainbows. He thinks it's true. His young friends, who learned about rainbows in school, know that the book was a fairy tale. They even know that just because it's in a book doesn't make something automatically true. The main lesson of the episode is about the science of rainbows, but with your guidance, children could also learn that different people can read the same book and interpret it differently because they have different levels of expertise on particular topics.

Just as children pass through predictable developmental stages, interpretive lenses will change as children grow. Our job as media literacy educators is to help each child adjust their lens as they go, so that with every new experience the lens becomes clearer and more useful.

When you teach children to recognize that each person has their own interpretative lens, you're socializing them to identify our commonalities—our shared lens—and also what makes our individual filters unique. They're learning to routinely look for, learn from, and value difference. It's great preparation for living in a democracy grounded in pluralism.

# 3. Media Shape and Are Shaped by Us

It's amazing how many people believe that they are immune to media influence. In one early study (Tiedge 1980, cited in Silverblatt et al.

2014, 6), 80% of respondents strongly agreed that media had an effect on society, but only 12% strongly agreed that media had an influence on them personally!

The truth is, we're all shaped by media, including those of us with sophisticated media literacy skills. Media are so intertwined in our culture that they are inescapable. If you live in the United States, chances are that shared pivotal moments with other Americans have been via media. Depending on your generation, you might recall the moon landing or the *Challenger* disaster, the Twin Towers being destroyed on 9/11, Barack Obama's inauguration as the first Black US president, or the more recent storming of the US Capitol building. These were events that some of us experienced in person, but most of us experienced through media.

Just as we can't ignore our culture or history, even those who choose not to include much media in their personal lives can't ignore media influences. At one level, the proof of media influence is obvious. If media didn't influence us, it's unlikely that companies would spend more than $500 billion on advertising globally each year.

Yet, with all their resources, advertisers still only dream of being able to design ads that guarantee results. That's because communication is two-way. Media owners and makers control only part of the interaction. That makes them powerful, but not omnipotent. And that's an important message to convey to children. People are certainly influenced by media in important ways, but they are not helpless victims.

## Media Shape Us

Media shape us through message and form. Both are a lot like a battery—there are positive and negative sides. That's what we'll explore in this section.

At their best, media present unbound possibilities. Documentaries and podcasts introduce new ideas by taking us to other continents, planets, and time periods. There are amateur athletes whose first encounter with their sport was watching a broadcast of the Olympics and concert pianists who heard their first symphony on a local public radio station. In movies, people can talk to animals, archeologists are heroes, and wizards show courage and leadership. And more than a few *Star Trek* fans credit the show with inspiring careers in science, engineering, or space travel. Perhaps you've had your own media-inspired "I want to go there or do that someday" moments?

Of course, the same facets of media that nurture our intellect and imagination also allow for the introduction of sinister ideas. Media that inspire people to military service can also glorify and sanitize the horrors of war. Social media sites help us stay connected but also proliferate posts designed to radicalize users into cults of hate or mislead them with conspiracy theories and unsafe health practices. And media that show a world of immense possibility can lead to depression when we discover that only a small percentage of people actually have access to the "lives-of-the-rich-and-famous" worlds they offer.

## Creating Norms

As Chapter 2's section on stereotypes explored, one important way that media shape us is by creating norms. Public relations professionals are paid to do just that. They use techniques like product placements in films, where branding specialists make sure that the hero drives their client's car or eats their client's cereal. But the really successful ones take it one step further. They don't just sell a particular brand or product; they sell an idea.

One of the most famous PR success stories was a campaign from the De Beers mining company. For millennia, rings have been a symbolic token of betrothal, but until the late 1940s, they rarely included diamonds. At the end of World War II, De Beers controlled 90 percent of the world's diamond supply. They bet that the growing American middle class would have money to spend on things like engagement rings and that the postwar spike in the number of marriages would create a large demand. Using publicity newsreels that featured glamorous Hollywood stars getting engaged, product placement in films, and advertisements featuring the now-famous tagline "A diamond is forever," they convinced people that a *diamond* ring was the only proper display of true love.

So, if you expect(ed) a diamond engagement ring, you've been shaped by a media-created norm. This type of cultural influence is a modest example of what Noam Chomsky and Edward Herman famously described as "manufactured consent," the idea that media convince the general population to accept and act on messages that reinforce the political, economic, and social status quos so those in power can stay in power (Herman & Chomsky 1988).

The more diverse the places that one receives a message, and the more often it is repeated, the more powerful the effect. That includes messages that aren't as direct as "buy a diamond ring."

## Mean World Syndrome

In the 1970s, media scholar George Gerbner drew on this concept of normalization to describe the observation that he dubbed the "mean world syndrome." He found that people who viewed a lot of TV were likely to think that the world was much more dangerous than it actually was in real life. It didn't matter that TV's normalizing of violence—both in news and in fictional programs—existed specifically because it was not the norm in real life (Gerbner et al. 1980).

The news, by definition, reports on what is unusual, not what occurs every day. And TV dramas would be boring if they showed us people pondering what to have for dinner, sorting laundry, or stuck in traffic. Violent action scenes and crimes draw audiences exactly because most of us don't experience them outside of media. How many times have you heard an interview with a real-life victim say, "We never thought it could happen to us. It's like something you only see on TV"?

Nevertheless, the mean world syndrome has had real-world impact on the ways that people raise children, making many families much more risk averse even though a child today is much safer than in previous decades (see, for example, the collection of statistics gathered by Lenore Skenazy at https://letgrow.org/crime-statistics). So, we see parents or guardians who live in safe neighborhoods drive kids to school instead of letting them walk or take public transportation. And many schools still offer "stranger danger" education, even though stranger abductions are exceedingly rare (accounting for just 0.3 percent of all missing children in the United States according to the Let Grow citation of a 2019 report from the Center for Missing and Exploited Children).

We see similar patterns of fear resulting from social media. Just as commercial television is structured to amplify drama, talk radio and social media algorithms are structured to amplify extreme views. With few real-life experiences to counteract the distortions, it's not surprising that people who spend a lot of time with these media are likely to demonize groups with whom they rarely interact personally—the ones they identify as "them" in contrast to "us."

## Representation

Making things seem normal can be a radically transformative act. For those who have been discriminated against or rendered invisible, seeing people like themselves on screen holds out the hope of greater acceptance and opportunity. The marginalized person is provided with a potential role model and everyone else gets accustomed to seeing marginalized people in positive roles. When in 2015 *Sesame Street* introduced a character with autism, for example, it not only let children on the autism spectrum know that they were worthy of inclusion, it also modeled ways that neurotypical children could befriend someone who might not always react in familiar or expected ways.

When Barack Obama was reelected president of the United States, a friend shared an anecdote about her Black preschooler who was excited and then paused to ask, "Can white people be president, too?" The child knew that a Black person could be president, but during their entire lifetime no White person had ever been president. It's easy to overlook how circumscribed young children's life experiences are and how much they are influenced by what they see—and what they don't see.

For young children, seeing someone who is like them expands their vision of what's possible (University of Pittsburgh School of Education Race and Early Childhood Collaborative 2016). Early childhood educators have opportunities to help children connect with media that show diverse role models. Knowing that *repetition* creates norms lets us understand why token examples won't satisfy the need.

Nor is simply counting the number of diverse characters in the media we use enough. We also need to analyze how characters are presented. For example, diverse casts are fairly common in children's media today, though White males are often still in the role of leader or central character. If all we do is count the number of times that characters from marginalized groups appear without examining their relationship to characters from groups in power, we may inadvertently reinforce the inequities we are trying to challenge.

By choosing to draw attention to some things while ignoring others, media don't so much tell us *what* to think as they shape what we think *about*. When we apply the concept to news and information, we call it *agenda setting*. It relies on our assumption that if a story is genuinely important, it will be covered by the news or talk shows. We tend to think that if journalists, media personalities, or influencers are talking about a topic, it must be significant and if they aren't, it must not be. That assumption is not entirely wrong—news media and talk shows often cover important stories. But it doesn't account for the profit (or sometimes political) motives involved in presenting some subjects while steering clear of others. Many vital topics remain hidden because they don't generate revenue or serve the interests of those in power. For example, we rarely see stories about child-care providers even though we know that child care is an essential service.

PAUSE TO **REFLECT**

Is there a topic that is important to you that you rarely see included in mainstream media? What action(s) could you take to get that topic on the agenda of media makers?

What's on the "agenda" in the media that the children you work with play, read, listen to or view? What do you wish was there that's missing? Is there anything you could do to fill the gap?

## Profit Motives

In addition to being shaped by media content, we are also shaped by its structures. By far the most impactful of those structures is corporate, for-profit ownership of the majority of mainstream media outlets, including social media platforms.

To generate income, commercial media rely on delivering our attention to advertisers. The more eyes and ears they deliver, the more money they make. The more time we spend on their sites, the more eyes and ears they can deliver. This construction governs our relationship with media as well as media makers' choices about topics, styles, and delivery of content.

### Preserving the Status Quo

Because they can't afford to alienate advertisers, corporate media tend to avoid content that businesses consider to be radical, controversial, or critical of sponsors' products or business models. So, most of the time, most commercial media preserve the social status quo. However, when companies decide that their interests are best served by promoting an ideological shift, they can use media repetition to influence social change. In recent decades, for example, media have normalized things that were once taboo, like interracial relationships or LGBTQ people as successful and healthy.

This system enables a relatively few powerful people and companies to have enormous influence. Once a few outlets portray something as acceptable, there will be more people and corporations that come to see it as normal. The more that society and businesses see something as normal, the more likely it is to be included in media. And so it goes.

If the changes reflect your values, you're likely to see this spiral as a good thing. If not, you might experience it as an attack by an entity beyond your control. Either way, media literacy education plays an important role in helping people make the connections between the particular values that media repeat and the financial interests that are served by that repetition.

## Mirror, Mirror

The concept of media as mirror refers to the role that media play in meeting our desire to belong and to know how we compare to others. We look to media for messages about who we are supposed to be or how we are supposed to act. We want to know who is the "fairest of all" and, racist implications not withstanding (because we hear "fairest" as meaning "attractive" rather than exclusively "light skinned"), we look for ways to make sure that it is us.

Media as mirror can be pro-social. For example, *Sesame Street* segments show little ones how to act in school, increasing chances for success by showing expectations for classroom behaviors that might be different from those exhibited at home. In this instance, messages available for free via mainstream media can be extremely important for new immigrant families or for children who have never been in formal child-care settings. They are an important tool as we work toward greater equity.

Efforts like social media Go Fund Me campaigns take advantage of the mirror phenomenon by posting the number of contributions and names of contributors, hoping that if you see others do it, you'll feel that you should contribute, too. It's why when you give to a non-profit or a political campaign you'll nearly always receive a follow-up email or text asking you to tell others in your social media networks. They even include convenient links and graphics to make it easy to share.

But when our relationship with media is primarily commercial, the reflection in the mirror is limited to what we look like as a consumer. As a value system, consumerism prioritizes individual identity over communal ties or societal well-being. It tells us that we should satisfy immediate needs rather than consider long-term well-being. And it promotes overconsumption. It's not an accident that the Pokémon theme song doesn't say, "Build a team." It says, "Gotta catch 'em all."

Advertisers don't want us to ask questions such as, "If ten million people decide to buy this, what's the impact on our shared environment?" because the answer to societal questions often leads to fewer purchases. So, for example, multinational corporations market bottled water as a convenient and healthy alternative to sugary drinks or contaminated water. They don't want us to think about what happens to all that plastic, or how the marketing of bottled water encourages mistrust or neglect of public tap water systems.

When young children look into commercial media mirrors, they are likely to see an image that links personal value with the ability to spend money: "If your parents really loved you, they'd 'treat' you to this fast-food meal" or "If you want to be popular, then you must buy x." They are looking at a mirror that owes its existence to an ability to monetize our insecurities.

Commercial media only occasionally present reflections that help us see ourselves as learners or responsible members of a world, nation, or community. Mister Rogers' famous reminder that "you're special just because you're you" stood out because it was unusual. There is no profit in people believing that they are fine as they are.

We can chip away at the corporate mirror by choosing ad-free children's media, but that's not enough. Media literacy's Act competency also asks us to zoom out and look at the system. For example, we don't just find an influencer who provides candid product reviews; we ask whose interests are served when we are encouraged to rely on influencers for "honest" information because we accept as normal that companies will misrepresent their products. We don't just critique the ads in women's magazines; we wonder who forces yearly fashion changes, so we feel compelled to purchase new clothes even when the old ones are still in good shape. We ask how commercial media profit from making it appear that these "norms" are just the way the world works (like De Beers did with diamond rings). And we ask how this system would change if we all really did believe that we are fine just as we are.

### Platform Design

Did you ever stop to wonder why your social media feed uses scrolling? Or why there are single-click options for certain responses but not others? Or sidebars that you can't shut off filled with additional content recommendations?

These design features are choices. Platforms use them, at least in part, because they keep us online longer than other types of designs. They have the same function as raising the tension in a TV drama just before the program cuts to a commercial so you'll keep watching.

Commercial imperatives often lead to the worst aspects of media platforms. Clickbait, the easy spread of "fake news" (more accurately termed "disinformation" or "polluted" information), the facilitation of perpetual FOMO (fear of missing out), and the promotion of conspiracy theories and extreme views are just a few of the negative consequences.

If the effects were exclusively negative, government regulation would be relatively easy. But of course, it's not that simple.

The same structures that erode privacy and enable tracking also allow us to connect with people all over the world, use GPS maps, get food delivered when we can't leave home, and call for help from a cell phone. The anonymity that facilitates cyberbullying also makes it easier to expose corruption and file whistleblower complaints. The advertising model that amplifies our fears and insecurities with a barrage of unavoidable messages also pays for some outstanding media productions and allows those with limited financial resources to connect for the cost of a device.

That low cost can help new artists find an audience, give voice to marginalized groups, allow protestors to organize resistance, and provide a way for alienated young people to find a supportive community. In some cases, low-cost access is literally life saving. Activists can stream arrests, making it difficult for governments to use secrecy to hide repression. Ostracized trans or gender nonconforming youth can connect with accepting peers, which decreases the likelihood of suicide.

Media are rarely all-or-nothing, completely beneficial or exclusively harmful. That can make teaching media literacy interesting . . . and sometimes a bit frustrating. It's always easier to teach absolutes than "it depends." But we live with contradictions, and our job is to prepare children to thrive in that complex reality.

## We Shape Media

The most obvious way we shape media is by making our own. Social media wouldn't exist without the videos, memes, GIFs, and posts that everyday folks create and share.

We also shape media through the ways we choose to engage as media consumers. Because our actions are tracked, what we click on, watch, listen to, search for, include in lists, play, purchase, or download all influence the content we're offered. If the system offered entirely free choice, that ability to choose would give us enormous power. But it doesn't. There are obvious constraints, like paywalls or apps that won't work properly for users who install an ad blocker.

In keeping with media literacy's Act competency, those limitations lead many media literate people to look for other ways to shape media. Here are just a few things they do:

### Ask big questions . . . and get others to ask them, too.

There are so many ways that media are intertwined with our lives and culture, and every one of them comes with a set of deep, important questions:

- Who collects our data and what do they do with it? Do we have a right to privacy?
- Should we be permitted to erase the things we've shared publicly or is it important for them to be part of the historical, public record, even years later?
- Who profits from the media we use? How would media change if it was created to serve the public interest instead of commercial profits?
- Is democracy possible in a world where deepfakes are also possible?

What's your "big question" about media? How/where might you create spaces to explore the societal implications of the things you notice? How might you engage policy makers in these explorations?

### Advocate for government regulation.

Government regulation can rein in harmful practices such as making it illegal to record users without consent, or prohibiting employers or law enforcement from using facial recognition algorithms that discriminate against people with dark skin. However, as long as we value free speech, regulation will be a limited option. Even if we could prevent certain types of content from reaching the general public or even just children, it isn't clear that government agencies or corporations would make the same calls that we would about what should be permitted and what should be out of bounds.

In a world that adds billions of new social media posts, tweets, and videos every day, even the best regulation won't guarantee the elimination of objectionable content, which underscores the need to equip people with media literacy skills.

### Act collectively.

In today's complex media ecosystem, we have some individual agency, but substantive change comes from joining with others. Anyone can use a site's reporting mechanisms to call attention to problematic content. A single report isn't likely to get results, but if 10,000 people report the same post, a platform is more likely to pay attention. When enough people are involved, strategies like boycotts and public pressure (ironically, including media coverage) can lead media companies and advertisers to change rules, business practices, or content.

### Become a media information resource.

The key to making collective action work is an educated public, and that's where media literacy education comes in. Early childhood educators aren't likely spend time with children discussing complex issues that are beyond kids' control, but they can follow the issues (perhaps subscribing to newsletters like Claire Wardle's First Draft (http://firstdraftnews.org) or Anne Collier's Net Family News (http://netfamilynews.org) and share what they learn. Tips might focus on the ways that big picture issues affect daily lives; for example:

- Just because a site or an app asks for your phone number, birthday, or location doesn't mean you have to give it. Even if they keep asking or tell you it's to help keep your account "secure."
- There are settings on your devices that allow you to reject tracking. However, many functions will ask you to override that settings preference so they can function (e.g., ride-sharing services or weather alert apps need to know where you are). Once you unlock permissions for one app, other apps may automatically also have access unless you explicitly block them.
- Discount cards and store memberships give you access to better prices, but you're swapping your personal data for the savings.
- Apps and services base the ads and recommendations you see on what you've already looked at or purchased. If you and your children use the same device, they are likely to see things based on *your* media choices. So be careful what you do on shared devices!

### PAUSE TO **REFLECT**

A quote often attributed to iconic media theorist Marshall McLuhan declares, "We become what we behold. We shape our tools, and thereafter our tools shape us." What do you think this means? Why might it be important for educators or families to understand?

One of the most consequential actions we can take is to teach the next generation to be media literate. In a few years, they will control media companies and systems, and those who are media literate will understand their power and have an ethical framework to guide their work.

## Sources


Boyatzis, C.J., G.M. Matillo, & K.M. Nesbitt. 1995. "Effects of the *Mighty Morphin Power Rangers* on Children's Aggression with Peers." *Child Study Journal* 25 (1): 45–55.

Delpit, L. 2012. *"Multiplication Is for White People": Raising Expectations for Other People's Children.* New York: The New Press.

Gerbner, G., L. Gross, M. Morgan, & N. Signorielli. 1980. "The 'Mainstreaming' of America: Violence Profile No. 11." *Journal of Communication* 30 (3): 10–29.

Herman, E., & N. Chomsky. 1988. *Manufacturing Consent: The Political Economy of the Mass Media.* New York: Pantheon Books

Lawrence, M. With D. Curtis. 2020. "'We Are Power Rangers!': Learning from Children's Dramatic Play." Look, Listen, Learn. *Teaching Young Children* 13 (2): 4–7.

Levin, D., & N. Carlsson-Paige. 1995. "The *Mighty Morphin Power Rangers:* Teachers Voice Concern." *Young Children* 50 (6): 67–72.

Masterman, L. 1985. *Teaching the Media.* London, UK: Comedia Publishing Group/Routledge.

NAMLE (National Association for Media Literacy Education). 2007. *Core Principles of Media Literacy Education in the United States.* New York: NAMLE. https://namle.net/wp-content/uploads/2020/09/Namle-Core-Principles-of-MLE-in-the-United-States.pdf.

Rogers, F. 1996. *Dear Mister Rogers, Does It Ever Rain in Your Neighborhood? Letters to Mister Rogers.* New York: Penguin Books.

Rogers, F., & B. Head. 1983. *Mister Rogers Talks with Parents.* New York: Berkley Books.

Tiedge, J. 1980. Cited in A. Silverblatt, A. Smith, D. Miller, J. Smith, & N. Brown. 2014. *Media Literacy: Keys to Interpreting Media Messages.* 4th ed. Santa Barbara, CA: Praeger.

University of Pittsburgh School of Education Race and Early Childhood Collaborative. 2016. *Positive Racial Identity Development in Early Education: Understanding PRIDE in Pittsburgh.* Report. Pittsburgh: University of Pittsburgh. www.racepride.pitt.edu/wp-content/uploads/2018/06/PRIDE_Scan.pdf.

Vasquez, V.M. 2014. *Negotiating Critical Literacies with Young Children.* 10th anniversary ed. New York: Routledge.

PART II

# Defining the Task Wrap-Up

PAUSE TO **REVIEW**

How would you explain the following to a colleague or friend?

- the major goals of media literacy education
- the idea that all media are constructed
- the relationship between repetition and societal norms
- the significance of the "mean world syndrome"
- the difference between engaging children in media literacy inquiry and sharing your own interpretations of media with them
- the distinction between media management, media literacy, and teaching with technology

___

___

___

PAUSE TO **REFLECT**

One thing I read that affirmed an idea I had before I started reading was ___________________?

One "hmmm moment," I had was ___________________

One new insight I had was ___________________. Now that I know it I will ___________________ when I work with children or families.

One question I have is _______________. I think I can find an answer if I _______________.

One sentence from Part II that I want to remember or further explore is:

___

___

PART III

# From Pedagogy to Practice

"Just tell me what to do."

I hear this at professional development sessions sometimes. Understanding complex pedagogy, differentiating instruction, accommodating children with diverse languages and "special" needs, even coming up with activity ideas can test the limits of educators' energy and expertise. It would be a relief to be handed a plan that already accounted for all the difficult decisions and creative challenges. Of course, the risk of off-the-shelf plans is that they may or may not match what your children and families need.

So this part of the book isn't a prescriptive curriculum. It's more like a showcase of ideas. You might approach it in a Goldilocks sort of way, looking for activity ideas and strategies that are "just right" for you and the children and families you serve. As you consider which ideas to try, ask yourself:

*What types of activities am I most comfortable doing and what is it about the activity and me that makes those activities feel like a good fit? What types of activities require me to stretch the boundaries of my comfort zone and what might I gain by experimenting?*

CHAPTER 8

# Integrating Media Literacy: Routines and Modifications

Chapter 2 explained how media normalize ideas by repeating them. Repetition works the same way in education. The things we do every day are, by far, the most powerful tools we have to nurture a culture of inquiry in which media literacy competencies bloom.

So, as you begin to think about the things you'll do to integrate media literacy into your teaching, it makes sense to start by looking for opportunities in current daily routines and the activities you do frequently. The suggestions in this chapter are intended as creative sparks. Let them help you find the places in your work with children that are natural fits for inquiry.

## The Things You Say

### 1. Share Offhand Observations

When adults share brief, spontaneous observations that include media-related questions, they give implicit permission for children to do their own wondering, noticing, and thinking about media. By showing that you are curious, you can convey the idea that asking interesting questions about media-related things in the environment is just what people do. Here's what that might look like in practice:

- Casually pick up and examine a candy package and say something like, *Isn't it interesting that even though candy isn't alive, the package features a piece of candy with eyes, arms, hands, and a mouth. Hmmm. I wonder why the candy makers decided to do that?* Then put the package down and continue with whatever you were doing.
- During an art project using sample cards from the paint store, note how interesting the color names are and wonder aloud why there is a paint color named "hot pink" but no "hot brown" or "hot blue."

You can follow up if children show interest in particular comments, but it's okay if they don't. The goal is to model inquiry, not to involve children in pursuing what's interesting to you.

### 2. Answer Questions with a Question

If you had a dollar for every question a child asked in a typical day, you'd be rich by now, right? When children ask questions, most of us reply and move on to the next thing demanding our attention. But what if nearly every one of those questions was an opportunity to reinforce critical inquiry? What if instead of giving an answer, you responded with a question of your own: *How could we find out?*

When our first impulse is to tell rather than ask, we rob children of the opportunity to learn how to find answers. So whenever possible, make the process of finding answers visible, coaching children through it. This transfers responsibility for learning to them and puts us in the role of guide rather than expert.

To get an idea of what this habit looks like in practice, imagine a child who is excited about an upcoming class performance. He asks you,

"Are we going to make our costumes tomorrow?" You could just say, *Yes, so be sure to remember your special hat*. Or you could ask, *How could you find out?* If he doesn't recall by himself, you could point him to the weekly task board and offer help as needed to find the correct day and interpret the pictures that indicate special activities. Next time he just might have the confidence and the knowledge to find the answer himself.

Or maybe a child who has just used a tablet to photograph her block tower asks you how to record her voice so she can describe her accomplishment. Instead of just tapping the correct button or instructing her to "tap this," you might point out the menu and ask if she sees any that seem to be related to recording voices. If she doesn't discover it herself, you can point to the microphone, explain what a mic is, and share that lots of devices and apps use a microphone icon to open the sound recording function. She will have learned that

a. Clues exist

b. There is a specific clue she can use in the future when she wants to use a device to record audio

c. You expect her to be capable of identifying and using such clues.

She will also hear media-related vocabulary like *menu* and *icon* and *mic* that she wouldn't have heard if you had done the task for her.

Or consider this scenario: During a read-aloud, a kindergartener who was enthralled by a recent class visit to a fire station asks: "Why is that fire truck red? The one at the station was yellow." Instead of providing an explanation, start a dialogue (Figure 8.1).

Children won't pick up on all the details of a single conversation, no matter how rich or skillfully led. But when such mini-dialogues are routine, they'll begin to internalize the questions and criteria that can help them find quality sources.

Of course, your response to children's queries will always depend on the question and the situation. If a child on their first day in your care approaches you sort of squirming and asks, "Bathroom?" it will never be appropriate to respond, "How could we find out where the people who built this building decided to put the bathroom?" But most of the time, a question is your best initial response to a question.

## 3. Narrate Your Process for Choosing Resources

We don't have to wait for children to ask a question to add to their evaluation skills. We can make visible the thinking process that we use when we choose sources or media.

For example, imagine that children have returned from outdoor play and one of them has an unusual insect. You explain that it's important to leave living things where we find them, but before they return it to its home outside, they can take a picture and use the picture to find out more about their discovery. The child who found the insect holds it while a friend uses a tablet to photograph the bug.

A teacher who doesn't use a media literacy education approach might go online to search for information while the children engage in another activity, and then later share search results with the group. At a site that has shifted to a media literacy education approach, the early childhood educator would involve the children in the process of seeking information, perhaps working with an interactive white board or gathering children around a computer screen so everyone can follow the steps. The quest starts by asking, *What questions do we have about the bug?*

Once a short list has been generated, the quest continues: *We can use a search engine to find answers. See this box with the camera icon? By dragging our image to this box, I can upload your picture and search the Internet for similar pictures. That can help us figure out what it is.* Looking at the grid of search results: *Do any of these look like the creature that you found? Which should I click on?*

**You:** That's a really good observation! You were paying attention to details. How could we find out about how people choose colors for fire trucks?

**Child 1:** [shrugs shoulders]

**You:** Who do you think might know a lot about fire engines?

**Several children [excitedly]:** The firefighters. Call the firefighters!

**You:** That's a good source. The people who work with fire trucks every day probably know a lot about them. Are there any other places we might find credible information?

**Children:** Ummm . . .

**You:** Is there anything in this building?

**Child 2:** [pointing to the book in your hand] A book!

**You:** Yes. Books can also be excellent information sources. This book doesn't answer our question, but there might be a book with information about fire engine colors. Our librarian might be able to help us find it. Anything else we could do to find an answer?

**Child 3:** Ask Siri.

**You:** That's an interesting idea. I wonder how Siri figures out the answer. Siri is a type of computer. I know of another computer that could help us find the answer. Let's use my laptop to log on to the Internet. What should we type into the search field?

Even if the children don't yet have the knowledge, they need to provide suggestions. Inviting them to consider what to ask a search engine involves them in the search process and highlights an important step when looking for information online. The level of detail you share will depend on their developmental level and prior knowledge. With little ones, you might quickly pause to show the magnifying glass icon and identify it as a clue they can use to find the place where they can ask a question. Grade school children might be ready for an explanation of the search engine, e.g., *Let's use my laptop to log on to DuckDuckGo. That's a search engine I like to use because it doesn't track what we do.*

Figure 8.1 Example of a dialogue in which the teacher answers a child's question with a question.

The group could do a compare/contrast analysis to help them come to consensus about which to choose, with the teacher noting that if their first choice doesn't give them an answer, they can always come back and click on a different choice. With children who are beginning to read, the leader might point to printed information that identifies the source of the photo and invite children to think about whether they are more likely to find the answers to their questions from, say, a private person's vacation photos or a library or museum site.

If nothing viable comes up, the provider might shift to a text-based search, asking which of the children's questions to type in the search bar. When the list appears, the teacher narrates the selection process: *The top sites are trying to sell me something—see this little "ad" icon? That's how I know. I'm not interested in buying anything right now, so I'm going to skip those. This one says it is a collection of pictures from a university where people specialize in studying about insects in our state, so I think that's a good place to start.*

For young children, it doesn't have to be any more complicated than showing that people apply criteria to distinguish useful from not-so-useful sources. Very little ones aren't likely to recall lots of specific criteria, but they'll internalize the norm that people engage in an inquiry process before selecting information sources.

With preschoolers and primary grade students, involving children in the research process provides an opportunity to reinforce vocabulary and debunk common "rookie" mistakes that children might encounter (e.g., the mistaken notion that .org, .edu, or .gov extensions are always okay and.com sites are always a problem). And we can intentionally expose children to a variety of information-sharing formats, expanding the possibilities they envision for presenting their own work beyond familiar options like books or video to things like an infographic or perhaps a Pinterest- or Padlet-style page.

Lots of common early childhood education routines provide an opportunity to explain source choice:

**Read-alouds:**

Introduce media by explaining why you picked them. It doesn't have to be more than a sentence: *I chose this book for our read-aloud because it's a story about something that really happened, and it's told by someone who was there who shares their own perspective and doesn't try to speak for everyone else.*

**Using apps:**

Explanations help children learn evaluation criteria that apply specifically to selected digital tools they use: *We're not going to use our tablets for art today because paint that we can touch lets us create many more variations when we mix colors than "painting" on a screen.* Or *I chose to add this new math app to our tablets because it was designed by people who specialize in teaching math to kids your age and it lets players save their game results so we can include them in our portfolios.*

As children learn more about digital media, we can include explanations about more complex choices like looking at data collection and privacy policies.

**Classroom guests:**

Guests (even via videoconference) provide a concrete opportunity to share evaluation criteria that can be applied to media experts and influencers. As you introduce the guest, add a sentence to two describing their expertise: *I invited Mr. Shemesh to help us learn how to take care of our garden because he grows organic strawberries that have won awards!* Organic *means he doesn't use chemicals to kill bugs or other things that could damage the plants. He can give us tips on how to keep our plants healthy without using pesticides that might hurt the bees. And he is Ariella's grandpa!*

If children prepare questions for the guest ahead of time, help them link their queries to the reasons that this person, given their expertise, might have an answer.

**Snack time:**

Don't forget about non-screen media. For example, when you take out a box of crackers for snack, you might explain how you chose this particular product: *Remember what we learned about food being halal? See this symbol? It tells me that specialists have checked to make sure the crackers are halal. I chose crackers that had this symbol to make sure we had a snack that everyone could eat.*

# Activity Modifications

Sometimes integrating media literacy is simply a matter of tweaking activities that you already do. This can be especially helpful if curriculum mandates make you feel like you're constantly fighting a time crunch.

## 1. Treat the Books You Read as Media

- Rather than always starting a read-aloud by reading the title, author, and illustrator, change it up sometimes and ask, *"How could we find out who wrote this story?" "Where can we find the book's title?"*
- In addition to comprehension questions, sprinkle in some queries from other media literacy question categories (p. 56). Talk about the pictures as if they are as important to the story as the words.
- Add checks for evidence to dialogic reading, asking, *"How do you know that?"* when a child gives you an answer to a predictive or open-ended question.

  With the youngest children, the specific responses aren't all that important. The goal isn't to elicit a "right answer" as much as it is to model inquiry and establish the habit of linking conclusions to evidence. As children begin to understand that link, you can help everyone learn what to look for by naming the type of evidence, for example, *Ah, you know that because you saw a clue in the illustration.* Or *You know what's going to happen next because you read this book before. You used evidence from your personal experience.*
- Model language for evidence-based comments, introducing if/then sentences and how to use the word "because," for example, *I was surprised when . . . because. . . .* or *I knew if they solved the puzzle then the gate would open.*
- Ask children to imagine what a character sounds like. Do heroes sound just like them and villains sound like other people? Do they have an accent (which can lead to a follow-up discussion on stereotypes)? Does a tiny character have a high-pitched voice and a large one a low-pitched voice (which you might later connect to a science lesson on sound)? What clues are they using? Why do we think certain characters would sound a certain way?

  Once children have done this with books, try it with comics. Then try it with media that move. Help children make the link to animated shows or video games and decisions that the director or creator makes about what each character will sound like. As part of introducing new shows or games, invite children to guess what characters sound like and then watch to see if they agreed with the director's choice. Help children understand that what we "hear" in our heads is part of our filter when we interact with media.

## 2. Approach Making Books as a Media Making Activity

Engaging children in inquiry about book covers and illustrations helps them improve their media creation skills along with their thinking skills.

- Explain that book covers have two purposes: to let people know what the book is about and to inspire a desire to read it (or purchase it—marketers really do want you to judge a book by its cover!). Ask children how their illustration will do these things. This type of inquiry lays a foundation for later analysis of media such as magazines or newspaper front pages.

- In the primary grades, you might extend the discussion by displaying each student's cover in a gallery walk or via a collaborative digital tool. Invite them to explain which they would want to read and why. Or invite them to guess the focus of their classmates' stories. You might even extend the discussion to talk about "target audience" and how the illustrator's choice might change if the book was intended for a different audience.

  Provide an opportunity for children to modify covers that didn't communicate their intention effectively. Model the types of "I" sentences we use to note details and give constructive feedback: *Really cool robot. It was holding a baseball and that made me want to read the book because I didn't think robots could play baseball.* Or *I liked the frog, but I didn't understand why it's in the sky. . . . Oh, I see; it's about a frog that jumps higher than everyone. Maybe you could add something to show it was in a contest?*

- Alternatively, you might assemble a collection of images and have a group discussion about which would be most effective. For example, the frog story might use a realistic photo, a frog in a funny outfit, a cartoon frog, a line drawing of a frog, or the frog from Arnold Lobel's "Frog and Toad" books. Prompt children to think through the strengths and benefits of each choice, for example, *Is using a realistic photo for a fictional story misleading? If you used a frog from a popular book series, would people expect that character to be in your book?*

- Lead similar discussions about book illustrations. *How do authors, artists, and publishers choose illustrations? What's important to illustrate? How do illustrations draw our attention to certain parts of a story?*

## 3. Use Name Tags or Group Names to Discuss Representation and Target Audience

Involve children in choosing a room, group, or class name and then in creating an emblem to match. The need for the group to choose a single name and emblem creates a conversation that is filled with opportunities to talk about how their name and emblem effectively represents them (i.e., tells people something important about their identity).

- When children make name tags to identify a space or possession as theirs, engage conversations that expand their thinking. In addition to printing their name, what could they include that would tell people something important about who they are? If they are taking "selfies," how does their target audience influence their pose? Would the silly face they make for friends also be the face they would make for parents or community elders?

  Or if they decide that the picture they'll use to designate their coat hook is their favorite superhero or sport, what happens if their friends like the same thing? What could they add to distinguish themselves from others?

  Older children could extend the discussion about representation to consider mascots and team logos, including whether it's okay for a sports team to use the name or image of a Native American tribe or should only that tribe be able to use it (e.g., the Florida Seminoles). What about a stereotype of Indigenous peoples (e.g., the Atlanta Braves tomahawk or the Kansas City Chiefs arrowhead, or any team being called "Indians" when they aren't Native American)? Is it ever okay to take someone else's name or symbol and use it when you're not representing them?

PAUSE TO **REFLECT**

If you were going to put something on a t-shirt to represent who you are, what would it be? Have you ever worn a t-shirt with the name of a brand, a band, a school, a team, or a political slogan? What were you communicating with that choice? Who was your target audience?

## 4. Add Media Tech (Pretend and Real) to the Other Toys or Materials in Play Areas

When toy (pretend) media devices are available, children can use their play to work out or rehearse media-related issues. That provides caregivers with an opportunity to observe. What might you learn about the ways that media devices are present in their lives?

When real media devices are available, a powerful and growing research literature on digital play indicates that children use them to enrich their play experience. They seamlessly go back and forth between devices and other hands-on activities, especially as they create stories. Little ones experiment, create, de-construct, and cooperate in ways that can contribute very effectively to critical literacy skill-building (e.g., Marsh 2016; Wohlwend 2013). Researcher Jackie Marsh (2016), a global leader in the area of digital play, writes, “It is clear that, even from a young age, children are able to operate effectively as digital authors and readers, navigating technological worlds with confidence and competence relative to their age” (211).

You can expect that children will start production projects and come back later to revise and continue their story. Action figures, dolls, or other toys may become the stars of a video or slide deck. Kids who understand that they can share what they’ve created with the outside world (like families) may begin to document moments in their play that they think are worthy of preserving and sharing (e.g., the triumph of a dominos run that works just right or first success at walking the full length of the balance beam).

Making devices available during free play also allows children who are less familiar with the technology to benefit from experience with peers and from a teacher’s ability to step in and provide some coaching to bring them up to the level of others, an important aspect of addressing digital divide issues (Marsh 2016).

Follow up with conversations about the production choices that children made. Did they tell the story of mastering the balance beam showing some failed attempts before their success? Did they just show their feet, or can the viewer see their whole body? Is there anything they could do to become an even better communicator? You can encourage them by oohing and aahing over how impressive it is that they made a video, and also help them improve the way they use the tools they have.

PAUSE TO **PRACTICE**

Make a copy of the gears graphic in Figure 5.1 (p. 38). Review each of the routines and modifications in this chapter and place their corresponding number next to each competency that the suggestion addresses. (Place an *S* next to the numbers for things you say to distinguish them from activity modifications.) Then go back to each competency and explain how the suggestion(s) you’ve listed address the competency.

## 5. Use Circle Time, Morning Meeting, or Show-and-Tell to Talk About Media

Let kids know that they can talk about media if that's what's on their mind. Perhaps even designate one day a week to take time to ask about games, videos, TV shows, and the like. Use the opportunity to listen to how children are making meaning from media and introduce a media literacy question or two that they might ask.

## 6. Use Media Examples and Framing to Explore Spatial Relationships and Practice Prepositions

Media provide excellent opportunities to explore concepts like next to, in front of/behind, over/under, above/below, or inside/outside:

- Use photographs, or still frames from films, TV shows, and games to play "find an example of ____________." Children will be learning to pay attention to details in media while also reviewing concepts and vocabulary.
- Introduce the words *choreograph* and *blocking* (what a theater director does with actors in a scene). Then give children a physical feel for spatial concepts by role playing scenes from familiar stories, copying dance moves from a TikTok video, or creating their own choreography and using prepositions to teach it to others. Help them connect what they're doing to media they watch by noting that what they see in media is planned, not accidental. That perfect dance routine where everyone ends up in exactly the right spot for the camera might have taken hours to plan, rehearse, and record!
- Use frames to teach inside/outside or above/below. Let children use cameras to capture things inside the frame or keep things outside the frame. Help children visualize the concept by sharing a "making of" video that zooms out to reveal production equipment and people on the set of a familiar show. (For a good example, see *Sesame Street: Behind the Scenes of PSA shoot* at https://youtu.be/Hbx1gpipO2w.)

  If technology isn't available, let children make frames by forming their hands into *O*s and putting one over each eye as if they were looking through binoculars. Help them notice what they can't see when they are looking through their "binoculars" and how it changes if they move their head. Or cut out shapes from the middle of index cards. Look through the frames by moving them side to side, up and down, or in and out to change what is included in the inside of a frame and what ends up outside the frame. Connect the frames with the idea that people who make media choose what to include or exclude. Help them apply the concept to the drawings or paintings that they create and how the edges of the paper create a frame.
- Use the image-layering functions included in most slide-making or word-processing programs to let children play with moving images to the front or back.

When you make explicit the connections to media, each of these strategies helps children understand that all media are constructed. They also provide great ways to practice prepositions for children learning the words in a new language.

## 7. Read Body Language

If you show pictures of facial expressions or body language to help children learn to recognize and name emotions, remind them that the actors and dancers in the shows and movies they watch have to learn how to use their faces and bodies to show what their character is feeling. Just a brief mention helps children notice that media are constructed.

## 8. When You Begin New Units of Study, Check to See What Children Already Know by Probing for the Sources of Their Ideas, Including Media Sources

Kids come to us with ideas gathered from everything they experience, including media. Some of those ideas are accurate and some are not. When I was growing up, if you had asked me what foods made people strong, I would have confidently answered, "Wonder Bread" because I repeatedly heard their slogan, "Builds strong bodies 12 ways." It wouldn't be until many years later than I would learn that "12" referred to the number of additives needed to compensate for the processing they did to transform whole grains into white bread!

It's likely that the children you teach have equally strong, and sometimes misinformed ideas from media. They may believe that there are no big cities in Africa because the only images they've seen of the continent are from films like *The Lion King*. Or that accidental exposure to radioactive slime can give someone superpowers. Or even that forests are scary because in so many fairy tales, forests are the site of dangerous events. If you're familiar with the media that children watch and play, you'll be able to better guess the sources of some of their ideas or misconceptions and then analyze the credibility of those sources with them.

If, in your current practice you use a K-W-L framework, you have an additional option: Add follow-up prompts to your existing questions:

> After asking *What do you **K**now?* ask, *And where did you get that idea/information?* (What were your sources?)
>
> After asking *What else do we **W**ant to know?* ask, *And where could we find answers?*
>
> After asking *What did we **L**earn?* ask, *And which sources were most helpful?*
>
> (Rogow & Scheibe 2017)

## 9. Invite Children to Analyze Holiday Decorations

Every season our media and our environment—public streets and businesses, homes and classrooms—are awash in the colors, fonts, and symbols associated with particular holidays. By engaging in media analysis, we can help children see that these are a reflection of constructed cultural "norms"—a mesh of heritage, community, and marketing.

We proceed with caution because some of the things that started as marketing have become treasured family traditions, and we don't want to use media literacy education to undermine family bonds. Instead, we help children notice and understand how our forms of public observance come from specific choices. The avenues for analysis are diverse:

- Why are orange and black colors for Halloween, but not Independence Day?
- Why do the same stores that make a big deal out of Valentine's Day or St. Patrick's Day not also tout Arbor Day or Constitution Day?
- Would Thanksgiving decorations feature turkeys if everyone was vegetarian?
- How do the people who produce the Macy's Thanksgiving Day Parade choose which floats and balloons to include?
- Are there holidays that are important to your family but that aren't given much attention in popular media or the community (perhaps Diwali, Rosh Hashanah, or Eid al-Fitr)? How does that feel? What could *all* the children do (those who observe and those who don't) to publicize these holidays and help people understand them?
- Who created holidays like Grandparents Day? If you could create a holiday, what would it be and why?

In addition to analyzing decorations and public observances, consider the following:

- Any holiday that involves costumes—Halloween, Mardi Gras, Purim—offers a chance to talk about what a costume is, how it differs from a uniform, how actors are wearing costumes even when they look like "regular" people, and how ads for costumes create expectations for what is gender appropriate (who you can and can't be). They can also provide an opportunity to talk about stereotypes, like the difference between dressing as a cowboy (which is a job) and an "Indian" (which is a sacred heritage).
- Any holiday involving gift giving can be an opportunity to explore stereotypes (e.g., comparing gifts suggested for fathers compared with those suggested for mothers).
- Holiday songs are filled with unique phrases. Take a few minutes to wonder aloud about what they mean. Do children who sing "Jingle Bells" know what a "one horse open sleigh" is? Are there three horse open sleighs? How about eight horse or no horse? Who uses sleighs anyway, and why would they use a sleigh instead of a car or bicycle?

  Discussing lyrics not only provides media analysis practice, it can also prevent the form of confirmation bias known as mondegreens—mishearing lyrics in ways that transform them into something that makes sense to our brains. For example, a child may sing the hymn "Bringing in the Sheaves" as "Bringing in the Cheese." They know what cheese is. They have no idea what sheaves are or why anyone would bring them in. They sing what they know. Can you think of lyrics that you mis-learned, only to find out the actual lyrics years later?

## 9. Assign Media-Related Class Jobs

Perhaps there could be a documentarian of the day, whose job it is to take pictures of important class moments, or a reporter who creates an "Ask me about . . ." text message that is shared with families at the end of each day so conversations can continue at home. For jobs that involve technology, start with a child who knows how to use the device, and as the job rotates, the current job holder can teach the next. Be sure to create space to talk about the assignments and what makes something newsworthy or fair and accurate—for example, *Why is this photo a good representation of what our class did today?* Or *Why did you decide that today would be a good day for families to ask about bubbles? Is that a question that would apply to everyone, or only a few kids?*

## 10. Talk with Children About Their Artwork as Communication

Most of the time you'll want to let children follow their artistic muse without interference, but every now and then you can boost their media literacy skills by engaging in a bit of conversation.

We start by asking children to tell us about their pictures. We might discover unexpected stories or representations. Maybe those thick black scribbles covering the page aren't an expression of anger but are, instead, the young artist "writing" the phrase "Black is beautiful" because that's what daddy always says and this picture is for him!

In addition to conversations about comprehension, we can take advantage of the fact that the edges of a canvas are a natural frame, even when the canvas is a piece of paper, a sticker, or a tablet screen. That makes children's drawings or paintings perfect opportunities to talk about framing.

For example, imagine that you and the artist jumped into the picture (á la the sidewalk chalk drawing scene in Disney's *Mary Poppins* movie). Point to a spot in a child's drawing and ask, *"What sounds would I hear if I was standing there?"* Follow up their answer with, *"Does anything in your picture tell me that's what I would hear?"* Or you might reinforce

## PAUSE TO **PRACTICE**

Go through this hypothetical conversation paragraph by paragraph.

What do you notice about:

- The ways that media literacy was connected to other curriculum goals?
- What specific media literacy concepts Sophie was learning?
- How Ms. Cruz used media literacy questions to facilitate Sophie's learning?

What else do you notice that is relevant to your own interactions with children?

Sophie and Ms. Cruz

1. As part of her effort to get to know her 4-year-old charges better, Ms. Cruz has asked that they draw a picture of where they sleep. When Sophie finishes her picture, Ms. Cruz invites her to have a conversation about it.
2. After Sophie shares a few details, Ms. Cruz asks, "What is outside the frame?" Sophie knows what this means because yesterday the class had done a project where they cut out the middle of an index card, held it up, and saw how they could move the "frame" to include certain things or to leave them out. Ms. Cruz smiles at Sophie's ability to transfer what she learned to this new task and is glad she planned the drawing activity to reinforce yesterday's lesson.
3. Sophie thinks for a minute and responds that she has left out her sister's bed, which is in the bedroom they share but isn't in the picture. Ms. Cruz asks, "How would someone know that this is your bed and not your sister's bed?" Sophie points to a blob with eyes that she identifies as her stuffed animal. Introducing some media-related vocabulary, Ms. Cruz offers that media makers include these kinds of "props" when they create "sets" so the viewer can tell where they are. Ms. Cruz wonders aloud if there are any other props that Sophie might want to add to her drawing that would help people understand that they are looking at her bed. Sophie pauses to consider the possibilities and returns to drawing.
4. Later, Sophie shows Ms. Cruz the things she added to her picture. She points to a new blob—this one with arms—and says that these are her pajamas. And she explains that she made the bed orange because her blanket is orange, but her sister's is pink. Ms. Cruz admired the thoughtful added "props," repeating the new vocabulary word.
5. Sensing that Sophie is ready to go a bit deeper, she asks, "Whose eyes are we seeing through?" Sophie knows this question, too. When the class watched an episode of *Clifford, the Big Red Dog*, they paused the video and noticed how different things looked from Clifford's point of view from up high than from T-Bone's point of view down low. And they made "binoculars" with their hands and looked around at how it changed what they saw when they looked around from their own perspective. Sophie proudly announced, "My eyes!"
6. Ms. Cruz was tempted to continue the conversation, either asking Sophie to compare her bed to where Clifford sleeps (which had been a focus of the episode they viewed because they were starting a health and culture lesson about sleep) or asking her what sounds they would hear if they were inside her picture. But she could see that Sophie was antsy, so she wrapped things up.

7. She invited Sophie to sign her artwork, helping her with some of the letters of her name when Sophie got stuck after "So . . ." and commenting that this was how other people would know who made this media.
8. Then Ms. Cruz asked Sophie if her picture was important enough to scan and e-mail to her Auntie. Ms. Cruz had the Auntie's e-mail address, because at the beginning of the year she had explained to families that she would introduce children to e-mail as a language tool, and asked for contact addresses for a few special people who might be interested in receiving messages from their child. Sophie's parents had provided their own e-mail addresses and also the address of an aunt who was close to Sophie.
9. Sophie agreed that this was an important piece of art and that she would like to scan it. They walked over to the computer. Sophie put her drawing on the scanner bed. Ms. Cruz helped Sophie open the correct software program, find the scan button, and save the file to Sophie's portfolio. Ms. Cruz asked Sophie what she should name the file: "What would be a good title so that people would know what this picture was?" Sophie was unsure, so Ms. Cruz moved on. She knew that not every question needed an answer. Part of her job was just to model asking questions so that children would eventually pick up on the habit and ask their own questions. Ms. Cruz labeled the file "Sophie's Bed Picture" and added the date while letting Sophie know that they could come back and change the file name later if Sophie decided on her own title.
10. They attached the picture file to an e-mail and Ms. Cruz asked Sophie if there was anything that she wanted to tell her Auntie about the picture. Sophie dictated a brief message and, with Ms. Cruz's help, pressed "send." Ms. Cruz made a note to herself to help Sophie check the e-mail for a response the next day and checked the clock to see if there was time for Sophie to share her drawing with the rest of the children and for others to share their drawings with her. She decided that sharing everyone's drawings would be the kickoff of tomorrow's lesson on sleep.

the concept of framing: *"What would I see if I was in your picture and looked up [or to the side]?"*

Once media literacy inquiry and reflection become a normal part of your routine, you may want to reinforce the learning with activities that address specific issues and competencies. These typically take more time and planning. That's what we'll cover in the next chapter.

PAUSE TO **REFLECT**

What's missing from this chapter? Do you have a standard routine or activity that wasn't listed that you could easily modify to include media literacy inquiry or reflection?

## Sources

Marsh, J. 2016. "The Digital Literacy Skills and Competences of Children of Pre-School Age." *Media Education Studies and Research* 7 (2): 197–214.

Rogow, F., & C. Scheibe, C. 2017. *Media Literacy in Every Classroom*. Quick reference guide. Alexandria, VA: ASCD.

Wohlwend, K.E. 2013. *Literacy Playshop: New Literacies, Popular Media, and Play in the Early Childhood Classroom*. New York: Teachers College Press.

CHAPTER 9

# Integrating Media Literacy: Planned Activities

Digital media often make it easy for us to slip into binary thinking. Everything is a 0 or 1, all or nothing, 👍 or, 👎 Democrat or Republican, Yankees or Red Sox. Integrating media technologies or banning screens.

Media literacy educators strive to stretch minds into more nuanced thinking. Instead of an off/on switch, think of a dimmer switch, or even better, multiple faders on a mixing board in a music studio. Things don't need to be either loud or soft—there are complex gradations and many inputs. As world events unfold, technology evolves, and children grow, the mix is ever changing. We are constantly called to adjust and readjust.

When we plan media literacy activities, we want to open space for that type of complexity. Rather than predetermining how we want kids to feel or think about media messages and then figuring out some entertaining way to present *our* beliefs, we focus on the skills we want children to acquire.

So, where do planned activities fit in? Their very nature is that they aren't completely open ended. You might think of their purpose as akin to the way a beginning music student is introduced to scales or a budding ballet dancer starts with the five basic positions. Planned activities can provide opportunities to learn and practice so children develop a "muscle memory" for foundational media literacy competencies, like linking conclusions to evidence, knowing that everyone looks at media through their own unique interpretive lens, or understanding that media are constructed and production choices are consequential. When these basics become automatic, they free children to engage with all sorts of media and pursue individual media interests and collaborative media projects at a deeper, more cognizant level.

The media literacy education purpose statement introduced in Chapter 5 presents "habits of inquiry" and "skills of expression" as touchstones for lesson planning. So, the ideas offered in this chapter will be organized under those two headings.

## Habits of Inquiry: Activities for Analyzing Media

Feminist academic and activist bell hooks (1994) wrote that teaching "is meant to serve as a catalyst that calls everyone to become more and more engaged, to become active participants in learning" (11). The most important word in that sentence is *everyone*. Leading children in analysis activities shouldn't be a one-way interaction. Look for the ways that the ideas offered here create a partnership with children so that they are doing more than listening to what you've learned, and you are doing more than telling them what to think.

### Play the Questions Game

Start with any media image in kids' environment—a t-shirt, the opening screen of a video game, a historical photo in a school display case, a toy package, and so forth. Invite children to quickly generate as many questions as they can about it. Play along with them, adding one or two of your own questions. If children are developmentally ready for team games, you might set a timer and let teams compete to see who can generate the most questions. Listen to, but don't critique, the responses. The purpose of the game is simply to practice asking questions. Hearing one another's ideas expands children's thinking about the types of questions they can ask, reveals differences in interpretive lenses without making anyone's lens "wrong," and makes the habit of inquiry fun. It can also reveal children's interests, important for later follow-up in class or when sharing updates about children with families.

## Play "What Happened Here?" and "Caption This"

Education entrepreneur Shimira Williams suggests using intriguing photographs from the news (like a city bus stuck in a sink hole) to invite imaginative thinking (*What do you think happened?*) and problem solving (*What would you do to fix it?*). After brainstorming, help older children link the activity to media analysis by noting that media companies and organizations put provocative photos on their cover, front, or home page because they think people will find the pictures fascinating and will want to know more. They depend on our curiosity to generate clicks or purchases that send cash from us to them.

With emergent readers, you might link this to a media-making activity by playing Caption This. Teach children about the purpose and construction of a caption by having them caption the photo (or any other picture in their environment, including book illustrations).

With older children, introduce the idea that captions can shape what we think about a picture. Illustrate with a pair of identical pictures bearing different captions (e.g., a photo of a colorful sphere—one version is labeled "Marble," the other is labeled "Planet"). Invite them to talk about why and when media makers use captions. Look for real-life examples from your own community that you can share and talk about. *When are captions helpful? Why might someone choose to use a misleading caption? If we're investigating a subject, why would it be important to read more than just a caption?*

## Dance

Let kids move with abandon to different styles of music. After that becomes routine, help them notice things about the music and how they move. What do they or their friends do differently with their body when music is slow or fast or happy or scary? Once you've done that a few times, help them notice the music and patterns in the media they use: *How does that soundtrack make you feel? What type of music does your game use? Why do you think it uses that style of music? Do all the games use that style of music?*

## Decode Food Packages

Introduce children to the idea that food packages are speaking to them and there are clues they can learn in order to understand what those packages are saying. In an excellent example, Project Look Sharp used this framing to craft a K–2 nutrition lesson about sugar and fruit. They asked, *Is there really fruit inside a Froot Loops box?* Some children initially said yes, because, as one girl responded, the name "said 'fruit.' Duh!" The children hadn't yet learned about the ways that marketers use spelling changes, and besides, the box featured pictures of fruit.

Instead of a lecture about how they'd been fooled, the teacher showed children how to determine whether a cereal has lots of added sugar by looking for specific clues on the box. In addition to the grams of added sugar listed on the nutrition label, clues signaling lots of added sugar included sparkles and the word *frosted* or *honey*. Children also learned that describing something as "fruit *flavored*" usually meant that a food was only pretending to be like the real thing—like the package was wearing a fruit disguise, but there was no actual fruit inside (Rogow & Scheibe 2017). By the end of the lesson, all the children knew that the cereal wasn't fruit and that this package didn't contain any fruit, but it did have lots of added sugar. And they knew clues they could use to analyze other food packages.

There are lots of food package clues that children can learn to spot: What do the colors tell us about what might be inside? What do words like *made with* mean? How about *artificially, all-natural, real,* or *whole grain*? What do all the numbers on a nutritional label mean? Or "100%"? What is a serving size? Does the food have a different name in other languages and does that tell us something different about the food than the English name (e.g., in Mexico, Frosted Flakes are marketed as Zucaritos—*azúcar* is the Spanish word for "sugar")? Food packages provide abundant real-world opportunities for the integration of media literacy and simple math, reading, vocabulary, and health science lessons.

## Analyze Games and Apps

Help children practice "noticing" (careful observation) and see games as media by talking about a video game or app.

- Teach children to use scoring as a clue that reveals the embedded value messages. What does the game reward? What do players score points for doing?
- Use video games or apps to practice listening skills. What do they notice when they listen to the game? How does the game use sound to signal winning or losing? What other messages are conveyed in the audio (voice-overs, music, sound effects)? How do the sounds influence the way the app makes them feel? This can work well with a small group gathered around a good player. Let the child who is skilled at the game play as others watch and listen. If your group includes several good players, let children switch roles, perhaps listening for different things each time the game is played. You could even invite observers to close their eyes and guess what's happening on screen by the sounds they hear.
- With older children who are beginning to play games in which they create an avatar, use the game to spark a conversation about media representation. Invite children to describe their avatar and show you how they chose its features. Are there features that a child always or never choses? Why? Are there features they'd like to add that aren't available? Limited selections mean that the game limits identity choices, that is, *some* choice of features isn't the same as *free* choice. Guide them to notice what features are always or rarely available and talk about how that relates to who feels included or left out.

## Use Media Analysis as an Assessment

To assess comprehension, provide pop culture examples of a subject the children have been studying. Invite them to spot inaccuracies or identify valid information. That's exactly what Joyce Pixley and Nicole Laura, a creative first grade teacher and library media specialist team did. As part of a Project Look Sharp science initiative, they used a cartoon that might generate misconceptions to assess comprehension of core first grade physics concepts:

> Students demonstrated that they understood the properties of liquids, solids, and gases by analyzing depictions of water in a Spider-Man cartoon that included a water-related villain, Hydro-Man. Students who understood the physics lesson were able to explain which of the scenes were realistic and which were not. The teachers then asked students to reflect on why people create cartoons like Spider Man and whether cartoons were credible sources for science information. Finally, the teachers asked, "What did we do during viewing that we don't normally do?" The students answered, "We asked questions." Then they complained that in class they only watched clips, but at home they could watch the whole show! (Rogow 2012—Full lesson plan available at: https://projectlooksharp.org/front_end_resource.php?resource_id=434.)

# "Skills of Expression": Making Media

The growth of affordable media technologies suitable for small hands, along with media-making apps that match the skill level of children with limited or no traditional literacy skills have produced a bloom of teachers finding ways to help children make media. These educators routinely share ideas in places like the International Society for Technology in Education's (ISTE) Early Learning Network, the National Council of Teachers of English's (NCTE) Early Childhood Assembly, and NAEYC's Technology Interest Forum, and the projects they describe are diverse. Some are simple and short; others are complex and stretch out over weeks. Children create videos, books, comics, photographs, infographics, game worlds, slide decks, plays, newsletters, songs, podcasts, tweets, blog posts . . . you name it, and somewhere little ones are engaged.

The common thread of high-value media production activities is that *children* make decisions about what they want to say and how they want to say it. The grown-ups invite conversations that explore little ones' choices, provide feedback, and offer opportunities to revise. Adults may also need to scaffold technology use. Some kids will feel comfortable using cameras and apps and recording devices right away; others need step-by-step prompting—just like any other activity.

Scaffolding never means telling children what picture to take or what stories to tell. It means we show them how to take pictures or use an app and then ask questions that clarify the task, for example:

- *We need to tell our families about the special things that happened today. What stories do we need to post to our blog? What would be the best illustration for the story about our special guest?*
- *If we wanted to show what the person in our picture was thinking, how could we do that?*
- *Our Internet "penpal" class has asked us to send a postcard that shows something about where we live. What should be on the postcard? Should we create a digital card or a paper one?*

Grown-ups also expand children's media universe—and their thinking—by using many, many types of media. We conceptualize differently when we're writing a paragraph, painting a picture, orally explaining instructions, performing a song or dance, drawing a comic strip, or consolidating information into an infographic. When we offer the chance to produce digital media, children learn that digital devices are tools that can do much more than provide entertainment.

You don't need to know how to use every available app or device, but it's helpful to have a general idea of what's possible so you can incorporate techniques into activity planning and then find what you need. There are apps designed to help children string together pictures and narrate a story, others designed to foster a collaborative discussion around a central text or image, and some that make creating a book or comic strip easy. Still others offer green screens so you can easily change backgrounds or add special effects. There are apps that allow you to attach resources to QR codes, lift images from books to create augmented reality versions that add dimension, or create music tracks. There are far more possibilities than can be listed here.

Start with what you know. Ask for suggestions from colleagues and professional learning communities.

Here are a few ways that you might integrate media making into your activities and routines:

## Open a Restaurant

Whether creating a pretend pizza place in a play area or an actual school shop that sells snacks, a restaurant or store offers opportunities to combine media making with media analysis. Involve children in all aspects of the decision making:

- What's the name of their restaurant? How will the name help people know what they sell/serve?
- What colors will they use and why? If restaurants are a part of children's routines, ask what they recall about the colors of the signs, furniture, decorations, uniforms, or food wrappers. Do they match? Teach them that there is a name for all that matching: *branding*. Will they choose to use branding in their restaurant, or do they think that customers will enjoy their food even if everything doesn't match? If they decide to pay attention to branding, which items need to use the designated colors (e.g., aprons, tablecloths, signs, dishware)?
- What will their logo look like? How about takeout boxes? Placemats?
- What will the menu look like? Take a look at real menus as examples. What information do they provide? Are some foods listed larger than others? Why do they think that is? Are there pictures for some foods? How might these help sell more of that item?
- Ask if they remember anything else that makes them want to go back to certain restaurants (like changing the toys that accompany kids' meals). Explore whether they want to include those things in their own restaurant. What parts of kids' meals are good for kids and families? What parts are included because they benefit the restaurant?
- Do they need to advertise their restaurant or store? What would be important to tell people? What sorts of things are included in ads they've seen?

Making decisions about what to include in their own establishment will help children notice the design of real-life restaurants they visit. Analyzing those choices will help them understand the marketing aspects of those restaurants. If you've already got a play restaurant or store set up, just reframe the discussion to present tense (e.g., How does the name of the restaurant help people know what food is available?) or involve children in adding new features.

## Create a Newspaper

Another way to easily combine analysis with production is to involve children in making a newspaper. Even a very basic single page with the major features of a paper will work. In addition to the language development involved in writing stories, children learn from making decisions about:

- Which stories are important enough to include?
- Who should tell those stories? Kids who were involved? Kids who saw an event but weren't involved?

  On a simple level it's possible to help children get a sense of the advantages and disadvantages of critical distance in covering a story. For example, a child covering their friends might approach the task with too much empathy, feeling like they always had to say nice things. An outsider who doesn't know anyone in the group, i.e., a reporter with critical distance, might tell the story more accurately. On the other hand, the outsider might not be aware of how amazing an accomplishment is because they weren't there for all the times that the story's subject tried and failed before they finally succeeded.
- What's important enough to say in a headline?
- How much space should they give to each story? (A simpler way to ask this is, *What should be the biggest thing on the page?*)
- Which stories should include pictures? Which pictures? What should the caption say?
- Should the paper include advertising? If so, what should the rules be about the types of things that can be advertised? Should things that are illegal or that hurt people be allowed to advertise? Why or why not?

It can help to bring in real world examples to help budding journalists visualize the components of a typical front page. They can look for the types of information included, the ways that various components are put together to create the distinctive look of a newspaper, and what the paper does to attract attention to particular stories. Considering such questions helps children strengthen their sense that media are constructed and that the choices about how they are constructed influence readers. They'll learn that news can be fair, but never objective; people are deciding what to report and how to report it.

Newspapers can also be a way to connect children to their community and the world. In Portugal, a pilot project involved kindergarten and primary grade students in creating a newspaper as a way of using media literacy to teach active citizenship. Notably, the teachers and the children began the project with simple, safe issues like interviewing grandparents about their childhoods. But as children grew comfortable as journalists, they devoted the publication to general social justice issues (like the human rights of children), and local issues like recommendations for changing their schoolyard (Tomé et al. 2019).

Each issue was distributed throughout the school and community, which helped children understand their responsibility and take the work seriously. The project was limited, however, because students contributed content and ideas, but the layout and distribution were left to adults. The more that tasks can be handed over to children, the deeper the learning will be.

Some early childhood professionals resist engaging children in anything having to do with the news, preferring to create a safe space that shelters little ones from the often-troubling realities that journalists report. Despite the good intentions, children hear about news stories anyway. In the Portugal project, kindergartners, on their own, encountered a news photo of refugees arriving in a small boat. It was important that they had a space to talk about and process that event. In fact, it was explicitly because there were disturbing elements to the story that it was important for children to be able to grapple with it in the presence of caring adults.

Ultimately, engaging children in decisions about what to report helps grown-ups understand what's on little ones' minds. And the final product, either printed or in digital form, can be shared with families and the community, who can then continue the conversations with their children about the stories.

There are also a couple of adaptations worth considering. If the newspaper is shared online, decide whether to include a "comments" function. For families with relatives across the globe, this can be a way to strengthen connections. Aunts, uncles, cousins, and grandparents can find out what a child is doing and post questions or comments. This would work best in a password-protected environment.

You might also consider regular blog posts instead of a full newspaper. This provides the benefits of creating reports and selecting headlines and pictures but allows for focus on specific activities, events, or topics without having to worry about potentially extraneous features like weather predictions or ads. And, like online newspapers, blogs can include a comments function.

## Make Media as an Assessment

Assessment is about providing little ones with a chance to showcase what they know. Tech can get in the way if children are struggling with a media tool. To be certain that you're assessing what you intend to assess (e.g., their subject area knowledge rather than their proficiency with media), be sure that children are thoroughly familiar with the features of the particular media form and/or technology that they'll be using. Once they are comfortable with the tools, they may reveal knowledge and skills far beyond what is possible on traditional tests. Here are just a few possibilities:

- Have children create an infographic, song, book, or video about a topic they have studied.
- Invite children to use the features of a familiar graphic organizer app (like Sketch Notes) to use arrows and highlights to show the sequence and main message of a story.

Or test comprehension by having children use those features to create a set of instructions for an important task.

- Make trading cards of favorite book characters.
- Create a 3D chart using LEGOs to sort, organize, and present data. Then take a photo to create a permanent record that's easy to share, and help children note the similarities to standard charts and graphs.

One increasingly common form of assessment is a portfolio that includes photos taken by teachers of children's actions or accomplishments throughout the day. These can be texted to parents, used to document change over time, or even serve as reminders for children to help them recall what they did. But they become even more powerful and valuable when children participate in creating them. As a project in New Zealand discovered, tablets and apps that let children comment or add highlights (e.g., using a finger to circle something important) can help children partner with teachers to make photographs into richer documents (Khoo, Merry, & Bennett 2015; Wright & Forbes 2015).

Even better in terms of media literacy skills, hand the cameras over to the children. Let them decide what is important to document. The benefits of having children act as photographers extend well beyond learning how to use cameras or apps. They improve communication skills and there is some evidence that little ones who take pictures share more details and recall more of what they did, even weeks later. That can improve conversations with families about what's happening in preschool and instill a sense of pride (DeMarie & Ethridge 2006).

Families can be prompted to do their own media literacy inquiry conversations, asking children questions such as, "Who made this picture? What was going on? Why was this important to document?" The process could even lend itself to a quick lesson about selfies—why we take them, when they are appropriate, and so forth.

## Use Photography to Strengthen Connections Between Home and School or Child Care

An increasingly popular activity is the "visiting friend." Preschoolers or primary grade students are given cameras to take home, along with a character that everyone in the group recognizes. Sometimes it's a stuffed animal or a cardboard cutout of the teacher or a favorite book character, or even a posable version of a school mascot. The children are encouraged to photograph the "visitor" in various places around their home or neighborhood, engaged in various tasks or attending special events.

The children add narration to their photos, either in person when they present them to classmates, or using apps that let them record and share voice overs. Teachers participate, too, sending pictures including the "visitor" when they are on vacation or on medical or parental leave.

Because everyone is sharing photos of the same "visitor," the photos are an obvious way to strengthen group bonds. Including the "visitor" in home routines also helps everyone get to know one another better and notice things that they have in common and things that are different. And because everyone has experience with the camera, little ones can give and get feedback from peers that improves image-based communication skills.

The activity also provides opportunities to develop language skills, use imagination (as children create storylines for the "visitor"), and welcome new members to their community (by letting newcomers take their turn with the "visitor"). It's also an easy way to include families that speak varying languages.

Another example of the power that comes from putting cameras into children's hands is shared by education researcher Arielle Friedman (2016). She describes an amazing two-year project in an Israeli preschool (3- and 4-year-olds) that intentionally made photography central to all areas of preschool learning.

The project involved three major interconnected types of activities: unstructured photography, analysis, and structured photography.

Teachers led children in analyzing all sorts of photographs taken by professionals and staff. Some were used to stimulate questions and discussion related to other areas of study. Others were intended to help children improve their own photography skills. For example, children were invited to compare four photos of a cat taken from different angles and focal lengths. After identifying similarities, the teacher asked them to speculate on why the cat looked different in each picture. Then they were left to experiment with the cameras as they saw fit. This type of experimentation, rather than direct instruction, was their primary means of learning to take photos. Through trial and error, and coaching each other, these little ones learned techniques such as not pointing the camera directly into a light source.

Unstructured opportunities were created by placing five advanced digital cameras on a shelf where the children could reach them. Though the project would have been successful with nearly any type of camera, in this case, the use of high-end cameras was intentional. It instilled in children the feeling that they were being taken seriously and that they were trusted to operate and care for the technology just as adults do. And, in fact, during the project, no child ever damaged a camera.

Children were free to take a camera off the shelf and use it as they wished. Friedman reports that, for example, children documented their friends' role-playing, playing in the schoolyard at recess, and participating in various social activities during the school day. Some of the photos would be displayed on the preschool's website. Each child's separate photo collection would be uploaded onto an accessible "shelf" and presented to each child as a gift at the end of the school year.

Slightly more structured prompts helped the children use photography to link home and school. Children were invited to document all their daily preschool activities and to share photos with families. The youngsters also took turns taking cameras home, where they recruited family members into photogenic themes, for example, a family meal, a trip, pets, and/or the nuclear and extended family. They shared these photos when they returned to preschool.

Both at home and at preschool, children became designated event photographers for birthdays, holidays, and other occasions. In one poignant example, children shot portraits of visitors from a nearby nursing home. They printed and framed the pictures and gave them as gifts to the elderly guests. They also photographed the gathering, showing the adults holding their portraits. These photographs were mounted on the preschool walls and a loop of the series of photos played on a large screen at a subsequent event.

The outcomes of the experiment went far beyond children learning how to take photographs. Parents were amazed at children's skill given their age, and impressed with the sense of confidence, responsibility, and pride their children exhibited. Parents also reported, "Photography and photographs become topics and texts that inspire conversations at home or on family outings" and that the activities created a "special connection" between parents and children and helped parents "get to know their children better" (Friedman 2016, 26).

Teachers reported that the problem solving, curiosity, and pleasure in learning infused all aspects of the preschool. They told Friedman that children exhibited independence and

> the ability to infer, think about and analyze the photographic image. As a case in point, the teacher describes the improvement in the youngsters' visual-literacy abilities as evidenced by how they converse about a picture: "When a picture is placed in front of them, right away they look for what's 'behind it'; right away they delve into it. They really say everything. Unlike another boy who sees a child and a house, they know how to talk about a picture [. . .] [to find] a common denominator among pictures, what's different, what's exceptional.

> Sometimes they also speculate about what happened before or after. They do it automatically by now [. . .]. They figure out how to ask questions about pictures rather quickly." (21)

Remember that these are 3- and 4-year-olds!

## Make a Documentary

If you make a camera accessible to children so they can record moments of their choice throughout their day, you're essentially encouraging them to make documentaries. You might even teach them the word *documentary* and set aside special screening times to share their productions with friends and families.

But mostly when we think about making documentaries, we think about much larger, more comprehensive projects. That's what two second grade teachers in upstate New York did when they decided to have students make a documentary as a capstone project for a major area of study. The project was undertaken as part of a Project Look Sharp media literacy initiative on environmental sustainability, and neither of the teachers, Julie Wells and Jennifer Goodmark, had any prior experience in video production. (*Note:* Project descriptions and quotes from participants, including teachers, aides, and students are taken from an unpublished evaluation of this project (Rogow 2016)).

The project is an especially valuable example because, although the ultimate outcomes were fabulous, there were instructive missteps along the way. The lessons began with analysis. The children analyzed book covers to learn about the ways that media makers choose images to appeal to particular target audiences. The intention was that they would eventually apply what they learned to creating the introduction of their video. Because covers were image based, teachers noted that the activity opened space for all the children to participate:

> They really shone, and not only the kids who shine every time because they can read and they can write. And so that was good.

There was also a lesson analyzing postcards that was intended to help children think about representations of place. This, however, turned out to be a significant challenge "because second graders had no idea what a postcard was or what it was for." After some prompting, some recalled buying postcards as souvenirs, but none had ever sent or received one. Though the lesson was saved by a teacher who found and showed a wonderful video about what a postcard is, it would have been better to design activities around media forms that were already familiar to children (Rogow 2016).

A third analysis component was intended to prepare children to create a documentary by showing them a documentary created by other children. This turned out not to work at all. The students were so engrossed in the content of the documentary (which was about butterflies), that they couldn't use it to examine form.

Eventually it was time to jump into production activities, with students writing, performing, and shooting their documentary about caring for the watershed that was behind their school building. Early stages did not go smoothly. Children lacked focus, seemingly unsure of what they were doing or how to accomplish the visions that were in their heads.

Project Look Sharp Director Cyndy Scheibe stepped in and helped students divide the task into smaller components. Based on that work, here's what I would recommend for issue-based documentary projects with young children:

> *Hello* (introduce who you are—this is basic information like name, what class you're a part of, where your school is—and also a "hook" that would entice people to want to watch the rest of the video)
>
> *Oh No!* (introduce the problem that the class is tackling)
>
> *Way to Go!* (what the class did and what the results were)
>
> *Info* (what else people should know about the problem and what they can do)

This format allowed the class to divide into groups with clear responsibilities.

Looking back, teachers also concluded that their activity prompt was too general. Rather than asking students to report on what they'd learned, they needed to start by guiding children to focus on why they cared. Then the class could move on to what they had learned about the function of watersheds and why it was important to protect theirs.

### Production Issues

The teachers wish they had known before hand, "That it takes about an hour to edit one minute of polished video. . . . This is a lot bigger than what we thought it was going to be. . . . I think without the two of us doing [a lot of the organizing and editing], it would've been a complete and utter fail." The project ended up relying heavily on the talents and goodwill of the school's technology specialist and on the help of a classroom paraprofessional. It turned out that children didn't need to do every single production task in order for the project to be valuable.

There were also small details that the teachers wish they had realized up front, like how to help kids shoot with iPads without shaking, and the need to teach them to use Google Drive to organize all their media files so they could easily find the shots they were looking for.

Everyone knew that it would be important to involve children in decision making about what to include (writing) and how to present the material (shot selection). And, indeed, the teachers reported that the need to select shots was especially valuable "because the kids critiqued one another, but in a very nice way."

However, several of the well-intentioned, adult-imposed scaffolds backfired. For example, Project Look Sharp provided prompts for scripting a PSA (public service announcement) as practice, but the teachers reported that "in reality what our kids wound up doing was finishing that sentence or finishing that thought and not really elaborating more. . . . I think the prompts for the script were meant to be helpful, but they wound up being more restrictive than anything."

And the storyboarding activity initially didn't work. "In part this was because the children were working in teams, but the act of drawing is individual. Ultimately, for this age group, drawing as planning was too distracting; the kids got caught up in the accuracy of the details in their pictures instead of the essence of the content. It might have worked better to have students focus on key questions—'What's our message? What would show that? and Where could we find a picture of that?'—and have them write or paste answers in a storyboard format" (Rogow 2016).

Eventually everyone got into the groove of production and children found themselves engrossed in decisions and filming. One controversy arose over a desire to show some of the pollution in the creek that flowed through the watershed. On the day the children were outdoors filming, there were no visible objects in the water. They decided to float a plastic water bottle down the creek, so it passed behind the student doing her stand-up explaining the problem. They caught the bottle before it floated away, but the scene raised the ethics of using reenactments as part of a documentary. Was it false because it wasn't a record of what they saw when they went out to shoot that day, or was it accurate because it showed the reality of what the children had encountered on many other days? You can see the result of their choice about 2:40 minutes into the final video, which is available for viewing here: www.youtube.com/watch?v=Q8ouwiML_gM.

The project culminated with the school hosting a community-wide "premiere" for families and guests—red carpet, fancy clothes, and all! These 7-year-old documentarians loved the attention as their accomplishment was celebrated.

### Outcomes

Despite the difficulties, the teachers were pleased with the results. One noted that they had done water as a case study before, but "this was different because of how it was really children's voices this time." The kids already knew a lot about water, but the media literacy and video production were new, and they made for a more powerful experience. "I think they felt part of something bigger than themselves."

What's more, children retained information about the science concepts central to the curriculum at a higher rate than normal, an outcome they attributed to the exceptionally high level of engagement:

> Everyone could talk, everyone could convey a point, in some way be part of the team. There was no one in the end who was excluded.

The requirements of making the documentary also "helped with commitment to the science content and to learning as much as they could so they could give reasons [for their conclusions]."

Media literacy outcomes weren't quite so predictable. The second graders had learned that book covers were meant to interest potential readers in a book's contents, but they didn't extend that to creating introductions for their video. However, when assigned to create an introduction for their video, they understood that their job was to "hook" the audience and they executed the task well.

Similarly, the youngsters didn't remember phrases like *target audience*, but could clearly identify the audience for whom they made the video. And the term *editing* failed to resonate, but they could talk comfortably about the process: "we had to choose the things we wanted."

So. media literacy vocabulary acquisition was less than successful, but other, more important outcomes were long lasting. The teachers reported that long after the video project was over, the children still saw themselves as activists: "So their battle cry in the fall was 'Save the water,' and now it's 'Save the bugs,' or 'Save the pollinators,' and I think they see themselves as having some agency."

These observations were affirmed by the children, themselves. Students were unanimous that their video about protecting water made a difference. One girl shared that her brother used to throw his candy wrappers all the time in the river, and "once he saw my video (at the school screening for families), now he doesn't do that anymore." Another applied the anti-littering and anti-pollution messages she'd learned to something that was never covered in class: she now makes sure her family uses a pooper scooper when they walk the dog! According to the teachers, "Parents were saying, 'They're coming home and they're talking about this . . .'"

Making a video also made students feel visible. One boy was especially excited to be in something that was posted on the Internet. The teachers added, "This may not sound like a huge takeaway, but they just felt so heard and validated. They're like, 'We're stars. We made something.'"

Overall, the project was so engaging and powerful that when the students were interviewed four months later about their video project, just that little reminder allowed them to recapture some of their original enthusiasm. As one teacher put it, "Some of that sparkle came back today."

Making the documentary made a positive impact on everyone involved—students, teachers, families, and even the broader school community. This was an outcome no one had expected.

It was so successful in terms of curriculum and engagement that the teachers, who had been skeptical and reluctant at the start of the project, chose to repeat it the following year. That class ended up taking their film to the school board, along with a request that the board allocate $5,000 to build a bridge that would help protect people and the watershed during the regular floods that occurred. The board granted their request!

## Thinking Big (and Small)

Media-making projects have a way of enabling us to combine lots of different subject areas and skills, which, of course, mirrors the real world. They link production and analysis, improving both skill sets.

Big projects work when they are based on something about which children care deeply, which also connects to the real world. When little ones have a sense of agency, they sustain interest.

This chapter has described photography, documentary, and current events projects, but there are so many other possibilities. Children can create digital art, public service announcements (PSAs), music videos, theater sets and performances, comics, banners, t-shirts, [pause for a deep breath] buttons, stickers, murals, games, maps—any media they encounter they can create. The possibilities are limited only by your creativity and energy.

## A Note About Coding

Calls to teach computer coding in early childhood have been around since MIT mathematician Seymour Papert first suggested it in the 1980s. He viewed the computer as an object to think with, the way that Montessori or Reggio Emilio environments might enable children to interact with certain objects because the objects spark learning. And he valued coding as a way to nurture computational thinking.

The digital world has evolved significantly since then. Touch screen interfaces, easy-to-use plug-in templates, voice controls, and the like make it possible to create websites, games, and more without ever mastering coding. Common coding jobs are no longer high skill or high wage, and specific coding languages in use now may very well be irrelevant by the time today's preschoolers enter the workplace.

So, it's worth asking if there is value in including coding in early childhood education. We can dismiss the many (often extravagant) claims by people selling specific coding products, but there are also many extraordinary educators whose work is worth serious consideration (e.g., Marina Bers, Kate Highfield, Idit Harel, Gail Lovely). They are figuring out how to teach coding in developmentally appropriate ways with ever-improving tools, like ScratchJr, Kodable, and a growing assortment of programmable robotic toys. For our purposes, the question isn't about whether these educators have established that learning to code in the early years is beneficial; it's whether learning to code helps children to become media literate. The answer isn't completely clear, especially for early childhood.

There are certainly overlaps between the logic, reasoning, and symbolic language acquisition involved in both coding and media literacy inquiry. But at this moment in time, it's also clear that it is possible to excel at media analysis, reflection, and creation without ever learning to code.

Whether coding activities hold the possibility of fostering media literacy will depend on how you do them. A series of rote programming tasks, or an isolated activity like programming a small bot to move on a grid or track, won't contribute much to media literacy. But if coding is included

› In response to children's curiosity about how games or certain toys or machines work

› In ways that highlight explicit ties to media being made by people (e.g., there is a special language that media makers use to make the game do all the different things it does)

› In ways that emphasize the thinking patterns on which all coding relies, including the logic and sequencing involved in getting things to work as intended

› In the context of considering the ethics of programming machines to do things that either help or hurt people

then coding activities can support media literacy education goals.

## Signs of Success

As you select strategies to translate media literacy education's big picture goals into specific early childhood teaching practices, keep expectations high and appropriate. We'll know we're succeeding when we see kindergartners and primary school children who

- Spontaneously notice, wonder about, and comment on media in their environment
- Ask media literacy questions on their own
- Know how to find credible sources that can answer their questions
- Provide evidence-based answers to media literacy analysis questions
- Are aware of their physical and emotional responses to media and media use
- Create media and explain their choices and target audience
- Understand that they can act, individually and with others, to challenge media that they see as unfair

It's worth pausing to note what isn't on this list. We don't measure success by whether children reject media entertainment that we don't like, or reduce their screen time, or cut down on requests for unhealthy food, or limit purchasing nags to things *we* think they need rather than the toys or game enhancements or brands they see in mainstream media. All of these things can be sparked by our media literacy efforts, but it isn't realistic to expect education—even fabulous education—to guarantee those outcomes.

It's easy to understand why if you've ever been at a meeting where you could choose to snack on an apple or a chocolate chip cookie and you chose the cookie even though you knew the apple was healthier. Despite the Maya Angelou adage, knowing better doesn't always mean doing better.

Human behavior is a complex product of a wide array of factors. Education is just one influence. It cannot guarantee that people—even media literate people—will always make the wisest choices, or treat everyone with kindness, or reject the negative values that are repeated in some media. What it can do is ensure that people can make informed choices and have the skills to act on what they know.

Effective teaching is always a combination of what you do and how you do it. So, as you're planning a media literacy lesson, look at the steps you've sketched out and use the Lesson Planning Guide in Figure 9.1 to ask yourself key questions.

## Choosing Activities

You probably noticed that these last two chapters include many suggestions that don't involve electronic media. These can be exceptionally important as a way to introduce media literacy when technologies are not available or when children need more concrete engagement than they can get from a screen or even when teachable moments that don't involve digital media crop up during the day. But they aren't a replacement for using digital media technologies.

At some point, if we want children to become literate in a digital world, we must engage them with digital media. Listen to children's

PAUSE TO **REFLECT**

Author bell hooks (1994) wrote, "Learning is a place where paradise can be created . . . [with] an openness of mind and heart that allows us to face reality even as we collectively imagine ways to move beyond boundaries, to transgress" (207). What does your education "paradise" look like? What obstacles prevent you from getting there? How might you use media literacy education to overcome those obstacles?

## MEDIA LITERACY LESSON PLANNING GUIDE

**Goals**

- ❑ I am doing this lesson because ___________.
- ❑ What's my big picture media literacy goal?
- ❑ How will the activity help children reach that goal?
- ❑ Which of the 10 media literacy competencies will children learn or practice?
- ❑ How will this contribute to creating an inquiry-rich environment or culture of inquiry
- ❑ Are there other curriculum or learning goals, besides media literacy, that the lesson will address?

**Design**

- ❑ How will the lesson content support children becoming confident thinkers and/ or communicators (habits of inquiry and/or skills of expression)?
- ❑ How will the lesson avoid telling children what to think and instead show them how to think?
- ❑ How will children know that I'm not trying to "fix" them and that I value their abilities?
- ❑ How will the lesson put me in the position me of guide and co-learner?
- ❑ What have I seen that lets me know that children are developmentally ready for and interested in this lesson?
- ❑ How will I help children connect this to other important things they are learning?

**Process**

- ❑ How will I start or introduce the lesson?
- ❑ What question(s) will I pose?
- ❑ How will I assess what children have learned?

**Logistics**

- ❑ How much time will we need?
- ❑ What materials, equipment, and/or space do we need?
- ❑ Are there other adults I need to ask for help or involve in the planning?
- ❑ Are there permissions I need to seek?
- ❑ How will I let families know about what we're doing?

**Figure 9.1 Media lesson planning guide.**

conversations and pay attention to when and where media technologies are available. What engages? What enrages? What opportunities are children already taking to think about the technologies they're using and when could they benefit from some guidance from you?

As you choose and implement activities, be clear about your goals and be mindful of how they relate to your existing curriculum. Perhaps there is a suggestion from this chapter that you'd like to try. Think through how it will help the specific children in your care or class acquire important knowledge or skills and also connect to big(ger) concepts, like society's struggle for fairness and the value of including multiple perspectives. As you help children find their unique voices and place in the world, you just might also find yours.

## Sources


DeMarie, D., & E.A. Ethridge. 2006. "Children's Images of Preschool: The Power of Photography." *Young Children* 61 (1): 101–4.

Friedman, A. 2016. "Three-Year-Old Photographers: Educational Mediation as a Basis for Visual Literacy via Digital Photography in Early Childhood." *Journal of Media Literacy Education* 8 (1): 15–31.

hooks, b. 1994. *Teaching to Transgress: Education as the Practice of Freedom*. New York: Routledge.

Khoo, E., R. Merry, & T. Bennett. 2015. "'I Want to Say . . .': Privileging Young Children's Voices in iPad-Supported Assessment for Learning." *Early Childhood Folio* 19 (1): 3–9.

Rogow, F. 2012. "Evaluation of 'Credibility, Information, and Science: Integrating Critical Thinking and Media Literacy into the STEM Curriculum.'" Unpublished evaluation of the LSTA BOCES/Project Look Sharp Partnership.

Rogow, F. 2016. "Evaluation of 'Greening the Core: Integrating Media Literacy into Sustainability Education.'" Unpublished evaluation for Project Look Sharp–Ithaca College.

Rogow, F., & C. Scheibe. 2017. "Sharing Media Literacy Approaches with Parents and Families." In *Family Engagement in the Digital Age: Early Childhood Educators as Media Mentors*, ed. C. Donohue, 183–96. New York: Routledge.

Tomé, V., P. Lopes, B. Reis, & C.P. Dias. 2019. "Active Citizenship and Participation Through the Media: A Community Project Focused on Pre-school and Primary School Children." *Comunicação e Sociedade* 36: 101–20.

Wright, N., & D.L. Forbes, eds. 2015. *Digital Smarts: Enhancing Learning and Teaching*. Hamilton, New Zealand: Wilf Malcolm Institute of Educational Research at University of Waikato.

CHAPTER 10

# Engaging Families

When early childhood educators suggest that parents or guardians give children crayons and paper, they know that families may not be aware of the connection between early scribbles and writing, but they can reasonably assume that families know what writing is, and most know how to do it. Not so with media literacy. Though efforts are growing, relatively few Americans have had much, if any, instruction in media literacy, especially as it applies to young children.

So, a good first step would be to check in with families. See what they know and make sure there is a shared understanding of what media literacy is and why you teach it. Pick an explanation that fits your situation.

You might share the media literacy education purpose statement from Chapter 5 or explain that media literacy expands traditional reading, writing, and thinking skills to include communicating with pictures and sounds. Or even something like, *"Kids will be learning to ask analytical questions about the media we use and make."* Help families understand the difference between media literacy and media management (Chapter 5) and let them know you'll be sharing tips about ways to support children's growing media literacy skills. This chapter suggests some possibilities for share-worthy tips along with sharing strategies. It also offers guidance on responding to concerns about media effects.

## Information Exchange

For many families, choices around media use are as much a reflection of culture and values as any aspect of their heritage or identity. So, it's important that conversations related to media are respect filled and judgment free. Here are some ways to translate that approach into action:

### 1. Ask Before You Tell

If you already use surveys to solicit family information or you have regular parent–teacher meetings, consider including a few questions about media. Avoid a judgmental or intrusive tone by keeping the questions positive. For example:

- *Help me get to know your and your child better. Is there a movie that your family viewed together that everyone really enjoyed?*
- *Does your child have a TV, movie, or game character that they're really fond of right now? Do you ever talk with your child about those shows or games? If yes, what have those conversations been like?*
- *Is there anything about your child and media that you want me to know? Or any questions you have about your child and media?*

You can also use survey questions to hint at future activities, for example, *We'll be creating digital books and artwork this year that children will be able to share with one or two people outside the Center (besides you). If you'd like to grant permission to share via email or text, please write in the person's name, relationship, and email address, or phone number. Of course, anything that is shared with others will also always be shared with you.*

## 2. Present Media Advice as Information About Child Development

As a professional, you have knowledge about children's development that parents or guardians may not have. You can share what you know and then let families decide for themselves where media fit into a healthy routine.

For example, instead of urging parents or guardians to avoid a particular TV series, a child care provider might write a newsletter blurb that says, *"Infants and toddlers use many learning strategies, including imitating things they see. This includes things they see on screen, so at this stage of your child's development, you might want to check to make sure that the things your child is viewing are things that are safe to copy."*

A parent who is struggling to get a child to put away their tablet when it's time to eat might benefit from an acknowledgement that it's often difficult to get children to stop doing anything that they find engaging and fun. Invite the parent to experiment with transition strategies that work for the child at school and report back on results.

Child development information can also sometimes help you respond when confirmation bias leads people to assume that media cause most of children's problems. I recall an incident when, as a consultant developing educational outreach for the original *Teletubbies,* a complaint came in about a child who had been speaking simple phrases suddenly reverting to baby talk. The family blamed the regression on the child viewing and mimicking *Teletubbies*. Looking through a child development lens, my question was, what do we know about the reasons that children revert to earlier stages of development?

I knew that regression was often a symptom of a physical problem or a sign of traumatic stress and that if the concerned grown-ups blamed TV instead of investigating possible sources of stress or ailment, that would be a mistake. What's more, if the child was stressed and *Teletubbies* was their source of comfort, taking away the opportunity to watch the show would have made things worse, not better.

### Real Versus Pretend

As we navigate what children watch and how they interact with media, it's important to understand what real versus pretend means to them. One of the things people love most about media is the imaginary worlds they create. Those same worlds can create dangers for young children who use imitation as a major way to learn about how the world works. We want them to know that in real life people can't fly like Superman or hit people without someone getting hurt. But trying to teach little ones to distinguish between real and pretend is likely to be an exercise in futility. Here's why:

- Many misconceptions are a product of early developmental stages. Children will grow out of them. Offering explanations before they're developmentally ready to understand is a waste of time and energy.
- Engaging in pretend play is vital to healthy child development. We don't want to give kids the impression that "real" is good and "pretend" is somehow bad.
- Blanket prohibitions against copying anything from media means that children will learn not to copy the good stuff along with the bad, like the role models in pro-social shows and games.
- Young children already distinguish between real and pretend, it's just that their definition of real is different than ours. They think of it more as "realistic." So, if a media scenario relates to their personal experiences, they process it as real, even if it is happening to a puppet or cartoon.

- We don't want to deny children the benefits of parasocial relationships. If you have ever heard about the death of a celebrity and felt grief or maybe even put a flower at a memorial site even though you didn't know the deceased personally, you have experienced a parasocial relationship. The celebrity touched your life in an authentic way, but in real life, you didn't know each other. As long as such relationships don't become obsessive, they have value.

  Children can develop parasocial relationships with media personas, including fictional characters. The experience of the relationship is authentic, even if the character isn't real.

  On the caution side, children may willingly share personal information with a parasocial "friend." Trying to explain that this "friend" isn't real won't be effective. Providing clear instructions about what's okay to share and what should not be shared outside of immediate family, school, or emergency personnel like doctors or first responders is a better strategy (e.g., *It's okay to tell media friends your first name, but not your last name, and it's never okay to share your phone number, your address, or the name of your school with anyone unless you get permission from your mama or papa first*).

- The concept of "real" is confusing, even for adults. We can't just say "look for the actual human beings." Lots of humans play characters that are every bit as much a fantasy as a cartoon: pro wrestlers; every actor in a sitcom; the model in the ad wearing a lab coat who says, "I'm not a doctor, but I play one on TV."

  And then there are the actual people who have been portrayed in animated series, like Bill Gates on the *Simpsons* or cellist Yo-Yo Ma on *Arthur.* Or try explaining that videos featured on *America's Funniest Home Videos* are "real," but if you tried to do some of what's in them, you'd get hurt, just like you'd get hurt copying pro-wrestling moves, though the latter is acting and not real. Or that the actor who plays a favorite superhero is real when they are being interviewed on the red carpet, but not real when they are in a movie.

  Confused yet? Imagine a preschooler trying to make sense of it all. And the lines between reality and fantasy or real and virtual continue to blur. Many people routinely meet and play with actual friends in the fantasy worlds created by online games. In fact, the 2020 US presidential race will go down as the first time in history that a candidate took a national campaign into a virtual game space. When the Biden campaign posted signs in Animal Crossing, they were hoping to generate actual, not fantasy, support.

Rather than attempting the impossible task of teaching young children to differentiate between real and pretend, the better strategy is to teach them to differentiate between their world and the media world.

Children learn at very young ages that some rules always apply and some change from place to place. There are things they can do at home that they aren't permitted to do in the car or at child care. Or things they can do at grandma's that they can't do at home. And we routinely ask children to keep the noise level down by using "inside" instead of "outside" voices.

We can use children's existing knowledge of these shifting expectations to contrast media with other places. So, for example, if a child copies Cookie Monster's messy eating habits, rather than saying, "Cookie Monster isn't real. In the real world we use table manners." try saying, *"Cookie Monster lives on TV and they can do different things on TV than we are allowed to do here. Here, we don't overstuff our mouths."* Or acknowledge that the child is engaging in imaginary play that includes their (parasocial) friend Cookie Monster. In that case, play along and hand them a pretend cookie. If they object, remind them that TV is a different place with different rules. Explain what they need to do in this place to get a real cookie.

## 3. Send Home "Ask Your Child About" Messages

Help families learn from and about the media literacy skills that their children are learning by sending daily text messages that say "Today we __________. Ask your child about __________."

- *Today we learned that food packages talk to us. Ask your child what "artificial flavor" means and how it helps them tell if the picture on the outside of the package matches what's inside.*
- *Today we learned about "point of view." Ask your child about how a camera can make something look bigger than it really is.*
- *Today we learned about photo-journalists and each child took a picture of something important that happened during the day that they wanted to document. Here's the picture your child took. Ask them why they thought this moment was important.*

This helps families continue media literacy conversations at home. It has the added benefit of avoiding the general "What did you do today?" which isn't specific enough for many young children to answer in a meaningful way. It can be done in whatever language the parents or guardians are comfortable speaking, and it models the inquiry process, giving families a way to start conversations with a question.

## 4. Help Parents and Guardians Learn to Make Media Decisions That Make Their Job Easier

Try this at your next family meeting: Say to the parent or guardian, "Picture your child at age thirty. They have grown up to be the perfect person you knew they would be. Make a list of the adjectives that describe their character [honest, generous, adventurous]." Have every household make their own list. This list is now a tool to help families evaluate their child's media.

Next, show a clip from a media example you know is familiar to most children and families. Ask people to put a check mark next to every value on their list that is actively affirmed, and a line through every value that is contradicted. At the end of the clip, ask the parent/guardian to look at their list. Explain that if they have lots of check marks, this media choice is supporting their goals and making their job as a parent easier. If there are lots of things crossed out, it's making their job harder. If there aren't any checks or lines, this media probably isn't undermining their efforts, but it isn't helping either.

The advantage of having each family create their own checklist is that the tool doesn't impose anyone else's values. Families can use it to decide for themselves which values they prioritize and what they are comfortable with in terms of how children spend their media time.

There are also useful sites that rate children's media (e.g., Common Sense Media [www.commonsensemedia.org/] or the Children's Technology Review/CTREX [https://reviews.childrenstech.com/ctr/home.php]). The best of them share the criteria they use, describe weaknesses as well as strengths, and include reactions from other families. These can be helpful timesavers for parents and guardians, but they shouldn't substitute for people learning the basics of how to evaluate media for themselves.

## A Note About Banning Particular Media

A common question that arises in conjunction with this activity is whether parents or guardians should ban media that don't measure up well on the checklist but that their children really love. Here are some factors to weigh before taking away entertainment that a child enjoys:

- For children old enough to understand and talk about ideas, it is better to engage in discussions about media than to ban them. Children who have regular conversations with parents/guardians will have that guiding voice (and values) as part of their filters when they are watching or playing with digital media on their own.
- Young children grow out of program preferences relatively quickly. How often do you still seek the media you enjoyed when you were a preschooler?! If a particular film or video series or game isn't creating a problem, let it go. There probably isn't a lot of reason for concern.

Still, it is the responsibility of parents and guardians to be gatekeepers for media content. It could be the right choice to ban shows or games if

1. There is clear evidence that a particular show or game is causing a problem for a particular child (e.g., a movie that gives them nightmares).
2. A program or game substantively contradicts a family's core values.

If the decision is to declare a game or show off limits, be sure it's for substance, not style. Developmentally appropriate programs for young children often contain pauses that foster interaction. To an adult this can make a video seem to be annoyingly slow. And grown-ups may not laugh at the things a 6-year-old finds uproariously funny. Take away a show because it's creating a problem, not just because the adults don't enjoy it. And be aware that if a show or game is banned and a problem persists, that's strong evidence that something else is going on that merits investigation.

## 5. Be Aware of the Ways That Your Own Interpretive Lens Influences Your Perceptions of Families' Media Use

Your experiences growing up and, if you are a parent, the media choices you've made for your own children influence the way you see the practices of others. If you strongly object, for example, to letting children use electronic devices at meals, confirmation bias may lead you to assume the worst about the parents of the kid engrossed by a digital screen at a restaurant.

But what if you told yourself a different story? What if you assumed that the child was on the autism spectrum and that if not for the electronic game, the child and family wouldn't be out in public together at all? Or perhaps the child is sharing their experience with a relative online. Or maybe an exhausted parent just needed a break that day, and distracting the child with the device was a reasonable coping strategy.

These are not the most likely explanations. There are plenty of families with less-than-ideal media habits. That's one of the reasons that universal media literacy education is so important. But letting a child use a tablet on a public outing might be a great choice for that child and that family on that day.

Changing the narrative in our heads can help us approach the families we serve with an open heart. From that place we can offer child development information, like a friendly reminder that kids learn from watching us, and that doesn't just apply to them copying our media behaviors. They also learn important social skills from observing how we interact with others. If they aren't watching or listening to those interactions because they are always using a handheld media device when they are with their grown-ups in public, or they're not engaging in conversations that help their language development, they're missing out on valuable learning opportunities.

The message isn't that parents or guardians shouldn't let children use media devices at a restaurant (or on the bus or visiting with a relative or wherever). The purpose of sharing is to draw awareness to the ways that simple choices, including choices about media use, can influence what children learn.

## 6. Let Families Know Which Media You Use with Children, Including Selection Criteria

Explaining the criteria you use to make your media selections can help parents and guardians learn clues they can use to spot authentically educational media. When they begin to understand what to look for, they'll also start noticing when those features are missing from media. More evaluation criteria are available on the author's blog (see Appendix C: Resources). If you're going to recommend media for home use, keep in mind paywalls, Internet availability, and families' capacity to purchase or access through a library.

You might also want to assure parents and guardians that you aren't using screens as a babysitter. Explain how you engage children in conversations that develop their analysis and reflection skills, noting that they can, too.

And share media that give *you* joy. Maybe you've created a playlist of pop songs that are family friendly and great dance tunes, or a relaxing soundtrack for transitions and nap time. This sort of sharing can deepen your connection with families.

Strong partnerships grow from two-way relationships, so it's important to be clear that you're not only interesting in sending information *to* families; you're also interested in hearing *from* families. They are experts in the sorts of media that interests their child. They can help you make home–school connections, find new resources, and facilitate families sharing resources with one another.

## 7. Select Apps or Learning Management Systems Carefully

Early childhood programs that use digital technologies to keep in touch with families are responsible for ensuring that the apps families are asked to use have explicit, easy-to-read policies indicating that the app does not collect, share, or sell personal data, and that rights to anything created with the app belong exclusively to the person who created it.

It's also important to make sure families know what to do in order to protect their personal information. This includes collection by third party apps (e.g., if families sign in using Facebook, then Facebook may be collecting data, even if the program management app, itself, is not). For a sample list of features to look for and talk about, take a look at how Common Sense Media determines its privacy ratings: https://privacy.commonsense.org/resource/privacy-ratings.

## 8. Share What You Know About Media on a Routine Basis

Don't be an information hoarder. Unless families also read this book, there are probably things that you know about media that they don't. Find ways to share that knowledge in a regular, ongoing way. To make the sharing effective,

- Don't wait for a problem to arise or exaggerate the importance of media compared with other factors in a child's life.

- Keep ideas realistic. Instead of "watch with your kids," which no one can do all the time, suggest that parents and guardians co-view often enough to be familiar with the media/games that their children are watching/playing. That way they can ask relevant questions even if conversations happen later. Or they can make a game of posing a question before a show, letting a child watch while they make dinner and then asking the question during the meal.
- Share strategies that you find useful, like starting conversations with an open-ended question and listening to the ways that children make meaning from media instead of assuming we know what messages they are absorbing.

As an early childhood professional, you are in a position to help families build skills so they can make their own informed choices.

# Answering Families' Questions About Media Effects

It's not unusual for parents to react to media literacy education initiatives with a version of "But what about [insert the latest claim about screen media ruining children's lives]." In my mind the answer typically starts with, "If you only knew [insert clarification about the nuances of media effects research], it would be so much easier to explain." Conversations could be so much deeper and more productive if there were certain things that everyone already knew. Over the years I've developed a wish list based on frequently raised issues.

## My Wish List

Parents and guardians typically get information about media effects from mainstream media: news features, pundits and author interviews, or a social media post by a friend or influencer. So, the first set of items in my wish list covers things that are helpful to know about the ways that popular media share research. I wish that every parent and guardian knew that

- Commercial media attract more viewers/listeners/users (and so generate more revenue) with the dramatic and sensational than with nuanced reports of research results. So, we get alarming headlines like "Screens Are Creating a Generation of Zombies!" instead of the more accurate but less exciting, "The Effects of Screen Time Are Complicated."

One of the most important consequences of this commercial imperative is that researchers who identify problems are given much more attention than researchers who provide evidence of benefits. To media decision makers, the latter can feel like the equivalent of saying, "Everything's fine. Nothing to see here." And that's boring, especially when you can ring an alarm bell instead.

So, unless you're a children's media researcher, you've probably never heard of the 2016 study by Viviane Kovess-Masfety and colleagues that found that high usage of video games was correlated with high intellectual functioning and playing video games may have positive effects on young children (Kovess-Masfety et al. 2016). Not a conclusive study, but given its inclusion of 3,000 children, certainly worthy of attention. Similarly, the work of Jackie Marsh and colleagues, has garnered relatively little notice in mainstream media, despite their study of more than 950 0-3 year olds concluding that, "tablets and apps can foster play and creativity in a number of ways," engaging children in many play domains, "holistically across cognitive (including linguistic), bodily/affective, social and cultural aspects of their development." (Marsh et al. 2015, 12). And there are dozens more that support similar conclusions whose authors remain unknown outside professional circles.

The need to couch everything in eye-catching headlines often obscures rather than informs. In one recent example, psychologist

Jean Twenge documented a correlation between screen time and increases in youth depression and suicide rates. What caught the attention of media reports was her suggestion that in terms of well-being, social media was worse for girls than heroin (Twenge et al. 2020).

Scholars Amy Orben and Andrew Przybylski (2019) responded with evidence that there was a greater negative link between eating potatoes or wearing glasses and well-being than the negative association between technology use and well-being. In other words, they were suggesting that Twenge's comparison of social media and heroin use was absurd. The exchange was entertaining, but the reporting missed an opportunity to explain substantive disagreements about statistical analysis methods and data collection. And it encouraged people to take sides instead of looking at the strengths and weaknesses of each researcher's work.

- Headlines, chyrons at the bottom of the TV screen, and promos are rarely written by reporters or researchers. They are a marketing tools designed to generate clicks or views, not part of the story. They may not even accurately reflect the content of the report.
- Repetition can give the impression that a claim is widely accepted. That makes it easy to internalize ideas without thinking much about them. This plays out in lots of ways:
  - Seeing a tease or hearing a promo a few dozen times can normalize overdramatic claims before you've ever heard the actual story.
  - Repetition across social media can make it seem like views are widely held when actually they are the result of a few voices who function as an echo chamber that amplifies, and thereby quickly spreads, its messages. For example, a study by the Center for Countering Digital Hate (2020) found that just 12 people were responsible for 65 to 70 percent of the millions of social media anti-vaccination messages.

  Sometimes a claim appearing in many different media is just the same claim by the same author on the same book tour being repeated over and over.

  - The content we see on social media sites is substantially influenced by data that sites have gathered about us from past online activity, so once you've clicked on a headline about media harm, you're likely to see many similar headlines. That doesn't make the headlines true.
- Speed matters. A screaming headline on social media can be shared thousands of times in mere minutes. But credible responses take time. And because they take time (and may contradict media hype around the original claim) they are often buried or ignored in the popular press.

  A case in point is neuroscientist Susan Greenfield's claim that 500(!) peer-reviewed studies indicated that screen time was literally destroying people's brains. It takes time to check 500 studies. Eventually, Dorothy Bishop (2014), Oxford University Professor of Developmental Neuropsychology, investigated and found that of the original 500 peer-reviewed studies, only 15 directly addressed the claims that Greenfield made, and not all of them supported Greenfield's position. By then the buzz had dissipated and Bishop's response garnered little media attention.
- There are some excellent science reporters working in mainstream media, but much reporting is done by journalists or media hosts with no science background or training in the statistical methods used by media effects researchers. The best among them will summarize an argument and a critique, but it's just as likely that they are trusting a press release issued by a research team's university or think tank.

  In one example of why this matters, Justina Schlund (2021) of CASEL (Collaborative for Academic, Social, and Emotional Learning) documents how even well-intended coverage ended up garbling the phrase Social Emotional Learning (SEL) so badly that today, many people object when school districts work to incorporate SEL because they have mistaken ideas about what it is.

Then there is the wish list of science concepts. I wish that every family knew that

- Correlation is not cause.
- Documenting change is not the same as documenting damage. For example, it's one thing to observe that children don't play the way they used to. It's another to conclude that the ways they play now are less beneficial than previous play activities.
- Cultural criticism has immense value, but it isn't scientific research. A provocative question isn't proof that the premise of the question is accurate.
- Confirmation bias can lead people, including researchers, to see what they believe to be true, not necessarily what is true.

As a workshop leader, I rarely have an opportunity for extended contact with families. That makes it difficult to transform my wish list into reality. But educators do have extended contact. So, what's on your wish list?

## Taking a Close-Up

The wish list examples briefly illustrate why the research about negative media effects is important, but it isn't unassailable. Taking a more detailed look at one example of a media effects claim can clarify.

Consider this common question: Doesn't screen time cause attention-deficit/hyperactivity disorder (ADHD)? Many people who think there is a link between screen time and attention problems trace their belief back to a single study. Dimitri Christakis and colleagues (2004) published research in the journal *Pediatrics* asserting that every 15 minutes of TV viewing time in a child's first 3 years reliably predicted an increased likelihood that they would exhibit ADHD by age 7. It's a great example of media grabbing a sensationalist headline and running with it before carefully examining the research. And many aspects of this research should have raised red flags.

Christakis is a well-respected researcher with substantial credentials, and the research was published in a major journal. From a media literacy perspective, the claim has all the hallmarks of being credible. But if you actually used more than just the *credibility* category of media literacy questions to examine the research (see Appendix B) you'd note several weaknesses:

- The researchers found a correlation, not a cause, but headlines (though not the researchers) often implied a causal relationship.
- The data set relied on self-reporting from mothers. Self-reporting is among the least reliable of data collection methods (Parry et al. 2021). It meant that the study relied on the perceptions of mothers, not clinical diagnoses of ADHD. And it never acknowledged the role of confirmation bias in that perception.
- Christakis did not explain why his research was stronger than studies contradicting their results, including why they found negative results starting at just 15 minutes of viewing when many other studies have found no ill effects until children reached a "heavy viewing" threshold (typically several hours a day).
- In science, accurate results should be replicable. These weren't (see studies by Stevens & Mulsow 2006 and Obel et al. 2004, both published in *Pediatrics*). A recent re-analysis of the same data that Christakis used found that, contrary to Christakis's conclusion, the "data do not provide compelling evidence of a harmful effect of TV exposure on attention" (McBee, Brand, & Dixon 2021, 497).
- Arguably the most important problem is that the study surmises that children's brains were being damaged by television's fast-paced,

rapidly changing images. But the Christakis team never looked at content, and at the time of data collection, not all TV fare was fast paced. The researchers had no way of knowing what children actually viewed. That means that the mechanism proposed to explain the results didn't match anything that was actually studied.

- Interestingly, Christakis and colleagues attempted to remedy this last flaw with a 2018 study measuring the impact of actual exposure to fast-paced content. As the researchers acknowledged, it is notoriously difficult to study such a hypothesis because it's not ethical to expose children to harmful experiences. So, the 2018 research "simulated" what a child's brain would experience by exposing mice to excessive sensory stimulation, such as flashing lights (Christakis et al. 2018). The problem with that approach, however, is that there is no reason to believe that mice make any particular meaning from random sensory stimulation. Children watching TV, on the other hand, are making meaning from what they see and hear, and their viewing experiences are occurring in specific social contexts that also convey meaning. That changes the brain activity, and therefore the effects. The results from the mice can't be extrapolated to children.

There is no disputing that the numbers of diagnosed cases of ADHD and other attention disorders have increased over the last few decades. What is unclear is why. Screen media might be a contributing factor, though there's no reliable proof of that. Nor is there reason to dismiss any number of other possibilities, including better diagnosis and reporting, changes in food and eating patterns, toxic exposure, and even unrealistic expectations that little ones ought to be able to sit still for long periods of time. With so many alternative explanations, it would be reasonable to pose the media literacy question, "Who benefits from the continued focus on screen time?"

This particular Christakis study doesn't stand up well to basic scrutiny, but that doesn't negate all of his work or all media effects studies. For example, a survey of the field would reveal a lot of consensus around conclusions about screen media at bedtime leading to sleep disruption, or that babies don't learn well from screens.

Covering all the topics that have been researched relative to children and media is far beyond the scope of this book. Instead, the lesson for media literacy educators is, before passing along a claim about media effects, do your homework. Ask the questions in Appendix B, do some lateral reading to see what other researchers think, and look for areas of consensus.

### Logic, Reason, and Common Sense

Diving deeply into the research is not likely to be the best way to engage with families. Fortunately, simple critical thinking can provide a lot of insight.

In the case of attentional disorders for example, it is interesting that many of the same people who claim that screen use is leading to attention problems also complain that children are so addicted to their screens that it's hard to pull them away. Clearly the kids are paying attention to something! It's a logical disconnect.

Or consider the common claim that screen media make kids dumber. These have been around for decades. That's long enough to actually assess the cohort about which the claims were initially made. Predictably, the alarmists were wrong. The early TV cohorts are now middle aged and have, by most measures, lived normal, productive lives. Even today, for every instance of young people who are struggling there are equally powerful examples of young people who are using media to do amazing work in the world.

## Understanding Media Effects: Four Factors

In addition to using logic and reason, there is a simple formula that families can use to understand that nearly media effects

**How much** time we spend using media

**What** media we're engaging with

**Who** we are

**Why** we are engaging with media

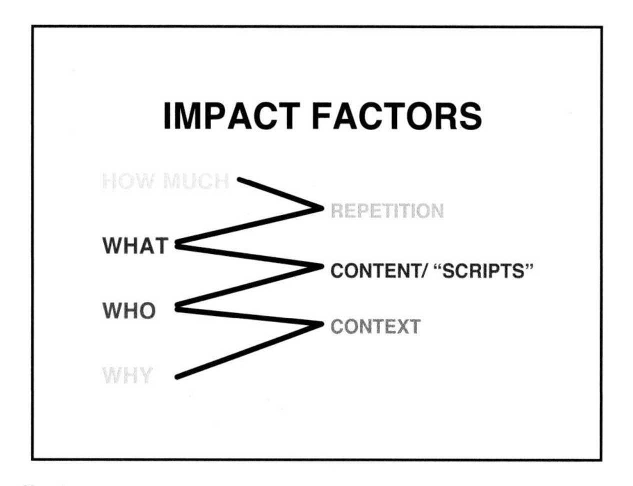


Figure 10.1 The four impact factors to understanding media effects.

every claim. The study of media effects is all about assessing whether there are real-life consequences of our media use, and if there are, what those consequences might be. More than just determining whether particular messages are benign, beneficial, detrimental, or all of the above, we want to know the results of the interactions with those messages and the systems that bring them to us. In that context, nearly all media effects can be explained by four interconnected factors (Figure 10.1).

## How Much

The amount of time we spend with media is significant for two reasons. The first is the possibility of displacement. Media time can crowd out other important activities.

Displacement claims need to be made with caution because

- There is evidence that children with relatively low levels of screen time aren't necessarily less sedentary than peers (e.g., Fakhouri et al. 2013), suggesting that there are factors other than screen time leading to sedentary time (e.g., more formalized academics at younger ages, suburban life requiring more time strapped into car seats, or increasingly organized and specialized youth sports that add expense and narrow opportunities for all but the best athletes).
- Active athletes also frequently play the video versions of their favorite sports.
- People regularly multitask—using media at the same time they do other things. They stream podcasts or music while jogging, listen to the news while doing the dishes, socialize with teammates while engaged in an online multiplayer game, and so forth.
- Some activities that once weren't counted as media time are now routinely accomplished using screen media (e.g., talking on the phone).

So, simply counting media minutes isn't always informative.

Still, when people are engaging with friends on social media they are probably not also playing with their children. Humans can't sleep or read novels and play video games at the same time, and if they're watching a movie they are probably not also simultaneously outside playing basketball. So, media time doesn't necessarily displace other activities, but it can.

Beyond displacement, there are effects from heavy use of screens. Definitions of *heavy* vary, and what constitutes heavy can depend on what someone is actually doing with the screen (Przybylski & Weinstein 2017). Four to five hours a day is not an uncommon threshold before significant problems begin to show up.

There is convincing evidence that children's (and our own) physical and mental health can suffer from an "always on" approach to media, even when it's only on in the background (Lapierre, Piotrowski, & Linebarger 2012; Pempek, Kirkorian, & Anderson 2014). It's clear that our brains need breaks to rest and recharge, and our bodies need to move, so if media use replaces physical activities, disrupts sleep, decreases conversation and face-to-face interactions, or eliminates quiet time, it's a problem. Still, there is a lot of leeway between "always on" and "never," so we need to be careful not to overgeneralize the effects of heavy use as if they applied to any use.

*How much* is also important because the power of media rests in its ability to repeat messages. The more media one consumes, the more media messages they see and hear. The specific effects of those messages depend on content choices, which leads to the second factor, *What* . . .

## What

Media include messages about nearly everything that matters in our day-to-day decision making and what we believe to be true about the world. Which messages we encounter depends on what we're interacting with. Consider the very different world views and vocabulary in, say, *Minecraft, Cat in the Hat, Toy Story,* or unboxing videos.

For young children, design, as well as content matters. For example, relatively slow pacing and uncluttered illustrations or backgrounds make it possible for little ones to follow the story and focus on what's important without overloading young brains with too much new information. Vocabulary that helps children stretch just a bit from where they are, but without an overwhelming number of new words, can make the difference between understanding media or misinterpreting.

It's important to know that not all media effects require comprehension. Usually when children don't understand they get bored and walk away. But an infant's mood can be affected by the "vibe" of music or a video's soundtrack, well before they are able to understand the words, even if they're in another room and can't see the screen.

Of course, as we've seen previously, the effects of any specific content on any specific individual depends on who they are, which brings us to the third factor, *Who* . . .

## Who

As the section on interpretive lenses in Chapter 3 explained, we come to media from particular vantage points, so our interpretations are never neutral or automatic. As author Anaïs Nin wrote in *Seduction of the Minotaur,* "We don't see things as they are; we see them as we are." Our own reasons for seeking entertainment and information influence how we are affected. That brings us to the fourth and final factor, *Why* . . .

## Why

What we take away from any media experience is based, in part, on our reason for engaging in the experience in the first place. For example, a pilot who logs on to a flight simulator for training has a very different mindset, and very different outcomes, than a preteen using the same app just for fun.

Prior knowledge magnifies the differences. A professional comes to the task already possessing a complex knowledge base on which to attach new information. A kid playing with the same app doesn't have as many prior knowledge receptors. They won't notice or recall nearly as much as the pilot.

We routinely apply varying degrees of attention to media. You are more likely to recall what you're reading if your purpose is to study for a test than to pass time at an airport. Gamers might pay close attention to which game strategies got them to the next level with the most "lives" still intact, but might miss subtle messages, or "Easter eggs," even in plain sight. A film student is likely to recall more details, especially about style and production techniques, from a film that has been assigned for class analysis than a movie they are watching on a date. We all make decisions about how attentive to be, and that influences how media affect us.

### Active Versus Passive

There is a common narrative that television viewing is passive in contrast to apps and digital games, which are active. This framing is misleading. It's not the media that are active or passive, it's us.

If you choose to approach TV actively, say, singing along, or looking for clues so you can solve the mystery before the detectives reveal the perpetrator, or calling out the answers to the game show questions, television can be more engaging than mindlessly playing a game like Candy Crush for the thousandth time.

Sometimes very young children can fool us into thinking they are "zoning out" in front of the TV because they are staring intently. That stare can mean "I'm in overload and not really processing any of this but I can't look away from the constantly changing pretty picture." It can also mean the opposite: "I am concentrating really hard so I can process this really interesting story."

Those who make the passive/active contrast suggest that there is a distinction between things we watch and interactive media that offer users opportunities to take actions that change what is happening on screen. Of course, by that definition, a play or concert or even a book isn't interactive. Neither is video that pauses for children to offer a response, like *Blue's Clues, Dora the Explorer,* or *Sesame Street* (which invented the technique). But in terms of learning, those television shows are likely more beneficial than playing with a poorly designed app that is repetitive and beneath a child's skill level to the point that they have memorized it and are just going through the motions.

Understanding our own role in active engagement explains why simply handing kids digital apps doesn't automatically contribute to becoming media literate nor does it guarantee a quality educational experience.

## Focus on the Skills

Debates about media effects aren't abstract. Families have to make decisions about children's interactions with media on a daily basis. They need good information. Fortunately, there have been many good books published in recent years that help families address media management issues. You might want to recommend works by Diana Graber, Lisa Guernsey, Devorah Heitner, Anya Kamenetz, Sonia Livingstone and Alicia Blum-Ross, and Jordan Shapiro, among others. Clearly, media is a topic of significant interest!

Written from a variety of perspectives and areas of expertise, they all respond to a version of the question, "Am I harming my child by allowing them to use screen media?" And they have all come to remarkably similar conclusions: It depends on what kids are doing, why they're doing it, and how old they are.

Lisa Guernsey (2012) shortened that conclusion to the "three Cs"—media effects depend on the content, context, and child. Translating that into actionable advice, Anya Kamenetz (2018) summarized, "Enjoy screens. Not too much. Mostly with others" (10).

These authors examined the research and reflect a growing consensus that heavy use of anything (including books) can lead to problems, but in families that make reasonably thoughtful media management decisions, the kids will be fine.

Sonia Livingstone (2019) observed, "Restricting children builds resistance, while guiding them builds judgment" (10:00). When families focus on media effects claims, especially when they learn about those claims from sensationalized media reporting, it's tempting to slip into restrictions. Every new report of a threat activates a natural desire to want to keep kids safe. As a media literacy educator, you can offer a different model. You know how to use media with children in ways that help them build judgment. And families can, too.

You and your children's grown ups share a mission that includes the goal of helping children become media literate. Media effects research will provide valuable guidance to help everyone reach that goal, as long as you distinguish between issues on which there is consensus and those that are contentious.

What we know for sure is that when you use media well, those media (and you) are enriching children's lives and helping them gain the skills, knowledge, and dispositions they'll need to be literate. That's why it's possible to acknowledge that researchers have identified some important things to guard against, but they don't outweigh the benefits of media literacy education that incorporates screens.

## Sources


Bishop, D. 2014. "Why Most Scientists Don't Take Susan Greenfield Seriously." *BishopBlog* (blog), September 26. http://deevybee.blogspot.com/2014/09/why-most-scientists-dont-take-susan.html.

Center for Countering Digital Hate. 2020. *Pandemic Profiteers: The Business of Anti-Vaxx*. Report. London: Center for Countering Digital Hate. www.counterhate.com/pandemicprofiteers.

Christakis, D.A., F.J. Zimmerman, D.L. DiGiuseppe, & C.A. McCarty. 2004. "Early Television Exposure and Subsequent Attentional Problems in Children." *Pediatrics* 113 (4): 708–13.

Christakis, D.A., J.S. Benedikt Ramirez, S.M. Ferguson, S. Ravinder, & J.-M. Ramirez. 2018. "How Early Media Exposure May Affect Cognitive Function: A Review of Results from Observations in Humans and Experiments in Mice." *Proceedings of the National Academy of Sciences* 115 (40): 9851–8.

Fakhouri, T.H.I., J.P. Hughes, D.J. Brody, B.K. Kit, & C.L. Ogden. 2013. "Physical Activity and Screen-Time Viewing Among Elementary School-Aged Children in the United States from 2009 to 2010." *JAMA Pediatrics* 167 (3): 223–9.

Guernsey, L. 2012. *Screen Time: How Electronic Media—From Baby Videos to Educational Software—Affects Your Young Child*. New York: Basic Books.

Kamenetz, A. 2018. *The Art of Screen Time: How Your Family Can Balance Digital Media and Real Life*. New York: PublicAffairs.

Kovess-Masfety, V., K. Keyes, A. Hamilton, G. Hanson, A. Bitfoi, D. Golitz, C. Koç, R. Kuijpers, S. Lesinskiene, Z. Mihova, R. Otten, C. Fermanian, & O. Pez. 2016. "Is Time Spent Playing Video Games Associated with Mental Health, Cognitive and Social Skills in Young Children?" *Social Psychiatry and Psychiatric Epidemiology* 51 (3): 349–57.

Lapierre, M.A., J.T. Piotrowski, & D.L. Linebarger. 2012. "Background Television in the Homes of US Children." *Pediatrics* 130 (5): 839–46.

Livingstone, S. 2019. "Parenting in the Digital Age." Talk presented at TEDSummit 2019 in Edinburgh, Scotland. www.ted.com/talks/sonia_livingstone_parenting_in_the_digital_age.

Marsh, J., L. Plowman, D. Yamada-Rice, D., J.C. Bishop, J. Lahmar, F. Scott, A. Davenport, S. Davis, K. French, M. Piras, S. Thornhill, R. Robinson, & P. Winter. 2015. *Exploring Play and Creativity in Pre-Schoolers' Use of Apps: Final Project Report*. www.techandplay.org.

McBee, M.T., R.J. Brand, & W.E. Dixon. 2021. "Challenging the Link Between Early Childhood Television Exposure and Later Attention Problems: A Multiverse Approach." *Psychological Science* 32 (4): 496–518.

Obel, C., T. Brink Henriksen, S. Dalsgaard, K. Markussen Linnet, E. Skajaa, P.H. Thomsen, & J. Olsen. 2004. "Does Children's Watching of Television Cause Attention Problems? Retesting the Hypothesis in a Danish Cohort." *Pediatrics* 114 (5): 1372–3.

Orben, A., & A.K. Przybylski. 2019. "The Association Between Adolescent Well-Being and Digital Technology Use." *Nature Human Behaviour* 3 (2): 173–82.

Parry, D.A., B.I. Davidson, C.J.R. Sewall, J.T. Fisher, H. Mieczkowski, & D.S. Quintana. 2021. "A Systematic Review and Meta-Analysis of Discrepancies Between Logged and Self- Reported Digital Media Use." *Nature Human Behaviour*. Advance online publication. doi:10.1038/s41562-021-01117-5.

Pempek, T.A., H.L. Kirkorian, & D.R. Anderson. 2014. "The Effects of Background Television on the Quantity and Quality of Child-Directed Speech by Parents." *Journal of Children and Media*, 8 (3): 211–22.

Przybylski, A.K., & N. Weinstein. 2017. "A Large-Scale Test of the Goldilocks Hypothesis: Quantifying the Relations Between Digital-Screen Use and the Mental Well-Being of Adolescents." *Psychological Science* 28 (2): 204–15.

Schlund, J. 2021. "5 Ways to Think About Social and Emotional Learning." *SmartBrief*, April 28. www.smartbrief.com/original/2021/04/5-ways-think-about-social-and-emotional-learning.

Stevens, T., & M. Mulsow. 2006. "There Is No Meaningful Relationship Between Television Exposure and Symptoms of Attention-Deficit/Hyperactivity Disorder." *Pediatrics* 117 (3): 665–72.

Twenge, J.K., J. Haidt, T.E. Joiner, & W.K. Campbell. 2020. "Underestimating Digital Media Harm." *Nature Human Behaviour* 4 (4): 346–8.

CHAPTER 11

# Taking the Next Step

Compared to other books on media and children, this book has asked you to do something unusual. It has asked you to see the challenge as illiteracy rather than media.

The distinction is about perspective. Effective media literacy educators are always well informed about media and media-related issues. And when we see media infringing on our individual or collective well-being, we act, engaging in media reform efforts the way we would any other vital civic endeavor. But those efforts, even when undertaken on behalf of little ones, center media, not children. No one would ever suggest measuring the efficacy of teaching or learning by how much media improved.

So, as educators, we focus on the *literacy* part of media literacy. That choice shapes the way we think about our responses and responsibilities.

PAUSE TO **REFLECT**

At the end of each part of this book, the Pause to Reflect box asked you to write one sentence that you want to remember. Take a look at what you wrote. What was it about the sentences you selected that caught your attention? Do they express messages that you want to share, and if so, with whom, how, and when could you make that happen? How will you explain why you think they are important enough to share?

If you are reading this book as part of a class or professional learning community, you might want to swap quotes and discuss everyone's choices.

## A Media Literacy Guild?

Since at least medieval times, people in the trades belonged to guilds that supervised training and designated skill levels: Apprentice, Journeyman, Master. I sometimes wonder what the levels would look like if media literacy education had a guild. Perhaps the titles would go something like this:

Curious Seeker

Apprentice Questioner

Adept Thinker

Reflective Maker

Wise Teacher

Or maybe the process is messier than a neat progression and we earn and hold several badges at once. As you come to the end of this book, what title(s) would you give yourself? What would you have to do to level up?

## Closing Thoughts

One of the media analysis question categories is *context*. And there is a very particular context for this book. In 1974 (the year of the interview, not of its publication), philosopher Hannah Arendt explained, "If everybody always lies to you, the consequence is not that you believe the lies, but rather that nobody believes anything any longer" (Errera 1978). Fast-forward half a century and, abetted by social media, where lies spread exponentially faster and further than facts (Silverman 2017), we are living Arendt's words.

In countries all over the world, educators at all levels are hearing from students and families who say, "I just don't know what to believe anymore." It's not unusual for teachers to encounter children and families who repeat (sometimes wildly outlandish) conspiracy theories. In some places, the very idea of evidence-based critical thinking is becoming anathema.

This context of conspiracy and mistrust has inspired increasingly urgent calls for universal media literacy education—a call which you are now more prepared to answer. Media literacy education, alone, can't bridge every division or stop disinformation campaigns from damaging democracy. But approached as literacy, with a focus on critical inquiry and reflection, it can prime young people to spot common ground and use it to engage in productive dialogue and community action.

It's difficult to imagine a successful democracy without citizens who have the will and skill to

- Engage respectfully
- Communicate effectively
- Evaluate sources and evidence with a logical and open mind
- Understand the experiences and values that have shaped their own perspective
- Recognize the experiences and values that shape others' perspectives

These are the central things that media literacy education brings to the civic table. Not screen time debates. Not special lessons about harmful media messages. Media literacy educators teach children to

- Use inquiry to become discerning, rather than mistrustful
- Become powerful, thoughtful, ethical, creative communicators
- Treasure the rich interpretations and human connections that result from hearing multiple perspectives.
- Use media technologies to create, rather than separate from community
- Seek adult guidance without expecting grown-ups to provide a single "true" interpretation or one right answer
- Have the confidence to answer, "How do you know?" and "How could we find out?" questions for themselves
- Consider the common good and value the principle of "justice for all"

In a digital world, these are as important to being literate as learning how to decode alphabetic text.

As the recent *Report of the NCTE Task Force on Critical Media Literacy* noted, "as society and technology change, so does literacy" (NCTE 2021, 7). For some, integrating media literacy education will require a re-assessment of many parts of the curriculum, not just the media they use. It's not viable to teach children how to find credible sources and also feed them versions of their nation's history that ignore those sources. It's unfair to tell them that they have the power to make things better and then refuse to challenge inequities that undermine that power. It's disingenuous to teach them to value reliable evidence and then dismiss the consensus judgement of the scientists who published ninety-seven percent of the climate research studies in peer-reviewed journals, all of whom agree that human choices are accelerating global-warming (see, e.g., Skeptical Science, https://skepticalscience.com/global-warming-scientific-consensus-advanced.htm). And if all of that sounds "too serious" for early childhood education, take comfort in knowing that it is possible to surround children with kindness while also recognizing that there is nothing kind about letting injustices stand unchallenged.

As early childhood educators, it is within our grasp to acknowledge that the world is complex without abandoning developmentally appropriate practice. Media makers like the *Sesame Street* team and Fred Rogers have modeled how to be simple without being simplistic. If they can tackle challenges like racism, disease, fear, and even death—then media literacy educators can help children learn to analyze and create media messages in developmentally appropriate ways. And no matter the media messages we explore together, we can ground the practice of media literacy education in the joys of discovery and learning that make working with children in their early years so amazing.

## Continuing the Journey

When I was an elementary school student growing up in a suburb of Chicago, nearly every year our class set out on a field trip to the massive Museum of Science and Industry. Our teachers and a tour guide took us through a few exhibits, set a few ground rules, and then freed us to roam as we pleased (with chaperones nearby) until it was time to meet up back at the bus. That free time was always the best part.

On your media literacy journey, you've now received the tour guide's introduction and are free to wander. And you aren't alone. You're joining a growing community of early childhood educators across the globe. Let yourself

> Explore. Re-imagine. Question.
> Listen. Create. Play. Share. Reflect.

And finally, we end with the most important media literacy question of all: *What else do you want to know?*

### Sources


Arendt, H. [1974] 1978. "Hannah Arendt: From an Interview," interview by Roger Errera. *The New York Review of Books,* October 26. www.nybooks.com/articles/1978/10/26/hannah-arendt-from-an-interview.

NCTE (National Council of Teachers of English) Task Force on Critical Media Literacy. 2021. *Report of the Task Force on Critical Media Literacy*. Report. Urbana, IL: NCTE. https://ncte.org/critical-media-literacy.

Silverman, C. 2017. *Lies, Damn Lies, and Viral Content.* Report. New York: Tow Center for Digital Journalism, Columbia University. doi:10.7916/D8Q81RHH.

PART III

# From Pedagogy to Practice Wrap-Up

PAUSE TO **REVIEW**

The book says, "In media literacy education, analysis isn't about showing children what they missed by pointing out what *we* notice." What do children learn when their teachers and child care providers assume the role of expert and provide interpretations for them?

What's the meaning of the following sentence: "We don't teach children to doubt, we teach them to investigate"? Why does making this distinction matter? How does it show up in lesson design?

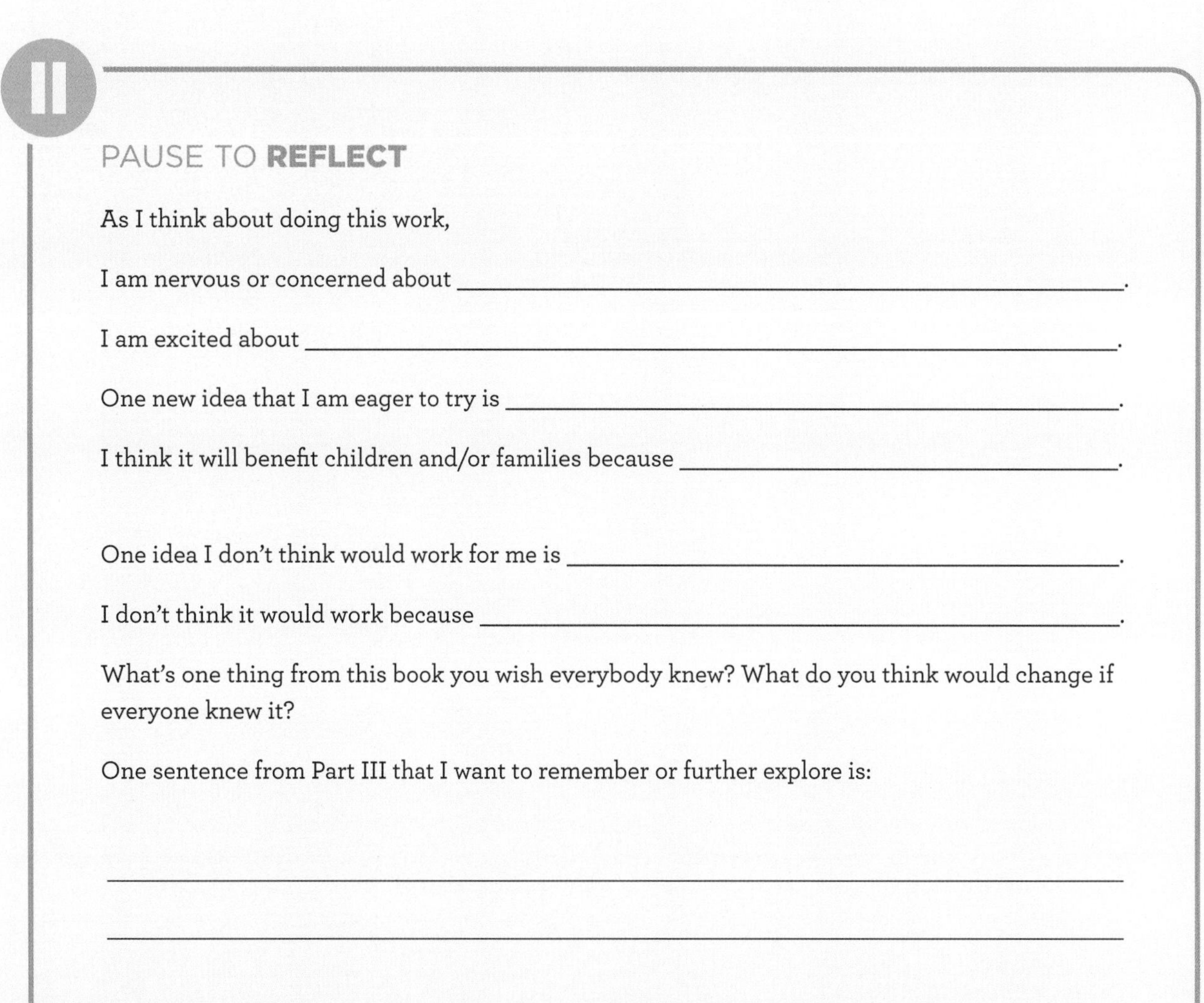

PAUSE TO **REFLECT**

As I think about doing this work,

I am nervous or concerned about ____________________________________.

I am excited about ____________________________________.

One new idea that I am eager to try is ____________________________________.

I think it will benefit children and/or families because ____________________________________.

One idea I don't think would work for me is ____________________________________.

I don't think it would work because ____________________________________.

What's one thing from this book you wish everybody knew? What do you think would change if everyone knew it?

One sentence from Part III that I want to remember or further explore is:

____________________________________________________________________

____________________________________________________________________

APPENDIX A

# 100 Words That Build Media Literacy Vocabulary

This Appendix is included because:

- We don't notice things for which we don't have language, and we can't analyze what we can't name, so words are important.
- Having a common vocabulary to describe and examine media improves collaboration and group discussion.
- Sometimes we need to explain complex concepts and we don't always have the developmentally appropriate language we need. This list is designed to help.

Because the goal is to help very young children understand, the explanations aren't always 100 percent technically accurate or comprehensive. And no list can cover everything. You'll want to add domain- or activity-specific words for the particular media you use.

Some of the words on the list won't apply to your situation at all. That's okay. You'll also notice that many of the words have multiple meanings. Suggested explanations relate only to the media-relevant meaning, and you may need to adapt for the particular media you are using.

In early childhood media literacy, vocabulary is best taught in context. So, think of this list as a reference for *you* to use, not a list to teach. And if you can easily demonstrate a concept or point to an example, that's almost always a better option that trying to explain with words.

1. **actor**—in media, when someone pretends to be someone else
2. **ad** or **commercial**—media made to try to sell us something
3. **animation**—what media makers do to create a cartoon—putting lots of drawings in sequence to make it seem like they're moving
4. **app**—short for *application*—it's what lets us do things on a phone, tablet, or computer
5. **audience**—the people who are looking at, listening to, reading, or playing a particular piece of media
6. **author**—a person who writes or creates media that they share with others
7. **background**—the things behind the main thing in a picture
8. **bias**—a way of thinking that makes us want to see things in a certain way or favors going in a particular direction, like the bias of a fabric
9. **buy**—trading money for something we want
10. **camera**—a tool we use to create photographs/take pictures
11. **choice**—making a decision, picking between options
12. **click**—what one does with a mouse
13. **close-up**—a picture that makes it feel like we are very close to the thing/person in the picture
14. **clue**—a hint that reveals something important about something we want to know
15. **coding**—the language we write when we want to make digital tools work
16. **color**—as noun and verb

17. **communication**—telling stuff to other people and listening to what they have to say
18. **compare and contrast**—looking for things that are the same and looking for things that are different
19. **connected**—linked; also, that we are online and able to communicate with other people there
20. **content**—noun; the things and ideas included
21. **costume**—the clothing that actors wear and what we wear when we're pretending to be someone or something else
22. **cursor**—the icon that blinks on a computer screen to let you know where you are
23. **decision**—making a choice
24. **design**—the set of choices we make that determines how something looks or how a game is played
25. **edit**—changing the media we make by replacing something, taking something out, or putting two frames next to each other
26. **emoji** - an icon that we use in text messages to communicate what we're thinking without using words, like a smiley face to show that we are happy
27. **emotion**—a feeling or reaction, like anger, joy, frustration, pride
28. **evidence**—the things that show that what we believe is true
29. **exaggerate**—making things seem much better/bigger/worse/and so on than they really are
30. **fact**—something that is true for all people, every time
31. **fair**—when we try to meet everyone's needs and everyone feels like actions or decisions are just
32. **focus**—making an image clear or blurry; or a thing draws our attention
33. **follow**—to select an option that notifies you when a particular person online posts something new
34. **frame**—the way we point a camera to include certain things and exclude other things, or the boundary we create to separate things that are included from things that are excluded
35. **friend**—in media, this is the word we use to describe letting people connect with us online and the people we connect with
36. **home page**—the first or main page of a website
37. **image**—a picture or things that are visible in a picture
38. **in app purchase**—the things that an app offers to you to buy that make play easier or more fun, or just because they think you'll like it and if you buy it they make more money
39. **in front/back; side/next to; on/under; inside/outside—any prepositions that describe spatial relationships**—best explained by demonstrating
40. **include/exclude**—what media makers do with things that they want/don't want other people to see, hear, or read
41. **influence**—when media affect what we think or the way we behave
42. **influencer**—a person who uses media to share what they know and has a lot of people who listen to/follow them
43. **intention**—our reasons for doing things; what we mean
44. **information**—the things we learn about a topic
45. **Internet**—the place we are at when we are online connecting to the world through our computers, tablets, phones, or voice assistants

46. **interpret / interpretation**—what we do/create when we're trying to understand or make sense of media

47. **landing page**—the part of a website we are taken to when we click on a link

48. **link**—a tool we use online that takes us from where we are to another place online

49. **message**—what media are trying to say to us; information we share with another person by texting on a phone or the act of sending that information

50. **microphone**—a tool we use to record sound or make sounds louder

51. **observe**—to look at something very carefully and pay attention to details

52. **online**—being in the digital world of the Internet

53. **opinion**—something we think or believe that others might see or think about differently

54. **original**—something new that no one has ever done before

55. **pace**—how fast the images pass by

56. **password**—a secret entry key we use so the computer knows it's us

57. **personal information**—important information about us, like our name, birthday, and where we live or go to school; information that can be used to find us and that we don't share with strangers

58. **perspective**—the way we look at things, using everything we've experienced and learned; or the way we look at things because of where we are sitting or standing

59. **persuasion/persuade**—convincing someone to believe something

60. **photograph**—the name for the type of picture that we use a camera to make

61. **pinch**—the motion on a touch screen when we bring our fingers together to make a frame smaller

62. **point of view**—a way of looking at things

63. **post**—as in posting something online

64. **private/privacy**—information that we don't want everyone to know/that we share just with the people who already know and care about us

65. **program**—something we watch on TV or the instructions people put into a computer when it is created to make it do what we want

66. **prop**—something included on a set or in a picture that helps us understand where the action is taking place and/or who the people are in the scene

67. **purpose**—the reason we have for doing something; our goal

68. **record**—the action we take to tell the camera or app that we want to keep what we are looking or hearing; also the toggle switch button that lets us turn that function on or off (as in "hit record")

69. **rehearsal/rehearse**—practice/practicing for a performance like a play, concert, dance, or video

70. **representation/represent**—included; something a media maker creates to stand in for the real thing, like an avatar, stereotype (for a group of people), or symbol (like a national flag)

71. **save**—an action we take on the computer so we can keep what we are working on

72. **scene**—one part of story

73. **scroll**—looking quickly through messages on a phone or tablet, or the text in a computer document

74. **search**—what we do when we look for information online, as in *"I'm going to do a . . ."*

75. **selfie**—a picture we take of ourselves, usually with a phone

76. **sell**—asking for money in exchange for something someone wants

77. **shot**—as related to cameras

78. **sound effect**—video and film cameras can't always record the sounds in a scene, or the scene is imaginary, so we aren't sure how something is supposed to sound, so we re-create the sounds using the things we have, like hitting shoes on a board to make the sound of a galloping horse or blowing air from our mouth to simulate wind

79. **sponsor**—people who pay to produce or share media, as in "and now a word from our sponsor"

80. **style**—the look or feel of some types of media, like something drawn in the style of an Eric Carle book or written in the style of a rap song

81. **subject**—the topic or star of a picture or story

82. **swipe**—sliding a finger up, down, or sideways on a touch screen

83. **tap**—lightly touching a certain place on a touch screen

84. **target audience**—the people we intend to talk to when we make media

85. **tempo**—the speed of music—fast or slow or in between

86. **text**—anything printed using words; using a phone to send someone a message using typed words, emojis, and/or pictures

87. **tracking**—the way a computer or voice assistant remember and shares what we do—it keeps an eye on us and writes down everything we do or say; with a camera, a shot that follows a character as they move

88. **true**—saying what really happened or describing something the way it really is

89. **trust**—believing a person because we know they tell the truth

90. **tweet**—a message we send using Twitter—it has to be short and it can include words, emojis, and pictures

91. **user**—a person who is using a digital or social media tool

92. **video**—one of the ways we can record images that move and have sound

93. **visual**—when media is made for us to interact with using our eyes

94. **voice assistant**—a type of computer that connects to the Internet and that we interact with using only our voice and that answer us using a voice, like Alexa or Siri

95. **voice over**—in video or film, a voice in the background that talks over an image or a voice that tells the story in a way that isn't part of what characters say to each other

96. **volume**—how loud or soft a sound is

97. **web page**—websites have pages, just like a book has pages, except you can go to them in any order

98. **website**—a space that a person or group creates online to share information

99. **writer**—a person who communicates with words that are written down

100. **zoom**—moving a camera lens so it makes things seem closer or farther away; zooming in makes the frame smaller so what we're looking at fills up more of the frame; zooming out does the opposite

APPENDIX B

# Using Media Analysis Questions to Draw Conclusions About Media Effects Research

Media literacy places a lot of value on evidence, so media literacy educators value evidence-based educational practice. But what do we count as evidence? Are we actually reading the research, or are we relying on media reports about the research? By calling attention to sources and the role of interpretive lenses (our own, the researchers, and the reporters), media literacy analysis questions remind us that science is not objective. What people choose to study, the way researchers frame their questions, and the ways that their findings are communicated influence how we think about the science, and how the science influences our work. And so, when claims about media effects influence our teaching, we ask . . .

## Authorship

- Who are the researchers and what are their credentials on *this* topic (institutional affiliation, publications, and so forth)?
- In book acknowledgments, whom do the researchers thank, with whom did they study, and what does that tell me about their approach?
- If I'm not reading the actual research, who are the reporters? What is their training in this field or research method?

## Purposes

- Why were the researchers interested in this particular research question? What do they think is important? Who might agree or disagree that the main research question is, indeed, important?
- Why are media outlets choosing to give time/space to this particular study?
- Who is the target audience?
- What do they want me to think (or think about) or do? Why would they want me to think or do that?

## Content

- What did the research actually find and how does that compare to the story about the research?
- How did researchers frame the task and how did that framing influence the work?
- Does the report include descriptions of the research methods? Do researchers or reporters identify shortcomings as well as strengths of the research methods (adequate sample and effect size; self-reporting versus observation; empirical or qualitative data collection, to name just a few possibilities)?

- Does the research actually support the explanation (e.g., identifying fast-paced video as a problem when the study only counted screen-time minutes and researchers don't actually have any way of knowing whether subjects actually viewed fast-paced videos)?
- Do they define important terms (e.g., what constitutes *fast-paced* or *screen time*)?
- Are conclusions over-generalized (e.g., a statistically significant finding for white college students is reported as if it applies to everyone, or a study of a small group of select children is treated as if it was a scientifically valid random sample)?
- What data are missing that might be important to know (e.g., did subjects have any prior media literacy education, and if so, what sort of exposure was it)?
- Did they measure attitudes and beliefs or actual behavior (e.g., did a survey find that parents *believed* that screen time was shortening children's attention spans, or did researchers conduct experiments that demonstrated actual decreases in attention span)? If research was conducted in a laboratory, can results reasonably be judged to also apply in real-life situations?

## Techniques

- What drew my attention to this story or this study?
- Which statistics did they choose to highlight and why?
- How is the story framed?
- Does the headline, CG (the text that appears on the bottom of a screen to identify a story), or promo tag accurately reflect the research?

## Context

- How does this compare to other research in the field?
- Where/how was it distributed (e.g., peer-reviewed journal, pay-to-publish journal, science magazine, pop psychologist podcast, column in an education newsletter, TV news segment)?
- When was the research conducted? Were there events of note that provide important context for understanding the research findings (e.g., a headline cites a frightening increase in the percentage of time children spend using phones, but the calculation compares a year when cell phones didn't exist to the first year that they were widely available to the public. The statistic is technically correct, but it's misleading because even a little time results in a large percentage gain if it is compared with zero.)?

## Credibility

- What do other credible sources think of these researchers? What else have they published and what do the reviews say (journal reviews, not sales outlet review comments or stars)?
- What can I tell about them from the sources they cite or from the sources who cite them?
- What specific evidence do I find convincing?
- Do the researchers explain why their conclusions override those of contradictory studies, or do they ignore critics or contradictory findings?

## Economics

- Who funded the research?
- Were there appropriate firewalls between financial backers and researchers (or were funders just paying for specific outcomes)?
- Who stands to financially benefit from this research and its conclusions?

- Who is making money from publicizing or distributing this work? (Don't forget to include researchers and their prospects for future grants, job promotions, book sales, or speaking engagements.)

## Effects

- Who stands to benefit from the study? Who might be harmed by it?
- Who is privileged or disadvantaged by presenting the research in this way?

## Interpretation

- Are reporters or interviewers accurately interpreting the research?
- Is the evidence convincing?
- Do I think they've drawn reasonable or unreasonable conclusions from the evidence (e.g., are they implying cause even if there is only evidence of correlation)?
- How is my interpretation influenced by confirmation bias or other aspects of my interpretive lens?
- How (and why) might others come to a different conclusion from the same evidence?

## Responses

- What else do I want to know / what additional questions do I have?
- What feelings does this evoke for me? How might confirmation bias be influencing my reaction?
- Now that I know this, what action(s) will I take? How will it influence my work with children and families?

### Try This

Name one research finding about media and children that you have shared with families or you wish every family knew. Trace the source of the claim. What is it about the research that you find to be particularly convincing?

APPENDIX C

# Resources

There are many high-quality media literacy resources available with more being created every year. So instead of trying to create a comprehensive list, this is my answer to "If you were really busy and only had time to look at a few things, which ones would be your priority? Where would you start?"

## General

### National Association for Media Literacy Education (NAMLE)

www.namle.net—*The* place to find media literacy education colleagues and keep up with the latest developments in the field. Convenes the annual National Media Literacy Week in the United States, a biannual national conference, and collaborative events with organizations across the United States and around the world. Also publishes the open-source, peer-reviewed *Journal for Media Literacy Education* (www.jmle.org).

Note—If you're not in the United States, many nations have their own media literacy education organizations. Though it isn't comprehensive, UNESCO's Media and Information Literacy (MIL) Alliance provides a place to start your search: https://en.unesco.org/themes/media-and-information-literacy/gapmil/members. Also of interest is the United Nation's Convention on the Rights of the Child "General comment No. 25 (2021) on children's rights in relation to the digital environment" at www.ohchr.org/EN/HRBodies/CRC/Pages/GCChildrensRightsRelationDigitalEnvironment.aspx.

## Research

### Sonia Livingstone's *Parenting for a Digital Future*

https://blogs.lse.ac.uk/parenting4digitalfuture—When I look for current research on children and media, I start with the work of Sonia Livingstone—one of the best researchers on the planet. This is her blog, which presents the research in a very accessible way.

### Joan Ganz Cooney Center

www.joanganzcooneycenter.org—Focused on the ways that children learn from digital media and how new media can serve children's needs, the Joan Ganz Cooney Center offers research summaries and blog posts that explore what's happening on the leading edge, just like visionary Joan Ganz Cooney did in the 1960s when she spurred the creation of *Sesame Street*.

### New America Foundation

www.newamerica.org/education-policy—With reports on media mentorship, bridging the digital divide, and much more, the Education Policy division of the New America Foundation, and especially the work of Lisa Guernsey, is an excellent resource for timely, research-based early childhood education policy analysis and recommendations.

## Lesson Ideas and Materials

### Project Look Sharp

www.projectlooksharp.org—Focused on integrating media literacy into existing core curriculum, this amazing team of educators offers a database of lessons—searchable by keyword, grade level, or subject area—all downloadable for free, including the media examples. Especially great resources for nutrition and health lessons.

## Tech Integration

### Kristi Meeuwse's *I Teach with iPads*

www.iteachwithipads.com/author/kristimeeuwse—If you've been handed a tablet and don't know what to do with it, start with this blog. There are plenty of ideas here, direct from a kindergarten teacher with three decades of experience. Dr. Meeuwse doesn't always integrate media literacy inquiry, but her excellent teaching-with-tech examples are easy to adapt to a media literacy approach.

### National Association for the Education of Young Children (NAEYC)

NAEYC.org/resources/topics/technology-and-media/resources—The 2012 joint position statement issued by NAEYC and the Fred Rogers Center for Early Learning, "Technology and Interactive Media as Tools in Early Childhood Programs Serving Children from Birth Through Age 8," and also the follow-up piece done five years later by Chip Donohue and Roberta Schomburg (NAEYC.org/resources/pubs/yc/sep2017/technology-and-interactive-media), both describe how to integrate technology in ways that support media literacy and children's general well-being.

If you're a NAEYC member, join the NAEYC Technology and Young Children Interest Forum, which offers webinars, hosts conference meetings, and shares resources via the NAEYC Hello online community.

## Cyber Safety/Digital Citizenship

### NetFamilyNews.org

www.netfamilynews.org—Anne Collier keeps track of the research on digital citizenship, cybersafety, and social media effects claims so you don't have to. Accessible, timely, and insightful.

## Counter Readings/ Confronting Stereotypes

### American Indians in Children's Literature

www.americanindiansinchildrensliterature.net Terminology, children's book recommendations (both what to read and what not to read), discussions of recurring issues (e.g., Thanksgiving, school mascots)—it's all here and curated in a simple, easy-to-find format.

### Woke Kindergarten

www.wokekindergarten.org—While not using an explicitly media literacy education approach, these abolitionist antiracism resources from a former kindergarten teacher include videos of read-alouds that demonstrate how to integrate serious social justice issues in age-appropriate ways.

### Teaching Tolerance Social Justice Standards/Anti-Bias-Framework

https://www.learningforjustice.org/frameworks/social-justice-standards—An outline of age-appropriate expectations divided into four domains: Identity, Diversity, Justice, and Action. Combine this with the NAEYC publication ***Anti-Bias Education for Young Children and Ourselves*** (NAEYC.org/resources/pubs/books/anti-bias-education) for a solid foundation.

### NAEYC Culture Interest Forums

NAEYC.org/get-involved/communities/interest-forums-culture—Members often share valuable teaching resources. Forums include: Asian; Black Caucus; Latino; Lesbian, Gay, Bisexual, and Transgender (LGBT); Men in Education Network (M.E.N); and Tribal and Indigenous Early Childhood Network (TIECN).

## For Parents

### Above the Noise

https://video.kqed.org/show/above-noise—Made for teens but relevant for everyone, this entertaining series of video shorts from Bay Area PBS station KQED provides accessible explanations of key media literacy concepts and their intersection with current events.

## For Kids

### Wonderopolis

www.wonderopolis.org—A website where kids can ask questions and get answers. The site shows where it gets its information for each answer, which helps youngsters build a bank of credible sources. It includes an immersive reader that allows users to listen to the answer while reading along.

## Books

**Vivian Maria Vasquez. *Negotiating Critical Literacies with Young Children*** (Routledge, [2004] 2014) and **Vivian Maria Vasquez & Carol Branigan Felderman. *Technology and Critical Literacy in Early Childhood*** (Routledge, 2013)—Hands down both are the best early childhood integration of tech, inquiry, social justice, and action that I have encountered.

**Kristin Ziemke & Kate Muharis. *Read the World: Rethinking Literacy for Empathy and Action in a Digital Age*** (Heinemann, 2020)—It can be helpful for our own teaching practice to know what will be expected of children at the next level up. For a vision of the logical next step (upper elementary with a bit of overlap for K–2), this is a brilliant resource for curriculum-driven, inquiry-based education that includes tech and some media literacy.

**Karen Wohlwend. *Literacy Playshop: New Literacies, Popular Media, and Play in the Early Childhood Classroom.*** (Teachers College Press, 2013)—This book introduces Wohlwend's groundbreaking Playshop model, which combines the power of free play, literacy, and digital technologies.

**Gayle Berthiaume & Gail Lovely. *Using an iPad with Your Preschooler*** (Suddenly It Clicks, 2014)—Still a favorite for explaining how to use a tablet in constructive ways with very young children. And if you're interested in integrating coding, Gail Lovely is one of the best. Keep up with her latest offerings at www.suddenlyitclicks.com.

**Ann Pelo & Margie Carter. *From Teaching to Thinking: A Pedagogy for Reimagining Our Work*** (Exchange Press, 2018)—Not explicitly a media literacy book, but a great follow-up for those who want to delve deeper into the pedagogies of reflection and inquiry. These veteran early childhood educators provide extraordinary insight along with practical suggestions.

## Additional Resources from Faith Rogow

### InsightersEducation.com

www.insighterseducation.com—The author's website includes a link to her blog, *TUNE IN, Next Time*, as well as other resources and contact information. You can also follow the author on Twitter @InsightersEd

## Finding Allies

### National Media Literacy Alliance

Anyone encountering resistance to integrating media literacy education might point opponents to this initiative spearheaded by the National Association for Media Literacy Education (NAMLE). Leading US education organizations have recognized media literacy as so important that they have joined together to form the National Media Literacy Alliance. Founding organizations include:

American Association of School Librarians (AASL)

International Society for Technology in Education (ISTE)

Journalism Education Association (JEA)

National Association for the Education of Young Children (NAEYC)

National Council for the Social Studies (NCSS)

National Council of Teachers of English (NCTE)

National Council of Teachers of Mathematics (NCTM)

National Science Teaching Association (NSTA)

National Writing Project (NWP)

Public Broadcasting Service (PBS)

Young Adult Library Services Association (YALSA)

Check the website of each organization for its particular policy statements and related resources in support of media literacy education. Also, several of the organizations have early childhood divisions or caucuses that are worth joining.

# Education Standards

A search of the phrase "media literacy" will come up "not found" in most education standards. But you can find substantial support for media literacy education if you . . .

- Look at the introductory goal statements, which often talk about various aspects of preparing students for a digital world.
- Look for media literacy concepts, like evidence-based inquiry or understanding perspective rather than only items specific to media.
- Refer to organizational statements of support for media literacy. In many cases, organizations that have published standards have also adopted position statements in support of media literacy education.
- Decouple the standards themselves from the standardized testing that has been attached to them. The standards have value despite tests being used as a bludgeon to coerce compliance and reinforce inequities.

Here are some places to start:

**Common Core State Standards** for English Language Arts & Literacy in History/Social Studies, Science, and Technical Subjects (2010)

www.corestandards.org/assets/CCSSI_ELA%20Standards.pdf

Though these standards clearly privilege print literature and information texts, they also call for relevant media literacy skills, expecting students to "reflexively demonstrate the cogent reasoning and use of evidence that is essential to both private deliberation and responsible citizenship in a democratic republic" (3). The Introduction further explains

> To be ready for college, workforce training, and life in a technological society, students need the ability to gather, comprehend, evaluate, synthesize, and report on information and ideas, to conduct original research in order to answer questions or solve problems, and to analyze and create a high volume and extensive range of print and nonprint texts in media forms old and new. The need to

> conduct research and to produce and consume media is embedded into every aspect of today's curriculum. In like fashion, research and media skills and understandings are embedded throughout the Standards rather than treated in a separate section. (4)

The K–5 Anchor Standards (10) say that students should be able to

> 4. Interpret words and phrases as they are used in a text, including determining technical, connotative, and figurative meanings, and analyze how specific word choices shape meaning or tone. . . .
> 6. Assess how point of view or purpose shapes the content and style of a text.
> 7. Integrate and evaluate content presented in diverse media and formats.

**Next Generation Science Standards**

www.nextgenscience.org/sites/default/files/K-2DCI.pdf

These standards don't directly address media, but their shifting of the focus from memorization of discrete facts and terms to understanding processes, connections, and reasoning when students explore the natural world provide significant intersections with the goals of media literacy education.

> In the kindergarten performance expectations, students are expected to demonstrate grade-appropriate proficiency in *asking questions*, developing and using models, planning and carrying out investigations, *analyzing and interpreting data*, designing solutions, *engaging in argument from evidence*, and *obtaining, evaluating, and communicating information*. Students are expected to use these practices to demonstrate understanding of the core ideas (*emphasis mine*, 4).

In addition, the K–2 standards emphasize observation skills and the understanding of concepts like cause and effect and noticing patterns (K-PS3-1, K-PS3-2, & K-LS1-1).

**National Council for the Social Studies/ College, Career, and Civic Life (C3) Framework for Social Studies State Standards**

www.socialstudies.org/standards/c3

The 2013 C3 Framework is built on an Inquiry Arc, emphasizing the ability to evaluate, analyze, and communicate. Its purpose is to "build critical thinking, problem solving, and participatory skills to become engaged citizens," and nearly every standard dovetails with the goals of media literacy education. Here are a few highlights:

> By End of Grade 2
>
> Construct compelling and supportive questions (24–25)
>
> D1.5.K-2. Determine the kinds of sources that will be helpful in answering compelling and supporting questions.
>
> D2.Civ.10.K-2. Compare their own point of view with others' perspectives.
>
> D3.2.K-2. Evaluate a source by distinguishing between fact and opinion.
>
> D4.1.K-2. Construct an argument with reasons.
>
> D4.3.K-2. Present a summary of an argument using print, oral, and digital technologies.
>
> D4.4&5.K-2. Ask and answer questions about arguments and explanations.

**Ontario Ministry of Education Kindergarten Program**

www.edu.gov.on.ca/eng/curriculum/elementary/kindergarten.html

For media literacy educators, these standards are exemplary. The word *inquiry* appears 196 times. In addition to the critical literacy sections cited in Chapter 6 of this book, the standards include a specific media literacy strand. Here are a few excerpts:

OE12: As children progress through the kindergarten program, they demonstrate an understanding and critical awareness of media texts

**Conceptual Understandings**

- Media texts are constructed to persuade and influence the reader or viewer.
- Media texts are everywhere.
- Media texts can influence our thoughts, ideas, feelings, beliefs, and wishes.
- We need to think about how media texts can affect us.

**Making Thinking and Learning Visible**

- Both children and educators are observers and inquirers

12.1 respond critically to animated works (e.g., cartoons in which animals talk, movies in which animals go to school)

12.2 communicate their ideas, verbally and nonverbally, about a variety of media materials

- Children demonstrate their learning by saying things like, "I learned that they put toys in cereal boxes because they want kids to buy the cereal."
- A small group of children make signs about how to be safe on the school bus.
- Educators ask questions such as: "Why did people make this cartoon?" "What is it about this cartoon that makes you want to watch it?" "Sometimes you buy cereal and there are toys in the box. Why do you think the people who made the cereal put the toys in there?"

Standards related to media literacy for other Canadian provinces can be found here: https://mediasmarts.ca/teacher-resources/digital-and-media-literacy-outcomes-province-territory

# Index

Page numbers followed by *f* refer to figures and those followed by *t* refer to tables.

## Q



## R



## S

# About the Author

Faith Rogow, Ph.D., is a media literacy leader, innovator, and founder of Insighters Educational Consulting. She was the founding president of the *National Association for Media Literacy Education* (NAMLE), a founding editorial board member of the Journal for Media Literacy Education, a founding advisor to Project Look Sharp, and a co-author of NAMLE's "Core Principles of Media Literacy Education in the U.S." (2007). For more than twenty years she has been one of the few people in the United States advocating for and creating media literacy education that is developmentally appropriate for early childhood. Her groundbreaking article "The ABCs of Media Literacy" (Telemedium, Spring 2002) has been widely circulated, as has her chapter – "Media Literacy in Early Childhood Education: Inquiry-Based Technology Integration" – in the Routledge/NAEYC anthology *Technology and Digital Media in the Early Years: Tools for Teaching and Learning* (Chip Donohue, ed., 2015). She also co-authored *The Teacher's Guide to Media Literacy: Critical Thinking in a Multimedia World* (Corwin, 2012).

**www.insighterseducation.com**